Lecture Notes in Engineering

Edited by C. A. Brebbia and S. A. Orszag

24

Supercomputers and Fluid Dynamics

Proceedings of the First Nobeyama Workshop
September 3-6, 1985

Edited by:
K. Kuwahara, R. Mendez and S. A. Orszag

Springer-Verlag
Berlin Heidelberg New York
London Paris Tokyo

Series Editors
C. A. Brebbia · S. A. Orszag

Consulting Editors
J. Argyris · K.-J. Bathe · A. S. Cakmak · J. Connor · R. McCrory
C. S. Desai · K.-P. Holz · F. A. Leckie · G. Pinder · A. R. S. Pont
J. H. Seinfeld · P. Silvester · P. Spanos · W. Wunderlich · S. Yip

Editors
Kunio Kuwahara
Institute of Space and Astronautical Science
Tokyo, Japan

Raul Mendez
Dept. of Mathematics
Naval Postgraduate School
Monterey, CA, USA

Steven A. Orszag
Applied and Computational Mathematics
Princeton University
Princeton, NJ, USA

ISBN 3-540-17051-0 Springer-Verlag Berlin Heidelberg New York
ISBN 0-387-17051-0 Springer-Verlag New York Berlin Heidelberg

Library of Congress Cataloging-in-Publication Data
Nobeyama Workshop (1st: 1985)
Supercomputers and fluid dynamics.
(Lecture notes in engineering; 24)
1. Fluid dynamics--Data processing--Congresses.
2. Supercomputers--Congresses.
I. Kuwahara, K. (Kunio).
II. Mendez, R. (Raul)
III. Orszag, Steven A.
IV. Title.
V. Series.
QA911.N63 1985   620.1'06'0285411   86-22089
ISBN 3-540-17051-0
ISBN 0-387-17051-0 (U.S.)

This work is subject to copyright. All rights are reserved, whether the whole or part of the material is concerned, specifically those of translation, reprinting, re-use of illustrations, broadcasting, reproduction by photocopying machine or similar means, and storage in data banks. Under § 54 of the German Copyright Law where copies are made for other than private use, a fee is payable to "Verwertungsgesellschaft Wort", Munich.

© Springer-Verlag Berlin, Heidelberg 1986
Printed in Germany

Printing: Mercedes-Druck, Berlin
Binding: B. Helm, Berlin

PREFACE

In the past several years, it has become apparent that computing will soon achieve a status within science and engineering to the classical scientific methods of laboratory experiment and theoretical analysis. The foremost tools of state-of-the-art computing applications are supercomputers, which are simply the fastest and biggest computers available at any given time. Supercomputers and supercomputing go hand-in-hand in pacing the development of scientific and engineering applications of computing.

Experience has shown that supercomputers improve in speed and capability by roughly a factor 1000 every 20 years. Supercomputers today include the Cray XMP and Cray-2, manufactured by Cray Research, Inc., the Cyber 205, manufactured by Control Data Corporation, the Fujitsu VP, manufactured by Fujitsu, Ltd., the Hitachi SA-810/20, manufactured by Hitachi, Ltd., and the NEC SX, manufactured by NEC, Inc. The fastest of these computers are nearly three orders-of-magnitude faster than the fastest computers available in the mid-1960s, like the Control Data CDC 6600. While the world-wide market for supercomputers today is only about 50 units per year, it is expected to grow rapidly over the next several years to about 200 units per year. The present supercomputer market is only about 1/10 of one per-cent of the world-wide computer market, but this market share has tremendous impact because it defines the state-of-the-art of computing and has great influences on future directions in computing. For example, the supercomputers of the mid-1960's, like the CDC 6600, were prototypes of what are now called RISC (Reduced Instruction Set Computing) machines, becoming popular now within the class of so-called mini-supercomputers (machines that perform and cost about an order-of-magnitude less than the biggest computers).

Supercomputers have much influence on computational mathematics. In recent years, we have seen the introduction of novel architectural features, like parallelism and pipelining, into supercomputer designs. The effective utilization of these architectural features requires the development of new algorithms for the solution of scientific and engineering problems. It is also interesting to note that the development of numerical algorithms has kept pace with the development of supercomputers. The operation counts and computational efficiency of new algorithms have improved at a rate of about a factor 1000 every 20 years.

On September 3-6, 1985, a unique workshop was held at Nobeyama in the Japanese Alps. At this workshop, 22 American and 36 Japanese computational scientists and supercomputer designers were able to interact with each other across a broad range of issues, from scientific applications to algorithm design to computer architecture. The scientific and engineering applications emphasized fluid dynamics, hence the title of this volume "Supercomputers and Fluid Dynamics." In this volume, 15 papers summarizing talks given at the Workshop are presented.

We believe that this forum gave an excellent way to establish communications between the hitherto distinct cultures of computational fluid dynamicists, computer scientists, and hardware engineers. This communication has opened new discussions and collaborations that we hope will lead to major new progress in computational science. In addition, the Workshop presented new opportunities for Japanese and American researchers to discuss joint areas of interest and initiate new studies. In fields as rapidly changing as supercomputing and computational fluid dynamics, this type of forum is essential to progress.

This Workshop, its organization and the present publication, were sponsored in part by the Institute of JUSE, Fujitsu, Ltd., NEC, Inc., Asahi Chemical Engineering, the New Jersey Commission on Science and Technology through the John von Neumann Center for Scientific Computing, the Air Force Office of Scientific Research, and the Office of Naval Research.

                                                  Kunio Kuwahara, Tokyo
                                                  Raul Mendez, Monterey
                                                  Steven A. Orszag, Princeton
                                                  January 10, 1986

LIST OF CONTRIBUTORS

Dr. B. J. Bayly
Applied and Computational Mathematics
Princeton University
Princeton, NJ 08544

Dr. Y. Chikada
Nobeyama Radio Observatory
Minamimaki, Mimamisaku
Nagano Pref., 384-13
Japan

Dr. J. H. Ferziger
Department of Mechanical Engineering
Stanford University
Stanford, CA 94305

Dr. K. Fujii
Second Aerodynamics Division
National Aerospace Laboratory
Chofu-city, Tokyo, Japan

Dr. K. N. Ghia
Department of Aerospace Engineering
and Engineering Mechanics
University of Cincinnati
Cincinnati, OH 45221

Dr. U. Ghia
Department of Mechanical
and Industrial Engineering
University of Cincinnati
Cincinnati, OH 45221

Dr. R. Himeno
Central Engineering Laboratories
Nissan Motor Co., Ltd.
Yokosuka, Kanagawa, Japan

Dr. K. Kamo
Department of Aeronautics
University of Tokyo
Hongo, Bunkyo-ku
Tokyo, Japan

Dr. M. Kiya
Department of Mechanical Engineering
Faculty of Engineering
Hokkaido University
Sapporo, 060, Japan

Dr. K. Kuwahara
Institute of Space and
  Astronautical Science
Komaba, Meguro-ku
Tokyo, Japan

Dr. C.K. Lombard
PEDA Corporation
Palo Alto, CA 94735

Dr. R.H. Mendez
Department of Mathematics
Naval Postgraduate School
Monterey, CA 93943

Dr. K. Miura
Mainframe Division
Fujitsu Limited
1015 Kamikodanaka
Nakahara-ku
Kawasaki, 211, Japan

Dr. T. Nakazuru
Mainframe Division
Fujitsu Limited
1015 Kamikodanaka
Nakahara-ku
Kawasaki, 211, Japan

Dr. S.A. Orszag
Applied and Computational Mathematics
Princeton University
218 Fine Hall
Princeton, NJ 08544

Dr. G.A. Osswald
Dept. of Aerospace Engineering
 and Engineering Mechanics
University of Cincinnati
Cincinnati, OH 445221

Dr. A.T. Patera
Dept. of Mechanical Engineering
Massachusetts Institute of Technology
Cambridge, MA 02139

Dr. R.B. Pelz
Applied and Computational Mathematics
Princeton University
218 Fine Hall
Princeton, NJ 08544

Dr. S.C. Perrenod
Cray Research, Inc.
5776 Stoneridge Mall Road
Pleasanton, CA 94566

Dr. C. J. Purcell
ETA Systems, Inc.
1450 Energy Park Dr.
St. Paul, MN 55108

Dr. R. Ramamurti
Dept. of Aerospace Engineering
 and Engineering Mechanics
University of Cincinnati
Cincinnati, OH 45221

Dr. A. Rizzi
FFA, The Aeronautical Research
 Institute of Sweden
S-161 11 Bromma, Sweden

Dr. T. Sato
Dept. of Mechanical
 Engineering
Faculty of Engineering
Hokkaido University
Sapporo, 060, Japan

Dr. S. Shirayama
Department of Aeronautics
University of Tokyo
4-6-1 Komaba, Meguroku
Tokyo, 153 Japan

Dr. E. Venkatapathy
PEDA Corporation
Palo Alto, CA 94735

Dr. T. Watanabe
Computer Engineering Division
NEC Corporation
1-10, Nisshin-cho, Fuchu
Tokyo, 183 Japan

TABLE OF CONTENTS

Secondary Instabilities, Coherent Structure, and Turbulence
S. A. Orszag, R. B. Pelz and B. J. Bayly   1

Bootstrapping in Turbulence Computation
J. H. Ferziger   15

Development of High-Reynolds-Number-Flow Computation
K. Kuwahara   28

Spectral Element Simulation of Flow in Grooved Channels: Cooling Chips with Tollmien-Schlichting Waves
A. T. Patera   41

A Vortex Ring Interacting with a Vortex Filament and its Deformation Near the Two-Dimensional Stagnation Point
M. Kiya and T. Sato   52

A New Three-Dimensional Vortex Method
S. Shirayama and K. Kuwahara   62

Multi-Cell Vortices Observed in Fine-Mesh Solutions to the Incompressible Euler Equations
A. Rizzi   77

Implicit Boundary Treatment for Joined and Disjoint Patched Mesh Systems
C. K. Lombard and E. Venkatapathy   89

Computational Study of Three-Dimensional Wake Structure
R. Himeno, S. Shirayama, K. Kamo and K. Kuwahara   98

A Semi-Elliptic Analysis of Internal Viscous Flows
U. Ghia, R. Ramamurti and K. N. Ghia   108

Simulation of Self-Induced Unsteady Motion in the Near Wake of a Joukowski Airfoil
K. N. Ghia, G. A. Osswald and U. Ghia   118

Viscous Compressible Flow Simulations Using Supercomputers
K. Fujii   133

The Scalar Performance of Three Supercomputers: Cray's X-MP/2, Fujitsu's VP-200 and NEC's SX-2
R. H. Mendez   148

NEC Supercomputer SX System
T. Watanabe   159

FX: A CMOS-Implemented Digital Spectro-Correlator System for Radio Astronomy
K. Miura, T. Nakazuru and Y. Chikada   165

The CRAY-2: The New Standard in Supercomputing
S. C. Perrenod   174

Introduction to the ETA 10
C. J. Purcell   184

SECONDARY INSTABILITIES, COHERENT STRUCTURES AND TURBULENCE

Steven A. Orszag, Richard B. Pelz and Bruce J. Bayly
Applied and Computational Mathematics
Princeton University, Princeton, 08544

Abstract

In this paper, we review recent progress on several problems of transition and turbulence. First, we explore the role of secondary instabilities in transition to turbulence in both wall bounded and free shear flows. It is shown how the competition between secondary instabilities and classical inviscid inflectional instabilities is important in determining the evolution of free shear flows. An outline of a general theory of inviscid instability is given. Then, we explore recent ideas on the force-free nature of coherent flow structures in turbulence. The role of viscosity in generating small-scale features of turbulence is discussed for both the Taylor-Green vortex and for two-dimensional turbulence. Finally, we survey recent ideas on the application of renormalization group methods to turbulence transport models. These methods yield fundamental relationships between various types of turbulent flow quantities and should be useful for the development of transport models in complex geometries with complicated physics, like chemical reactions and buoyant heat transfer.

1. Introduction

Numerical solutions of the Navier-Stokes equations have now been used with much success in the analysis and simulation of transition and turbulence in fluid flows. Analysis refers to the use of numerical solutions to isolate dynamical mechanisms and thus to simplify and organize our understanding of these complex flows. For analysis, computation offers the advantage over classical theory in that it allows the solution of rather general nonlinear problems in complicated geometries. Retaining the essence of complex phenomena like transition and turbulence seems to yield equations that are just too complicated for classical analytical techniques. However, numerical methods seem to fit the problem well and it has been possible to use large-scale computations to obtain insights into these problems.

On the other hand, simulation involves the generation of complex flows on the computer as a "numerical wind tunnel". Here computation offers the advantage over classical experimental methods that complete flow field data is available as part of the numerical solution and the solution can, at least in principle, be probed without disturbing the flow.

In this paper, we review progress on some problems of transition and turbulence that have been made possible by access to supercomputers. In Sec. 2, we discuss the role of so-called secondary instabilities in transition in wall-bounded shear flows. In the classical pipe and channel flows, classical linear, viscous instabilities are much too feeble to explain the robust processes of transition to turbulence. However, secondary instability provides a prototype of the kinds of instability that can exist in these flows and that can lead directly to disordered chaotic flow states and eventually to turbulence.

In Sec. 3, we contrast the secondary instability of wall-bounded shear flows with those of free shear flows. The major difference is that free-shear flows are inflectional so they can support strong inviscid linear instabilities. The result is a competition, often delicate, between several classes of strong instabilities. The resulting flow evolution depends sensitively on initial and boundary conditions.

In Sec. 4, we describe some recent results on the structure of eddies in turbulence flows. It is found that, away from walls, much of turbulent flows are nearly force-free or Beltrami in character. Some putative ideas on the stability of these flows are described.

Then, in Sec. 5, we survey new numerical tests of theories of two-dimensional turbulence. In the evolution of high Reynolds number chaotic flows, vortex layers develop and coalesce in time, giving rise to qualitatively distinct spectral features.

Finally, in Sec. 6, we review recent ideas applying renormalization group (RNG) methods to the generation of transport approximations for turbulent flows. These methods should be useful for the development of transport approximations to turbulence problems with both geometrical and physical complexity (as with chemical reactions, buoyancy, etc.).

2. Transition in wall-bounded shear flows

The classical problem of transition to turbulence in shear flows is to determine the nature of the breakdown of a laminar flow to turbulence. Two prototype wall-bounded flows are plane channel flow and boundary layer flow. The boundary layer case represents a situation intermediate between the essentially bounded channel flows and the completely free shear flows which will be discussed in the next section. In addition to their importance in their own right, these flows are instructive as prototypes of a large class of more complex flows whose behavior is nonetheless governed by essentially the same physical processes. Indeed, the main importance of the study of transition in simple, wall-bounded shear flows lies in the elucidation of the basic physical mechanisms by which all the more complex flows that are seen in the real world become turbulent.

The classical theory [1] of the stability of steady flows was initiated by Rayleigh, Kelvin, and Helmholtz roughly a century ago. On the basis of linearized stability analysis, Rayleigh demonstrated that any planar shear flow which does not possess an inflection point is necessarily stable, assuming purely inviscid flow. The inflection-point theorem is manifestly violated by the instability of plane Poiseuille flow (parabolic profile) and plane Couette flow (linear profile), and it was realized that even in the most highly inviscid flows, viscosity may yet exert a controlling influence on the stability of the flow. Incorporating viscous effects into the linear stability theory led to the study of the Orr-Sommerfeld equation [1], which was the central theme of transition theory for much of this century.

The stability analyses for the Orr-Sommerfeld equation generally concluded that the most dangerous instabilities were two-dimensional waves (Squire's theorem), that the critical Reynolds numbers for plane Poiseuille flow was ≈ 5772, and that Couette flow appeared to be stable for all Reynolds numbers. These conclusions are in poor agreement with experience for real flows, in which transition appears in both Poiseuille and Couette flows at a Reynolds number of about 1000. Furthermore, the growth rates predicted by the Orr-Sommerfeld theory are very small on the convective timescale of the flow [2], the latter being the timescale observed for the breakdown process, and the breakdown has a complex three-dimensional nature, in contrast to the two-dimensionality of the fastest-growing Orr-Sommerfeld modes at onset.

The crucial elements of the fast (convective timescale) transition are its nonlinear and three-dimensional characteristics. The Orr-Sommerfeld analysis for linear, two-dimensional disturbances to plane Poiseuille flow has been extended into the nonlinear regime by means of expansions in powers of the wave amplitude, and by direct simulations of the full nonlinear two-dimensional equations [2]. These analyses show that there exist steady finite-amplitude wave disturbances which can exist in the flow at Reynolds numbers much less than the critical value from linear theory. However, such flows (see Figure 1) are stable to two-dimensional disturbances, and it is necessary to take account of three-dimensional effects in order to explain the violent changes the flow suffers during transition.

Although the steady finite-amplitude waves are stable to two-dimensional disturbances, it turns out that they are strongly unstable (on a convective time scale) to three-dimensional perturbations [2]. This conclusion has been demonstrated by two distinct methods of analysis. First, the formal stability problem may be solved by finding the eigenvalue with largest real part of the Navier-Stokes equations linearized about the steady wave. Because of the two-dimensional, non-parallel nature of the basic flow for this *secondary instability* analysis, the stability matrix is often too large and unwieldy for application of the usual matrix eigenvalue routines. Special methods [3] have been developed for efficiently finding the most dangerous eigenmodes of systems like these. Results from this type of calculation are shown in Figure 2, which shows the maximum instability growth-rate as a function of the Reynolds number and the amplitude of the two-dimensional wave. The smallest Reynolds number at which there can exist a three-dimensional instability is seen to be slightly below 1000, which is in agreement with experimental observations of the point at which Poiseuille flow undergoes transition. The results of the eigenvalue analysis are corroborated [2] by performing a direct simulation of the full equations, using as initial conditions the two-dimensional wave 'seeded' with a very small amount of random three-dimensional noise. The disturbance rapidly becomes dominated by the fastest-growing mode, whose structure and growth- rate can be easily observed.

Because the three-dimensional instability grows on the convective rather than the viscous timescale, it seems likely that it is essentially an inviscid phenomenon, whose dynamics are only slightly affected by a small viscosity; in contrast, the Orr-Sommerfeld instability which has a viscous growth rate is essentially viscous. A theoretical understanding [6] of the phenomenon may be pursued by developing an inviscid stability theory analogous to the classical theory for plane, parallel shear flows. Although the stability problem is now much more complicated, the basic physical interpretations of the Rayleigh, Fjortoft, and Howard theorems as statements of momentum conservation, energy conservation, and phase-matching, respectively, remain valid. These theorems supply conditions on the flow that must be satisfied if an instability is to occur, and have important implications for the stability of complex three-dimensional helical flows (see Sec. 4) in addition to these two-dimensional waves.

Unlike the two-dimensional waves, the three-dimensional instability does not seem to saturate at some finite amplitude. Numerical studies [4] of the nonlinear evolution of the three-dimensional instability show that the flow quickly develops the characteristic one-spike structure that is typically observed in experiments [5] (see Figure 3). Subsequently, the flow becomes more and more disordered and, finally, turbulent.

The three dimensional instability is not just a characteristic of plane Poiseuille flow. Three-dimensional instabilities with the same general behavior are found in boundary layers, plane Couette flow, pipe flow, and even in free shear layers. The particular nature of three-dimensional secondary instability in free shear layers will be discussed in the next section.

3. Transition in Free Shear Flows

Inflectional free shear flows, like mixing layers and jets, are inviscidly unstable to two-dimensional disturbances. Squire's theorem implies that these instabilities are strongest when two-dimensional; when these two-dimensional instabilities evolve in time, they saturate into ordered laminar-flow states characterized by large-scale vortical flow structures. These vortical flows may themselves be unstable to subharmonic (pairing) instabilities, in which two (or more) vortices are paired and generate a new large-scale vortex motion [7].

We have found that the pairing process is *the* process that is responsible for positive transport coefficients (like eddy viscosity coefficients) in evolving two-dimensional shear flows [8]. In the direct numerical solution of the Navier-Stokes equations (using a spectral code), the periodicity length in the streamwise direction controls the number of allowed vortex pairings (*i.e.*, if the primary vortex has wavelength λ and the flow domain has periodicity length 4λ imposed on it, then just two vortex pairings are allowed). For a limited number of allowed pairings, the results show that the Reynolds stresses remain positive while the pairing process continues, but then, when pairing stops, the Reynolds stress changes sign and energy is transferred from the perturbation field back into the mean flow. Since the eddy viscosity, ν_{eddy}, is related to the Reynolds stress, $-u'\,v'$, by

$$-u'\,v' = \nu_{eddy}\frac{\partial \overline{U}}{\partial z}, \qquad (1)$$

it follows that the eddy viscosity is negative when pairing is artificially suppressed by the numerical boundary conditions.

Three dimensional secondary instability also occurs in free shear flows [9] but, in contrast to non-inflectional, inviscidly stable flows, this secondary instability no longer dominates the laminar instabilities. Indeed, the relative strength of pairing modes and the three-dimensional secondary modes depends strongly on the parameters of the flow [8]. However, the three-dimensional secondary instability is effective at much smaller spanwise scales than is the primary inviscid instability and seems to lead directly to chaos rather than ordered laminar flow states [8]. The secondary instability seems to persist to scales smaller by a factor of order $\sqrt{R}$ than the scale of the shear layer (which determines the scale of the shortest wavelength classical instability). It has also been found [8] that growth of the three-dimensional modes occurs mainly by energy transfer from the mean flow with the primary vortex acting as a 'catalyst', as in wall-bounded flows. The three-dimensional instability only disappears when viscous dissipation grows to balance transfer out of the mean flow (*i.e.*, at wavenumbers of order $\frac{1}{\sqrt{R}}$).

When pairing modes and secondary instability modes compete, the resulting flow evolution is quite sensitive to details of initial conditions. It has been shown [8] that when three-dimensional modes dominate pairing modes, the three-dimensional components grow to finite amplitude and lead to small-scale three-dimensional chaos. On the other hand, when pairing modes reach finite amplitudes, the positive transport coefficients they generate are so efficient at extracting energy from the mean flow that the growth of three-dimensional modes is suppressed. When pairing is stopped, the reversal of sign of the transport coefficients quickly leads to rapid growth of the three-dimensional small-scale secondary instabilities. This interaction process between Reynolds stresses and modal growth was first observed numerically and seems to provide an explanation of the experimentally observed tendency of certain free shear flows to remain essentially two-dimensional at large Reynolds numbers. A corollary of this analysis of free shear flow transition is that small scale mixing may be enhanced (suppressed) by suppression (enhancement) of pairing modes (*e.g.*, by action of suitable splitter plates in mixing layers).

As the three-dimensional modes achieve finite amplitude, they tend to form spiral flow structures. In Fig. 4, we show the region of large vorticity in an evolving mixing layer flow undergoing secondary instability. It is apparent that there are regions of large streamwise vorticity that connect large two dimensional primary vortex 'rollers'. The flow seems to tend to one in which the vorticity rotates from an orientation perpendicular to the flow direction in the primary vortex state to one in which the vorticity and velocity are nearly parallel in the finite-amplitude pre-turbulent flow. This result will be explored in Sec. 4.

4. Coherent Structures and Turbulence

In this section, we shall discuss some recent ideas on the description and dynamics of organized flow structures in turbulent flows. Results are taken exclusively from recent high resolution, numerical simulations [10,11] in which detailed pictures of complete flow fields are possible.

It is believed that if coherent structures exist in turbulent flows, they will be helical in structure [12,13]. Indeed, for a structure to exist for a reasonable amount of time it must retain a large portion of its energy. The term responsible for the cascade of energy into higher wavenumbers (dissipation) is $v \times \omega$ which is at a relative minimum when v and ω are aligned. Hence it is reasonable to expect that the structure will be helical in nature. Furthermore, the normalized helicity density, $v \cdot \omega / (|v| |\omega|)$, which is the cosine of the angle θ between v and ω, should be useful in locating coherent structures.

A helical coherent structure will not participate in the dynamical energy cascade. This may be one of the main reasons for the anisotropy of large scale motions as well as for departures from the Kolmogorov spectrum in the inertial-range. Regions where there are fluctuations of the helicity density ($v \cdot \omega$) should have high levels of small-scale intermittency.

Numerical experiments [11,14] have been conducted to investigate these ideas on the role of helicity fluctuations. The two problems considered were the evolution of turbulent channel flow and the Taylor-Green (TG) vortex flow [10]. For the channel flow data was examined after the flow had reached a statistically steady state at a Reynolds number of 6000; for the Taylor-Green vortex flow data was collected at R $=1500$ when the dissipation range was well developed.

In a single realization, at a single time, the non-normalized probability density of the normalized helicity density $P(\cos\theta)$ is shown in Figure 5. In Figures 5a and b, conditional sampling in regions were the dissipation was greater than 30% of the maximum was done for the channel and Taylor-Green vortex flow respectively. An essentially flat distribution suggests that there is no preferential arrangement of angle. However, Figures 5c and d show the probability for the conditionally sampled regions where dissipation is less than 5% of the maximum; there is a strong probability of v and ω being aligned. The helical structures exist where the dissipation is low.

Along with the numerical evidence for the presence of helical structures, there is the result [15,16] that purports to show that there exist a large variety of steady, helical Euler flows with chaotic streamlines. These flows are Beltrami or force-free flows with their vorticity parallel to their velocity fields. More precisely, for any given streamline topology, there is a steady (possibly singular) Euler flow with the same topology. The argument is to consider a perfectly conducting, viscously dissipating magneto-hydrodynamic flow with zero initial velocity field and with the initial magnetic field chosen to have the same field line topology as the required streamline topology. As $t \to \infty$, this flow settles down to a motionless state in which $(\nabla \times B) \times B = \nabla p$ -- identifying v with B and ω with $\nabla \times B$ gives the required steady Euler flow.

Recently, it has been argued [6] that, as a consequence of the streamlines being chaotic, there are regions of the flow that are dynamically stable to inviscid disturbances. Thus it is thought that an initial helical structure will break up in the regions where there are unstable (periodic) streamlines but in the regions where the streamlines are chaotic, the helical structure will persist. These inviscidly stable regions of chaotic streamlines are probably typically unstable to viscous disturbances.

In order to gain further understanding of the basic physics of the generation of small-scale turbulent flow features, the TG vortex is a nice model. This flow is that which develops in time from initial conditions that consist of excitation in basically a single Fourier mode. Because of nonlinear interaction, the flow becomes strongly three-dimensional and develops excitation at all spatial scales. The TG vortex has been used to study such fundamental questions as the enhancement of vorticity by vortex line stretching, the approach to isotropy of the small scales, possible singular behavior of the Euler equations, formation of an inertial range and analysis of the geometry and intermittency of high-vorticity regions. The TG flow is advantageous for these studies because its special symmetry has allowed the development of numerical algorithms that are a factor 64 more efficient in both memory and storage than conventional periodic-geometry spectral methods. For a three-dimensional flow, this factor 64 translates into a factor 4 increased range of spatial scales -- it is now possible to compute the TG vortex flow with 512^3 Fourier modes for each velocity component (or more than $4 \cdot 10^8$ effective degrees of freedom!).

One of the more exciting results to emerge from our studies of the TG flow is the suggestion that viscosity may play an essential role in the development of small-scale turbulence and not just play a role in the dissipation of turbulent kinetic energy. Indeed, we find that the development of the turbulent flow seems to require viscosity to induce instabilities of vortical structures in which the initial large-scale nonturbulent vorticity undergoes an explosive redistribution in space(see Figure 6). These viscosity-induced instabilities are probably effective because viscosity allows vortex line reconnections prohibited in inviscid flow. Further study of viscosity-induced instabilities should clarify the development of intermittent flow structures in turbulence.

5. Two-dimensional turbulence

Two-dimensional turbulence is a good testing ground for ideas on turbulence, first because it is unlikely to be more complicated than three-dimensional turbulence, and secondly because two-dimensional turbulence is likely to be approximately realized in many flows of geophysical importance. In addition, computations can be performed with higher resolution on flows in two dimensions than in three, so that numerical experiments can be used to discriminate between different theoretical turbulence models.

Two models which have been in apparent conflict for a number of years are the Batchelor–Kraichnan and the Saffman models for the high wavenumber behavior of the energy spectrum in fully-developed two-dimensional turbulence. Batchelor [17] and Kraichnan [18] independently proposed that the high wavenumber behavior of the spectrum would be governed by a cascade of the enstrophy, which is an inviscidly conserved quantity, to the smallest scales, where it would be dissipated viscously. Assuming that the enstrophy dissipation rate tends to a constant value as the Reynolds number goes to infinity, dimensional analysis gives a Kolmogorov-type power-law decay for the energy spectrum $E(k)$, which goes like k^{-3} as $k\to\infty$.

Shortly afterward, Saffman [19] argued that there was no particular reason why the enstrophy should cascade to the smallest scales, and proposed that viscosity would have very little effect on the structure of the flow. Instead, the large-scale flow would advect smaller-scale regions around the flow domain, and bring regions of different vorticity into close proximity. The resulting flow would have large regions of smooth vorticity distribution separated by comparatively narrow viscous layers across which the vorticity would jump abruptly. Geometric considerations then imply that the high- wavenumber spectrum has the form $E(k)\approx k^{-4}$ as $k\to\infty$ within the inertial range.

For a decade or so, there was no atmospheric data of sufficient quality, nor numerical simulations with enough resolution, to resolve the debate between the two theories. Recently, however, Brachet et al [20] extended earlier computations [21] that showed a tendency for the Saffman theory to be correct at relatively low Reynolds numbers and for the Batchelor-Kraichnan ideas to hold at high Reynolds numbers. Brachet et al [20] performed very-high resolution integrations of the Navier-Stokes equations at high R using random initial conditions for the velocity field and concluded that both Saffman and Batchelor-Kraichnan are correct, each for part of the time.

Saffman's argument is correct for relatively short times after the initiation of the computation. Figure 7a shows the early-time evolution of the flow. Notice the relative motion of regions of piecewise smooth vorticity; at these times the energy spectrum has the k^{-4} form (see Figure 8). However, these regions retain their identity only for rather a short time as the flow evolves. The viscous layers separating different regions are rapidly stretched and contorted by the large-scale straining motion of the flow, and quickly develop a highly convoluted structure. At roughly the same time as the convolutions develop, the energy spectrum switches from k^{-4} asymptotic behavior to the Batchelor-Kraichnan k^{-3} form (see Figure 8). After the switch to the k^{-3} spectrum, the flow reaches an approximate dynamical equilibrium in which the vorticity contours are continually being stretched, convoluted, and reconnected by the large-scale motion with the small viscosity playing an essential role in the reconnection process (see Figure 7b).

6. RNG Transport Models of Turbulence

For the engineering design of aerodynamical and hydrodynamical shapes in turbulent shear flows, it is currently impractical, even on the most advanced available supercomputers, to solve the full Navier-Stokes without approximation at large R. Because of the enormous range of scales in turbulent flows, the complete simulation of the turbulent flow would be extremely costly if not impossible even for one realization. For this reason, engineering calculations of these flows are done, and probably will be done for some time, using Reynolds-averaged Navier-Stokes equations (or some modification of these equations) with a turbulence model. The nature of the turbulence model is crucial to the success of these calculations. It is particularly important to have transport models that work well in the wall regions of the flow.

Recently, we have used dynamic renormalization group (RNG) methods to treat this problem [22]. The idea of the infrared RNG method is to use perturbation techniques similar to those used in the direct-interaction approximation [23] to eliminate all spatial scales smaller than the large eddies of the Navier-Stokes equations. This is done perturbatively by eliminating narrow bands of wavenumbers from the dynamics, rescaling the resulting equations into the form of a k-ε transport model, and then repeating the process iteratively until all the required scales are removed.

The key approximations made in this procedure are as follows:

1. While the perturbation expansion is asymptotically exact for the elimination of an infinitesimally narrow band of wavenumbers at the ultraviolet end of the spectrum, it is not exact when iterated an infinite number of times to remove a finite band of wavenumbers. We neglect this iteration error (mostly on the grounds that similar types of approximations work well on other kinds of hard physics problems!).

2. The flow is assumed to be locally homogeneous and isotropic in pursuing the perturbation theory. In the neighborhood of walls, this restricts one to eliminating only those degrees of freedom small compared to the distance from the wall and the large eddies of the flow. It is also assumed that the retained wavenumbers and frequencies are negligible compared to those in the eliminated band so that suitable markovianization of the equations can be made.

Once these approximations are justified (or believed on the basis that they seem to give results that compare favorably with observations), it is possible to derive RNG closures for a variety of turbulence problems. If only those scales smaller than a finite-difference (or spectral) grid scale are removed by the RNG procedure, then one obtains a large-eddy simulation model. The RNG large-eddy model has the advantages that it has built-in wall function behavior without making additional *ad hoc* approximations and that it generates a random force that drives the turbulence through its action in the buffer layer. If one applies the RNG procedure to multi-phase or chemically reacting flows [22], one obtains new forms of closure approximations that seem to fit well available data without further adjustment. Since data acquisition can be very difficult for these turbulent flows, the RNG procedure seems to have much appeal.

As an example of the RNG results, we give the equations here for the RNG form of the k-ε equations for pure kinetic turbulence. The resulting equations are:

$$\frac{Dk}{Dt} = \frac{\nu-1}{\nu}\left(\frac{\partial u}{\partial y}\right)^2 - \bar{\epsilon} + \frac{\partial}{\partial y}\left(\alpha\nu\frac{\partial k}{\partial y}\right) \qquad (2)$$

$$\frac{D\bar{\epsilon}}{Dt} = a\frac{\nu-1}{\nu}\left(\frac{\partial u}{\partial y}\right)^2 - Y + \frac{\partial}{\partial y}\left(\alpha\nu\frac{\partial \bar{\epsilon}}{\partial y}\right) \qquad (3)$$

$$\frac{\nu d\nu}{(\nu^3+C-1)^{1/2}} = \frac{1}{1.59}d\left(\frac{k}{\sqrt{\epsilon}}\right), \quad (C\approx 100) \qquad (4)$$

$$d\left(\frac{a}{\sqrt{\epsilon}}\right) = -0.2122\frac{d\nu}{(\nu^3+C-1)^{1/2}} \qquad (5)$$

$$d\left(\frac{Y}{\epsilon^{3/2}}\right) = -0.3246 \frac{d\nu}{(\nu^3+C-1)^{1/2}} \quad (6)$$

$$\left|\frac{\alpha-1.2627}{0.2627}\right|^{0.6418} \left|\frac{\alpha+2.2627}{3.2627}\right|^{0.3582} = \frac{\nu_0}{\nu} \quad (7)$$

Some key results from these equations (in which the constants that appear are basically geometrical in character and *not* free parameters) are that the von Karman constant is 0.42 and the normalized turbulent kinetic energy level is $1/\sqrt{0.0989}$.

Finally, to illustrate the application of the RNG method to problems with complex physics, we give some results for buoyantly driven convective shear flows. The key change from the above equations is that there is an inverse turbulent Prandtl number, $\alpha_{eddy} = \frac{\kappa_{eddy}}{\nu_{eddy}}$, determined by the relation

$$\left|\frac{\alpha_{eddy}-1.2627}{\alpha_0-1.2627}\right|^{0.6418} \left|\frac{\alpha_{eddy}+2.2627}{\alpha_0+2.2627}\right|^{0.3582} = \frac{\nu_0}{\nu_{eddy}} \quad (8)$$

where subscripts 0 indicate laminar quantities. In a fully turbulent region, the *inverse* turbulent Prandtl number is asymptotically 1.2627, in good agreement with the Reynolds-Colburn analogy. Another key feature of the RNG method for buoyant flows is that there is a modified buoyancy force; asymptotically, in fully turbulent unstable regions, the RNG correction to the buoyancy force is to reduce it by a factor 0.27 from its laminar value. This feature is due to small-scale turbulent mixing.

The resulting equations lead to impressive results for buoyant flows. In Fig. 9, we plot the scaled velocity profile in stratified shear flow, for both stable and unstable stratification, for the RNG transport approximation compared with experimental data. Then, in Fig. 10, we plot the heat transport as a function of Rayleigh number in Benard convection for the RNG transport model and for the experimental data of Krishnamurti.

Acknowledgements

This work was supported by the Air Force Office of Scientific Research under Contract F49620-85-C-0026, the Office of Naval Research under Contracts N00014-82-C-0451, N00014-83-K-0227, and N00014-85-K-0201 and by the Atmospheric Sciences and Mechanical Engineering Programs of the National Science Foundation. Computations reported here were performed on the Cray 1 computers at the National Center for Atmospheric Research which is sponsored by the National Science Foundation.

References

[1] Drazin, P.G., Reid, W.H. Hydrodynamic stability, Cambridge University Press, Cambridge 1981.

[2] Details and other references are given in Orszag, S.A., Patera, A.T., J. Fluid Mech., **128** (1983), 347.

[3] Goldhirsch, I., Orszag, S.A. An efficient method for computing the leading eigenvalues and eigenvectors of large asymmetric matrices, to be published (1986).

[4] Kleiser, L., Schumann, U. Laminar-turbulent transition process in plane Poiseuille flow, in <u>Proceedings of the Symposium in Spectral Methods</u> (Philadelphia, PA, 1984), 141.

[5] Nishioka, M., Iida, S., Kanbayashi, S. An experimental investigation of the subcritical instability in plane Poiseuille flow, in <u>Proceedings of the 10th Turbulence Symposium</u> (Tokyo, 1978), 55.

[6] Bayly, B.J. Kinematic and dynamical properties of complex three-dimensional flows, Ph.D. thesis, Princeton University (1986).

[7] Patnaik, P.C., Sherman, F.S., Corcos, G.M., J. Fluid Mech., **73** (1982), 215.

[8] Metcalfe, R., Orszag, S.A., Brachet, M.E., Menon, S., Riley, J. Secondary Instability of Free Shear Flows, submitted to J. Fluid Mech..

[9] Pierrehumbert, R.T., Widnall, S.E., J. Fluid Mech., **114** (1982), 59.

[10] Brachet, M.E., Meiron, D.I., Orszag, S.A., Nickel, B.G., Morf, R.H., Frisch, U., J. Fluid Mech., **130** (1982), 411-452.

[11] Pelz, R.B., Yakhot, V., Orszag, S.A., Shtilman, L., Levich, E. Velocity-Vorticity Patterns in Turbulent Flow, Phys. Rev. Lett., **54** (1985), 2505.

[12] Levich, E., Tsinober, A. On the role of helical structures in three-dimensional turbulent flow, Phys. Lett., **93A** (1983), 293-297.

[13] Tsinober, A., Levich, E. On the helical nature of three-dimensional coherent structures in turbulent flows, Phys. Lett., **99A** (1983), 321-324.

[14] Shtilman, L., Levich, E., Orszag, S.A., Pelz, R.B., Tsinober, A. On the role of helicity in complex fluid flows, Phys. Lett., **113A** (1985) 32-37.

[15] Arnold, V.I. The asymptotic Hopf invariant and its application, in <u>Proceedings of Summer School in Differential Equations</u>, Erevan Armenian SSR Academy of Sciences, (1974).

[16] Moffatt, H.K. Magnetostatic equilibria in viscous, perfectly conducting fluid and analogous Euler flows of an incompressible fluid: I. Fundamentals, J. Fluid Mech., **159** (1985) 359-478.

[17] Batchelor, G.K. Phys. Fluids **12** (1969), 233.

[18] Kraichnan, R.H. Phys. Fluids **10** (1967), 1417.

[19] Saffman, P.G. Studies in Applied Math., **50** (1971), 377.

[20] Brachet, M.E., Sulem, P.L. Free decay of high Reynolds number, two-dimensional turbulence, in Ninth International Conference on Numerical Methods in Fluid Mechanics, Lecture Notes in Physics, **218** Springer (1985), 103.

[21] Orszag, S.A. in Fifth International Conference on Numerical Methods in Fluid Dynamics, Lecture Notes in Physics, 59, Springer (1977), 32.

[22] Yakhot, V., Orszag, S.A. Renormalization group analysis of turbulence I. Basic theory, J. Sci. Comp., 1 (1986) 1.

[23] Kraichnan, R.H., J. Fluid Mech., 5 (1959), 497.

Figure 1 : Streamlines of the steady (stable) finite-amplitude two-dimensional traveling wave for plane Poiseuille flow at R=4000, plotted in the rest frame of the wave (from ref. [2]).

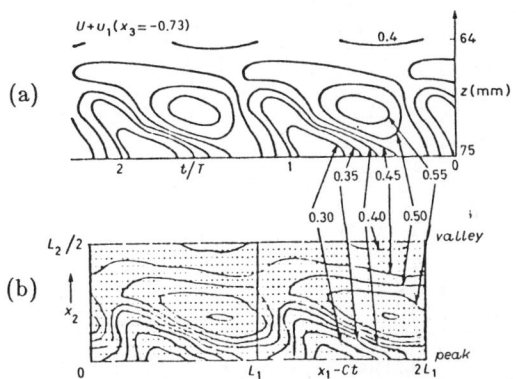

Figure 3 : Contours of x velocity in the (x,y)-plane at the one-spike stage in the laboratory experiments of Nishioka *et al.* (a) and in the numerical simulation of Kleiser and Schumann (b) [from ref. 4].

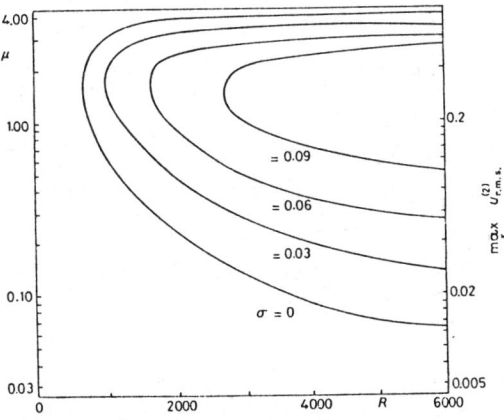

Figure 2 : Contours of constant growth rate (labelled by growth rate) as a function of R and the amplitude of the background two-dimensional nonlinear wave (see right-hand scale) (from ref. [8]).

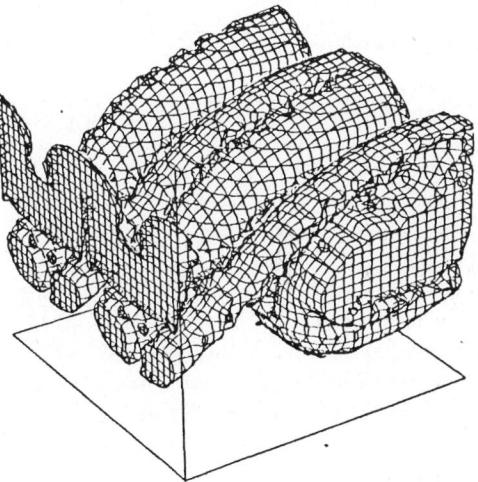

Figure 4 : A plot of the region of large vorticity in the secondary instability of a mixing layer flow (from ref. [8]). The ribs connecting the large rollers are regions of significant streamwise vorticity in which ω is nearly aligned with v.

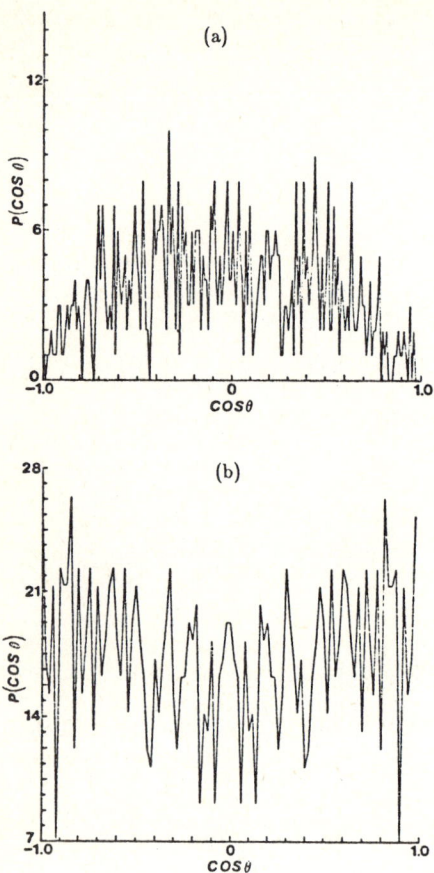

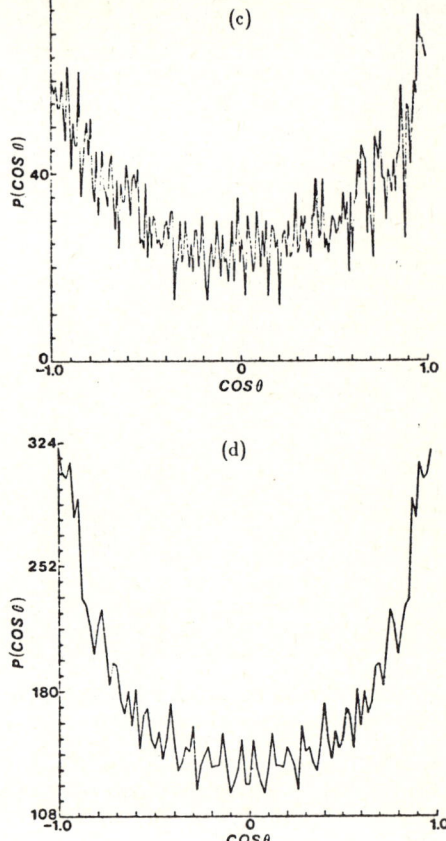

Figure 5 : The probability density for the distribution of the angle between velocity v and vorticity ω conditionally sampled in the region where dissipation is (a) greater than 30% of its maximum value in the outer part of the channel ($15 < z_+ < 100$); (b) greater than 30% of its maximum value in the Taylor-Green vortex at t=8.6. (c) less than 5% of its maximum value in the outer part of the channel ($15 < z_+ < 100$); (d) less than 5% of its maximum value in the Taylor-Green vortex at t=8.6 (from ref. [11]).

Figure 6 : A plot of the distribution of large-vorticity regions in the TG vortex flow as a function of time t and distance d away from the side-walls of the impermeable cube in which the flow takes

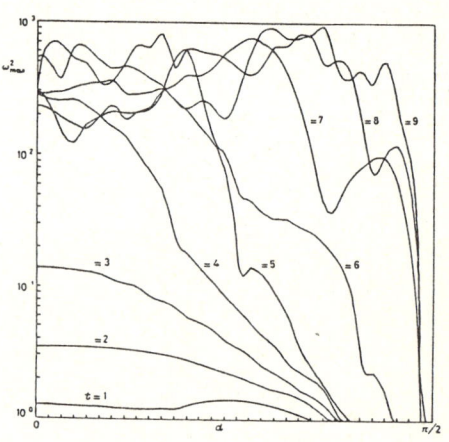

place. Observe how vorticity explodes in towards the center of the cube between t=4 and t=8 (from ref. [10]).

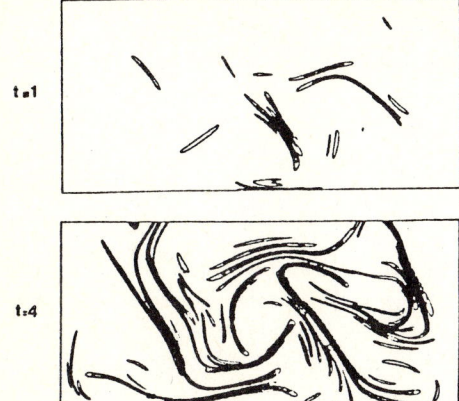

Figure 7 : Contours of squared vorticity gradient in a high resolution, two-dimensional turbulence run (from ref. [18]). Notice that at t=1 the vortex gradient sheets are well separated from each other in contrast to t=4 when they are much more densely packed.

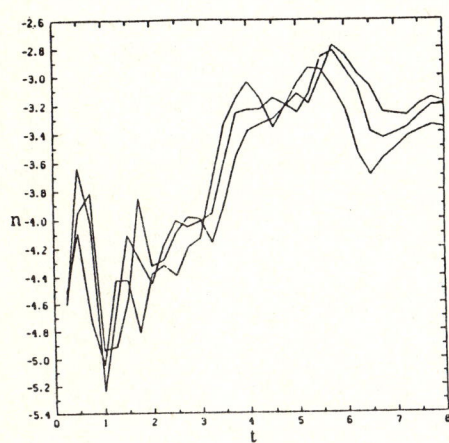

Figure 8 : The best fit to the inertial exponent, n, as a function of time for a high R, two-dimensional turbulence run (from ref. [18]). These results were obtained from a 1024^2 spectral code, fitting the results of the form $E(k) = ck^n e^{\beta k}$. The k^{-4} regime occurs near t=1 when the inertial exponential flattening of the vortex gradient sheets is started by viscous effects.

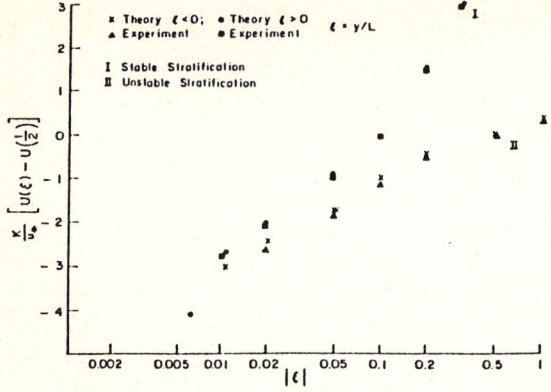

Figure 9 : A comparison between the RNG transport model predictions and experiment for the mean velocity profile in a stratified boundary layer for both stable and unstable stratification. Here the flow variables are scaled using Monin-Obukhov scaling.

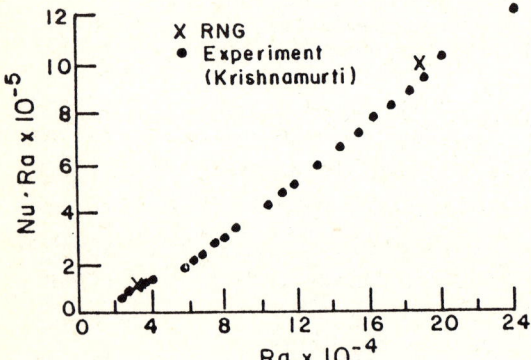

Figure 10 : A comparison between the RNG prediction and experiment for the heat flux in a Benard convection.

BOOTSTRAPPING IN TURBULENCE COMPUTATION

Joel H. Ferziger
Department of Mechanical Engineering
Stanford University
Stanford, CA USA 94305

I. Introduction

Classification schemes for methods for predicting turbulent flows were presented by Kline et al. (1978) and Ferziger et al. (1981); this scheme is given in Table 1. At each level in the scheme, a single method or model is more broadly applicable than a method at the preceding levels. This allows data for one flow to be used to predict other flows, an advantage of obvious importance. The primary disadvantage of the higher levels is that they cost more than the preceding levels; the data required to fix a model or correlation is also more difficult to acquire.

Table 1
Approaches to Turbulent Flow Prediction

1. Correlations
2. Integral Methods
3. One Point Closures
4. Two Point Closures
5. Large Eddy Simulation
6. Full Turbuence Simulation

The ability of a method to compute more detail and a wider range of flows allows it to produce data required to test models at lower levels. Indeed, working engineers often use simulations made with sophisticated turbulence models to construct correlations for optimizing designs; it is not unusual for engineers to move up and down through the levels (and from computation to experiment) in the design process.

The main goal of this paper is to demonstrate that it is now possible to use full turbulence simulations (FTS) to study models for large eddy simulation (LES) and to use both of these methods to test and develop one point closure turbulence models. This bootstrapping procedure makes it possible, at least in principle, to use turbulence simulations to predict turbulent flows without reference to experimental data; this procedure is not recommended but the possibility is interesting.

II. Full and Large Eddy Simulation

We begin with short descriptions of the methods. Full turbulence simulation is simply the numerical solution of the Navier-Stokes equations for the complete details of a turbulent flow; such simulations are necessarily three-dimensional and time-dependent. Large eddy simulation, which is also three-dimensional and time-dependent, explicitly simulates only the largest eddies; the small eddies are modeled. Both FTS and LES are currently too expensive to be widely used as engineering design tools. However, a few pioneering applications to high Reynolds number flows have been made recently [Kawamura and Kuwahara, 1983, 1985; Murakami et al., 1985]. These are similar to meteorological simulations in that only the small fraction of the turbulence energy residing in the very largest eddies is resolved. More commonly, FTS and LES are used as adjuncts to experiments for studying the physics of turbulent flows and testing turbulence models.

The output of a simulation is an enormous database containing all three velocity components and the pressure at as many as two million points at, perhaps, several thousand instants of time. These data contain more spatial detail than typical experimental data. However, the time simulated is typically no more than a few seconds and, even with the large number of spatial points, the Reynolds number range for which simulations can be made is severely restricted. Experimentalists are not as severely limited. Each generation of new computers may provide an order of magnitude more speed and memory but this yields only a factor of two increase in the Reynolds number.

In the choice between FTS and LES, FTS ought to be used whenever possible because it is essentially exact. LES must be used in cases for which FTS is not practical.

Since FTS is not directly applicable to flows of engineering interest (and will not be in the foreseeable future), the best use to which it can be put is one suggested above--testing and developing engineering turbulence models. This paper is directed at demonstrating how this can be achieved and describing what has been accomplished.

We now describe the bootstrapping process for a particular case, the flow between parallel plates (plane channel flow). It is now possible to fully simulate this flow at Reynolds numbers up to 5000, a low value by engineering standards. Accepting the results as valid data, we can use them to develop subgrid scale models for LES. With such models, it is possible to apply LES at Reynolds numbers an order of magnitude higher. One can increase the available Reynolds number range by yet another order of magnitude by developing model boundary conditions to represent the wall region. Empirical boundary conditions of this kind were used by Deardorff (1970) and Schumann (1973). FTS data can be used to put the models on a firmer footing; this program is being attempted; cf. Piomelli and Ferziger (1986).

The remainder of this paper will give two examples. The first demonstrates the application of FTS to the determination of models for LES. The second uses FTS to test and develop one point closure models.

III. Subgrid Scale Models and their Testing

A number of SGS models are based on Reynolds averaged turbulence models. The simplest of these is an adaptation of the commonly used mixing length model. It was given by Smagorinsky (1963):

$$\tau_{ij} = (c_s \Delta)^2 |S| S_{ij} \tag{1}$$

Here τ_{ij} is the subgrid scale Reynolds stress tensor, S_{ij} is the strain in the large-scale field:

$$S_{ij} = \frac{1}{2} \left(\frac{\partial \bar{u}_i}{\partial x_j} + \frac{\partial \bar{u}_j}{\partial x_i} \right) , \tag{2}$$

$|S| = (2 S_{ij} S_{ij})^{1/2}$ and Δ is the width of the filter defining the resolved scales. In contrast to the Reynolds averaged equations, LES does not require a model for the length scale.

As we shall see, Smagorinsky's model does not match the subgrid scale Reynolds stress distribution very accurately. For this reason, Bardina et al. (1981) proposed a scale similarity model based on the notion that the most important interactions between the large and small eddies involve those closest to the cutoff on either side. This model is:

$$\tau_{ij} = \overline{\bar{u}_i \bar{u}_j} - \bar{\bar{u}}_i \bar{\bar{u}}_j \tag{3}$$

where the bar indicates a filtered variable. This model matches the distribution of the subgrid scale Reynolds stress much more accurately than Smagorinsky's model but does not dissipate much kinetic energy. For this reason, Bardina et al. suggested that it be combined with Smagorinsky's model.

Finally, we note that Kawamura and Kuwahara (1983, 1985) have performed what they call full simulations of flows about airfoils and cylinders, achieving rather interesting results. These calculations used a third-order upwind finite difference method for the convective terms. They cannot be true full simulations because they do not resolve all the details of these flows. However, this work can be given another interpretation: that it is actually large eddy simulation with a fourth-order eddy viscosity subgrid scale model implicitly provided by the truncation error of the finite difference approximation. Use of finite difference error as an implicit subgrid scale model has been used earlier [Deardorff, 1970; Shaanan et al., 1975].

These results suggest consideration of a fourth-order eddy viscosity as a subgrid scale model. Further justification for this idea is provided by the theoretical demonstration (for isotropic turbulence) by Chollet (1983) that a fourth-order dissipation subgrid scale model is preferable to the second-order Smagorinsky model, by the successful application of this model to homogeneous flows by Bertoglio and Mathieu (1983) and by the successful application of fourth-order dissipation models in aerodynamic calculations. Further testing of this idea is required.

Now let us turn to the testing of subgrid scale models. Suppose that a flow has been fully simulated on a fine grid and that we wish to large eddy simulate the same flow on a coarser grid. The filtered velocity field that is the goal of the LES can be obtained by filtering the FTS results, while the subgrid scale field is obtained by simple subtraction. All quantities that need to be modeled in the LES can be computed exactly. Since the models compute the SGS Reynolds stress from the filtered velocity field, we can also determine the model values of these quantities. Direct comparison of the model and exact quantities can be made.

An easy method of comparing the two sets of data is to plot them against each other in a scatter plot. A perfect model will yield a straight line through the origin whose slope provides the model constant. A scatter plot testing the Smagorinsky model is given in Fig. 1. The data are more or less randomly distributed about the origin, indicating that the model is poor; the correlation coefficient for this data is approximately 0.35, meaning that only ten percent of the data is predicted by the model. A similar plot for the Smagorinsky-scale similarity combination model is given in Fig. 2. The improvement is obvious; the correlation coefficient is now 0.76. Tests of this kind have bene performed by Clark et al. (1975) McMillan et al. (1981), and Piomelli and Ferziger (1986). The approach has been validated but more remains to be done.

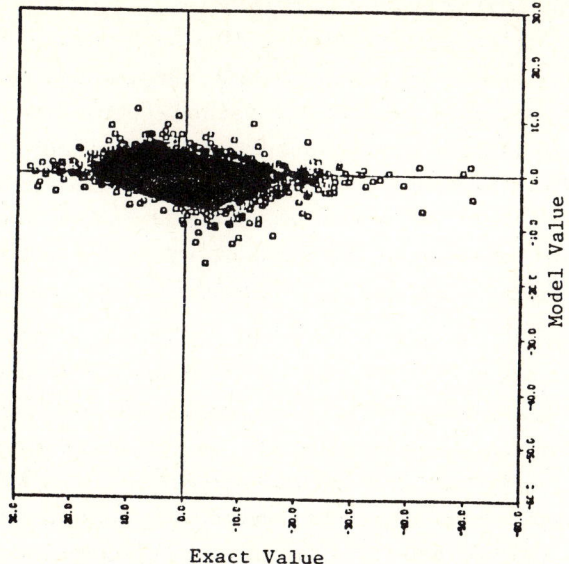

Fig. 1. Scatter plot of exact vs model subgrid scale Reynolds stress for the Smagorinsky model. From Bardina et al. (1981).

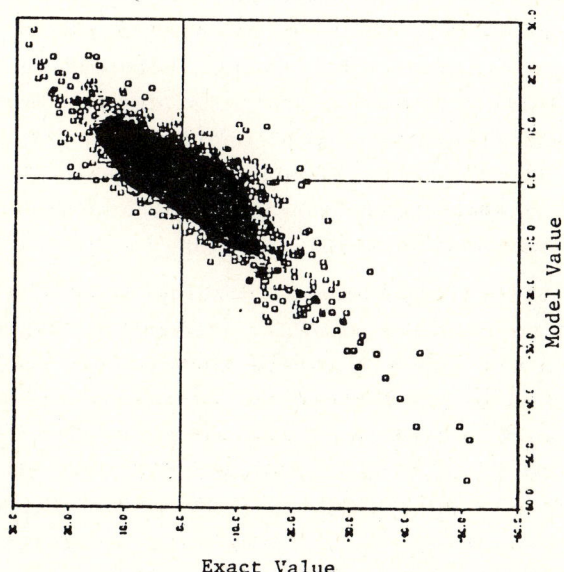

Fig. 2. Scatter plot of exact vs model subgrid scale Reynolds stress for the combined model. From Bardina et al. (1981).

IV. Tests of Reynolds-Averaged Models

As noted above, LES and FTS are too expensive for direct application as design tools. Integral methods were long the standard design tools and are still widely used. They are currently being replaced with the more flexible one point closure models, especially the two equation k-ε model. Reynolds stress models are receiving serious consideration for their ability to deal with the anisotropy of turbulence but require more computational time. At present, they are not often used in applications.

The k-ε model is capable of producing qualitative predictions of a wide range of flows but it is doubtful whether a single universal version of this model can deliver the accuracy needed in high technology applications. In the author's opinion, models tailored to particular zones of a flow (rather than to flows) will be required. To fix the parameters in models of such zonal models, a great deal of detailed data is required. Part of that need can be filled by FTS and LES.

Currently, FTS is best applied to homogeneous turbulent flows but it has been used to study channel and free shear flows. As homogeneous turbulence is also an excellent testing ground for Reynolds stress models, use of FTS for testing these models is a match of strengths. The unresolved issues are whether information gained at the low Reynolds numbers of the simulations can be applied at the higher Reynolds numbers encountered in applications flows and whether homogeneous and inhomogeneous flows can be treated with the same models. Nonetheless, the approach provides insight into the effects of extra strains on turbulence and its modeling.

Use of FTS of homogeneous turbulence for testing Reynolds stress models dates to the early 1970s. The number of papers devoted to this issue is now too large to allow coverage of all of them in a short section. We merely refer readers to the latest work in this area by Lee and Reynolds (1985) and the work of Wu et al. (1985) reviewed below. In nearly all of these cases, it was found that significant changes in the models were required. We shall use the compressed turbulence case of Wu et al. as an example in the next section; it is a fairly typical case.

V. An Example: Compressed Turbulence

Knowledge of the effects of compression on turbulence is needed for its application to internal combustion engine flows and shock-boundary layer interaction. Experimental data are difficult to obtain for this flow and the available data disagree on the whether the turbulence intensity increases or decreases as the fluid is compressed. The models disagree with respect to the constants.

In the cases of interest, the fluid is strongly compressed (up to 25:1) but the Mach numbers are small (< 0.1). This allows density fluctuations to be neglected and the flow may be treated as incompressible with an extra strain provided by the compression. Two cases were considered: isotropic and one-dimensional compression. As they are qualitatively similar, we shall present only the results for isotropic compression.

The turbulence intensity as a function of the total strain (essentially the linear compression of the flow) is given in Fig. 3 for various compression rates. For strong compression, which is well predicted by rapid distortion theory, the turbulence intensity increases as the fluid is compressed; in this case, each eddy is compressed and there is no time for eddy interactions or for viscosity to play a role. As the compression rate is decreased, the effects of nonlinear eddy interaction and viscosity become more important and act to reduce the intensity of the turbulence. The relative importance of these two effects, which is measured by the nondimensional ratio Sk/ϵ, where S is the strain (compression) rate, k the turbulent kinetic energy, and ϵ the dissipation rate of the turbulence, determines whether the turbulence intensity is amplified or diminished during the compression. It turns out that all the experiments are correct--they differ in the values of this parameter.

The integral (large) and Kolmogoroff (viscous or small) length scales of these flows are shown in Figs. 4 and 5, respectively. Under rapid compression, the integral scale decreases in proportion to the linear size of the fluid element; the Kolmogoroff scale decreases even more rapidly due to the effect of a decrease of the kinematic viscosity with the heating caused by the compression. When the compression rate is reduced, the effects of eddy interactions and viscosity act to increase the length scales and, the overall behavior is again determined principally by the parameter Sk/ϵ.

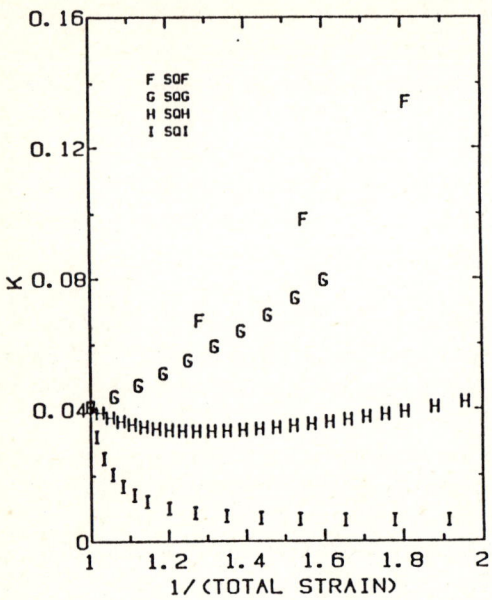

Fig. 3. Intensity vs total strain for turbulence undergoing isotropic compression. From Wu et al. (1985).

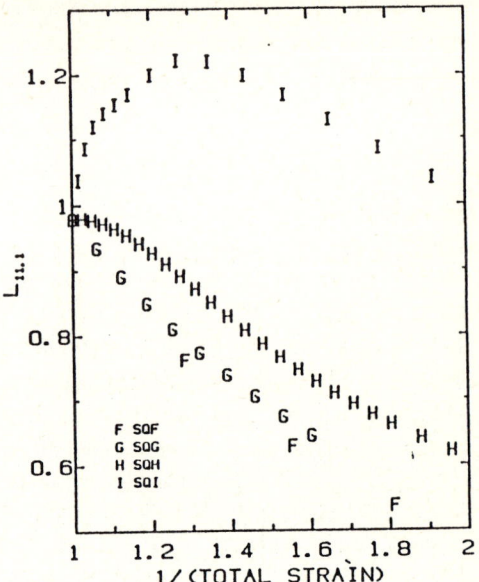

Fig. 4. Integral length scale vs inverse total strain in turbulence undergoing isotropic compression. From Wu et al. (1985).

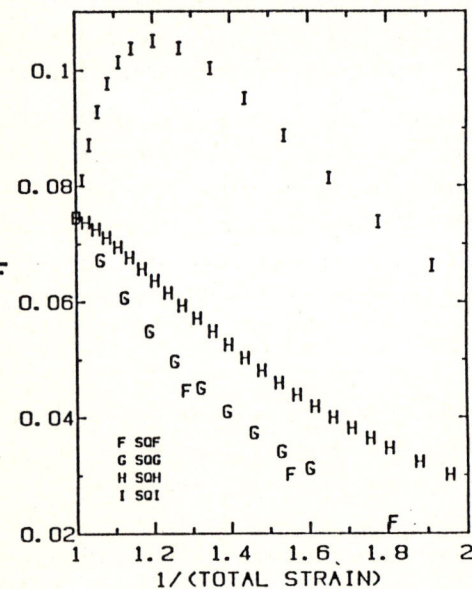

Fig. 5. Kolmogoroff length scale vs inverse total strain in turbulence undergoing isotropic compression. From Wu et al. (1985).

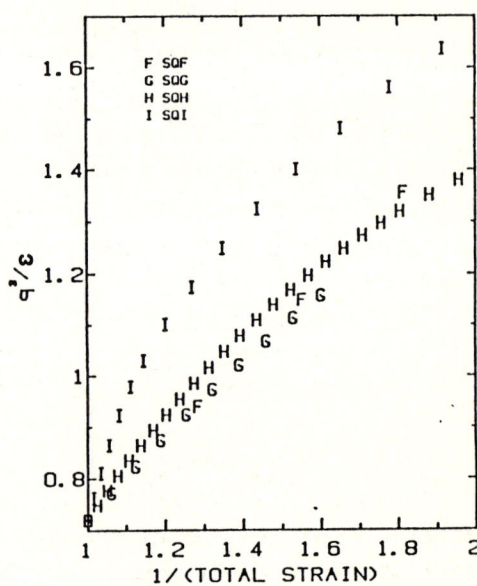

Fig. 6. Model length scale (q^3/ε) vs inverse total strain in turbulence undergoing isotropic compression. From Wu et al. (1985).

Now let us turn to the modeling of this flow. One of the most accepted concepts in turbulence theory is that the the length scale of the turbulence is related to the dissipation rate by:

$$L = q^3/\varepsilon \tag{4}$$

Using the data derived from the simulations, it is easy to test this relationship. q^3/ε is plotted against the total strain in Fig. 6. Comparing this with Fig. 4, we see that the relationship (4) is not valid in this flow for large Sk/ε. (In most flows this relationship holds quite well.) This may be a consequence of the change in viscosity under compression and the low Reynolds numbers of the simulated flows. However, no systematic variation of the ratio $q^3/\varepsilon L$ with Reynolds number was found in the results.

The dissipation, which is both the rate of destruction of turbulent kinetic energy and the determinor of the length scale in most turbulence models, cannot do both tasks simultaneously under strong compression. This explains the differences among the models: one model was adjusted to give the correct dissipation while the other was tuned to give the proper length scale.

Simulation results can thus explain the discrepancies among both the experimental results and the models. We now turn to the construction of a more accurate model for compressed flows. The evidence given above demonstrates that the two roles of the dissipation ought to be given to separate variables. Wu chose to introduce a time scale as the new parameter.

If the model is simply fit to the simulation data, we will have done little more than curve fitting. To avoid this, the following strategy was followed. The strain tensor for one-dimensional compression can be decomposed into an isotropic compression component and a component representing axisymmetric strain of the type produced in a diffuser:

$$\begin{pmatrix} S & & \\ & S & \\ & & S \end{pmatrix} = \begin{pmatrix} S/3 & & \\ & S/3 & \\ & & S/3 \end{pmatrix} + \begin{pmatrix} 2S/3 & & \\ & -S/3 & \\ & & -S/3 \end{pmatrix} \tag{5}$$

Models were constructed for each of the component flows in such a way that they could be combined to produce a model for the one-dimensional flow.

Construction of the model proceeded as follows. The dissipation equation was modified to include the new time scale, τ, and a differential equation for t was introduced. First, the decay of homogeneous isotropic turbulence was modeled. Since dτ/dt is dimensionless, it is a constant for isotropic turbulence at high enough Reynolds number. Tests showed this model to be unstable, so a stabilizing term was added. Next, appropriate terms were added to the dissipation and time scale equations and constants were selected to fit the FTS isotropic compression data. Finally, a similar treatment was applied to axisymmetric strain data supplied by Lee and Reynolds (1985). In this case, the Reynolds stress tensor is not isotropic and the usual k-ε model predicts an incorrect sudden rise in the anisotropy of the Reynolds stress when the strain is applied. To avoid this, it is necessary to introduce a Reynolds stress model (only one component is needed in this flow). For details of the model, see Wu et al. (1985).

The resulting model was applied to the prediction of the one-dimensional compression results. The results are shown in Fig. 7. As can be seen, the results are excellent. It is encouraging that the model could be built component by component. If this procedure can be applied to other flows, it will provide a systematic means of putting together models for complex flows.

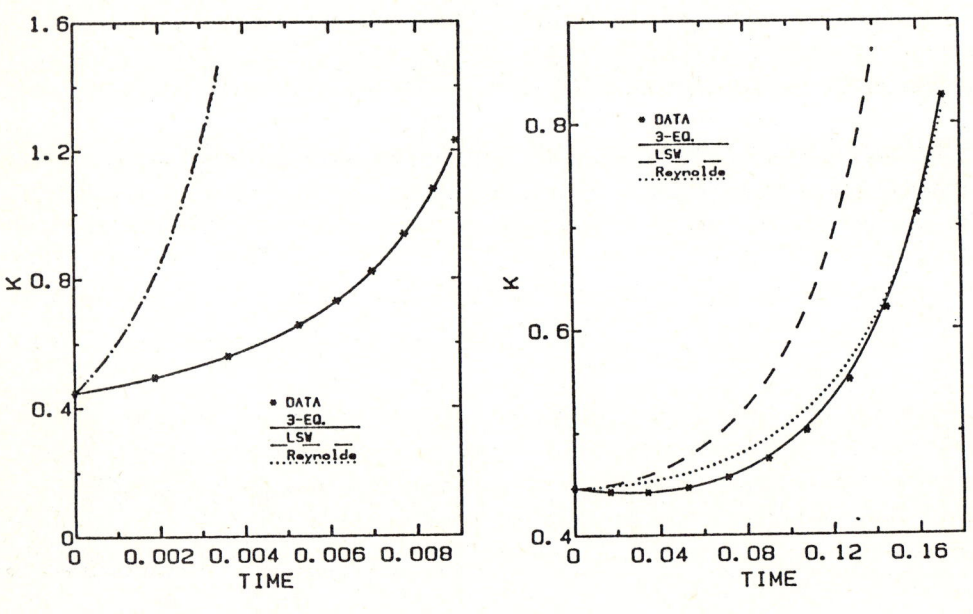

Fig. 7(a) Fig. 7(b)

Fig. 7. Turbulence intensity vs total strain according to the three equation model of Wu et al. (1985) for various values of Sk/ε. (a) 25, (b) 2.5, (c) 0.5, (d) 0.1.

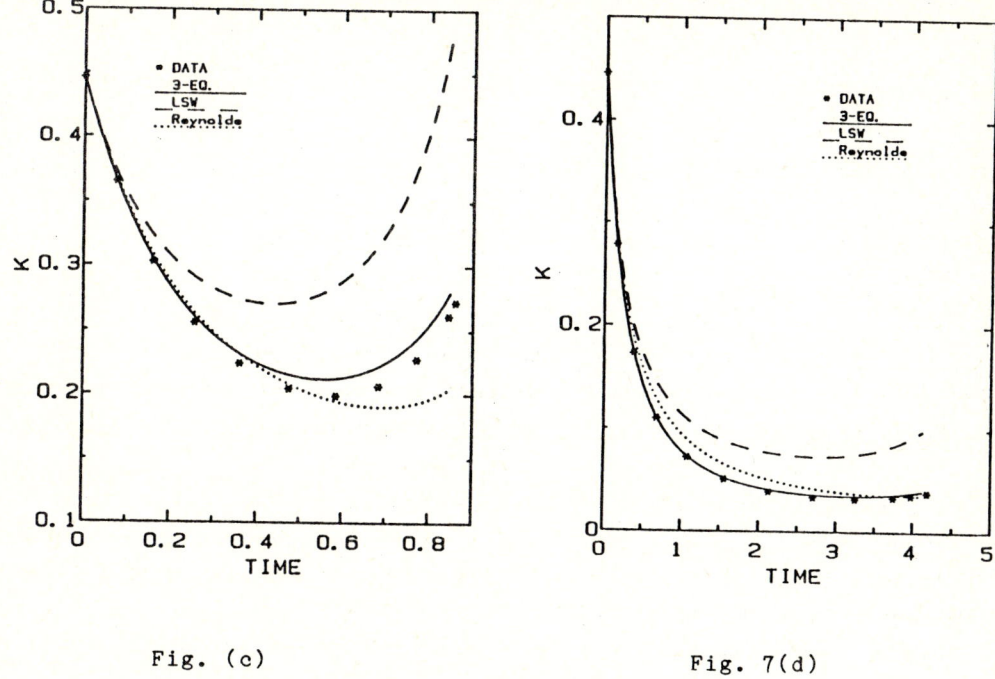

Fig. (c)   Fig. 7(d)

VI. Conclusion and Discussion

Turbulence is a complex nonlinear phenomenon for which exact governing equations and material properties are known. Consequently, given computers of large enough capacity, it should be possible to simulate any turbulent flow. The large range of scales in turbulent flows makes it unlikely that this will ever happen. In the absence of such computers, we are forced to use approximations--turbulence models.

Turbulence models can be thought of as sophisticated engineering correlations. Their construction relies on the accumulation of accurate data from either experiments or computer simulations of turbulent flows. Useful simulations can be done on computers smaller than those described in the preceding paragraph. Indeed, a bootstrapping process, which relies entirely on computer-generated data, is conceptually feasible. (Practicality is another matter.)

In this paper, we have shown how full simulations of simple flows at low Reynolds numbers can be used to create models for large eddy simulations which permit simulation of flows at still higher Reynolds numbers. Both FTS and LES can then be used to construct models used to simulate flows of engineering interest.

This approach is in its beginning stages. It would be foolish to suggest abandoning experimental work; the need for experiments will probably never disappear. However, we have reached a stage at which the two approaches complement each other. This suggests that a cooperative effort between laboratory and computer experimentalists can produce results beyond the capability of either; such efforts are beginning. It also suggests that laboratory experiments of the future will differ in kind from those done in the past.

Acknowledgments

The author wishes to thank a number of people who have helped in developing the ideas in this paper. Foremost among these are my colleagues Prof. W.C. Reynolds and S.J. Kline. Dr. C.T. Wu is responsible for most of the material in Chapter 5. A number of other students have helped in various ways; I especially want to mention K. L. Tzuoo, R. K. Avva, and U. Piomelli.

References

Bardina, J., Ferziger, J. H., and Reynolds, W. C., "Improved Subgrid Models for Large Eddy Simulation," AIAA paper 80-1357, 1980.

Bertoglio, J. P., and Mathieu, J., "Study of Subgrid Models for Sheared Turbulence," Proc. Fourth Symp. on Turb. Shear Flows, Karlsruhe, 1983.

Chollet, J. P., "Two Point Closures as a Subgrid Scale Modeling for Large Eddy Simulations," Proc. Fourth Symp. on Turb. Shear Flows, Karlsruhe, 1983.

Deardorff, J. W., "A Numerical Study of Three-Dimensional Turbulent Channel Flow at Large Reynolds Number," J. Fluid Mech., 41, 452, 1970.

Ferziger, J. H., Bardina, J., and Allen, G., "Overview of Taxonomy: Morphology of the Flows and Computational Methods," in Kline et al. (1981), Vol. 2.

Kawamura, T., and Kuwahara, K., "Computation of High Reynolds Number Flow around a Circular Cylinder with Surface Roughness," AIAA paper 84-0340, 1984.

Kawamura, T., and Kuwahara, K., "Direct Simulation of a Turbulent Inner Flow by a Finite Difference Method," AIAA paper 85-0376, 1985.

Kline, S. J., Ferziger, J. H., and Johnston, J. P., "Turbulent Flow Computation--Status and Ten Year Outlook," J. Fluids Engr., 1978.

Lee, M. J. and Reynolds, W .C., "Simulation of Homogeneous Turbulence and its Application to Turbulence Modeling," Rept. TF-22, Dept. of Mech. Engr., Stanford Univ., 1985.

McMillan, O. J. and Ferziger, J. H., "Tests of New Subgrid Scale Models in Strained Turbulence," AIAA paper 80-1339, 1980.

Murakami, S., Mochida, A., and Hibi, K., "Numerical Simulation of Air Flow Around Cubic Model," Proc. Intl. Symp. Comp. Fluid Dyn.,

Tokyo, p. 728, 1985.
Piomelli, U., and Ferziger, J. H., "Subgrid Scale Models for Channel Flow Simulation," AIAA paper 86, 1986.
Schumann, U., "Ein Untersuchung über der Berechnung der Turbulent Strömungen im Platten- und Ringspalt-Kanelen," Dissertation, Karlsruhe, 1973.
Smagorinsky, J., "General Circulation Experiments with the Primitive Equations. I. The Basic Experiment," Mon. Wea. Rev., **91**, 99, 1963.
Wu, C. T., Ferziger, J. H. and Chapman, D. R., "Simulation and Modeling of Compressed Turbulence," Rept. TF-21, Dept. of Mech. Engr., Stanford Univ., 1985.

Development of High-Reynolds-Number-Flow Computaion

Kunio KUWAHARA
The Institute of Space and Astronautical Science
Komaba, Meguro-ku, Tokyo, Japan

Introduction

Finite-difference computaion of the Navier-Stokes equations has a long history. One of the earliest work was done by M. Kawaguti[1] by using mechanical hand calculator in the early fifties. He computed a steady flow around a circular cylinder at Reynolds number 40 (Fig.1). He says in his paper "the nummerical integration in this study took about one year and a half with twenty working hours every week, with a considerable amount of labor and endurance". With the appearance and development of electronic computers, this type of computation became easier and easier. However, the high-Reynolds-number-flow computation had remained difficult. The Reynolds numbers of the computed flows were less than 1000 in most cases.

At high Reynolds numbers, the computation become very unstable numerically; this difficulty is mainly due to the very small viscous diffusion. One way to overcome the numerical instability in high-Reynolds-number-flow computation is to use an upwind scheme. The stability of the first-order upwind scheme is quite good, but it has a strong diffusive effect similar to the effect of molecular viscosity. Thus, it is not suitable for our purpose. The second-order upwind scheme is better in this sense, but it is more unstable and causes undesirable propagation of errors.

By using a third-order upwind scheme, the flow around a circular cylinder in the critical regime was successfully simulated[2]; in this case, leading numerical error terms are the fourth-order-derivative terms. For the compressible flow computation, the Beam-Warming method[3] or its modifications are widely used. All of these schemes have a fourth-order numerical diffusion to stabilize the computation and which seems capable to compute high-Reynolds-number flow.

These works suggest that high-Reynolds-number-flow computation may be possible if the computational scheme is stable and if its numerical diffusion does not conceal the effect of viscosity. In other words, they can be computed with the methods which have fourth-order numerical diffusion, where second-order numerical diffusions are carefully removed. Keeping these in mind, series of computations have been done, and they are summarized in this paper.

Finite-Difference Schemes

The unsteady incompressible full Navier-Stokes equations written in generalized coordinates are solved. All spatial derivatives except those of the nonlinear terms are approximated by central differences. The nonlinear terms are approximated by a third-order upwind scheme[2].

$$(u \frac{\partial u}{\partial x})_i = u_i(-u_{i+2} + 8(u_{i+1} - u_{i-1}) + u_{i-2})/12h$$
$$+ |u_i| (u_{i+2} - 4u_{i+1} + 6u_i - 4u_{i-1} + u_{i-2})/4h \tag{1}$$

From this expression, it is clear that this scheme has a numerical diffusion approximately expressed by a fourth-order derivative.

The computational schemes for compressible flow are based on the implicit factorization method with improved accuracy. An artificial diffusion term of fourth-order difference is added to the explicit term, as it is usually done, to remove the aliasing errors and to stabilize the computation. Three types of different schemes are used for the inversion of the matrix for the implicit part. These are a bidiagonal scheme[4] and a block tridiagonal scheme[5] and a block pentadiagonal scheme[6] according to the accuracy of the implicit terms. The bidiagonal scheme is most efficient while the block pentadiagonal one is most accurate. The block tridiagonal scheme is essentially the Beam-Warming-Steger's[7]. The explicit part is the same in all schemes, thus all of them should give the same steady state solution.

For the convective terms on the right hand side, fourth-order differencing like Eq.1 is used in order to improve the accuracy. The Jacobian and the metric terms are also formed by using fourth-order differencing.

Flow around a Circular Cylinder

Figure 2 shows the streamlines at Reynolds numbers Re = 2000 and 60000, illustrating the flow patterns before and after the drag crisis. The roughness is equally distributed on the surface with 200x100 grid points. The typical flow pattern after the drag crisis is clearly shown for Re = 60000. Figure 3 shows the flow around a circular cylinder without any roughness for Re = 670000. The number of grid points is 500x100. Even without surface roughness, the drag crisis is well captured.

At very high Reynolds numbers, the flow speeds become high and sometimes the compressibility may have some effect on the flow structure. Therefore, the same flow was simulated by solving the compressible full Navier-Stokes equations. The Mach number is 0.3 and the Reynolds number ranges from 1×10^5 to 7.83×10^6. The scheme is essentially what is used in the Beam-Warming-Steger method, but the accuracy is improved by using fourth-order differencing in the nonlinear terms. The second-order artificial diffusion terms are not employed at the sacrifice of the stability. Also, thin-layer approximation was not employed but full viscous terms were evaluated. The drag coefficients are shown in Fig.4 together with data of some experiments. The agreement between the calculations and the experiments is excellent up to the Reynolds number 10^6. Figures 5 and 6[8] show the comparison of the flows at four different Reynolds numbers. The drag crisis of a smooth circular cylinder is clearly obtained. The transition to the transcritical regime is also obtained. No essential difference was found between incompressible computation and the compressible one at Mach number 0.3.

Although at high Reynolds numbers, the grid spacing needed to resolve the smallest eddies in the boundary layer is too fine for the computers available at the present time, the above computations have captured a global qualitative structure of the flow.

Fully-Developed Turbulent Flow in a Duct

A turbulent flow in a duct was simulated by integrating the incompressible Navier-Stokes equations without any subgrid modeling[9]. The initial and boundary conditions are essentially the same as those of Deardorff[10]. In most cases the number of mesh points is 30x20x30. The Reynolds number, based on the distance between the two walls and mean velocity at the center of the duct, is 20000. The average velocity, the Reynolds stress $u'v'$ and the turbulence intensities are shown in Fig.7. All profiles agree reasonably well with experimental results and with the computational ones obtained by Moin & Kim[11].

Transition to Turbulence

The transition to turbulence is simulated without any subgrid modeling, which is very difficult by LES.

Figure 8 shows space-averaged velocity profiles from impulsive start to turbulence[9]. Up to the non-dimensional time of t=560, the flow is almost laminar and the velocity distribution is becoming parabolic, but near t=620 an asymmetry indicating the beginning of the transition develops.

Fig.9 and 10 show the transition at different Reynolds numbers. The initial condition is the flow at t=575 of the previous case; it is just the beginning of the transition. At Reynolds number 5000 (Fig.9), a similar transition takes place, but for Re = 2000 (Fig.10) the transition is very slow and we can not observe any symptoms of transition from the velocity profile. The turbulence intensity, however, suggests the development of the disturbance. These findings correspond well to experimental observations.

Figure 11 shows the contour lines obtained by the computation using a larger number of grid points (60x40x50); the initial condition was determined by using the data observed by Laufer with a disturbance twice as large as that observed by him.

Flow around an Airfoil at Low Angle of Attack

Figure 12 shows the solutions for the flow around an NACA 0012 airfoil at an angle of attack of 2 degrees[12]. The range of the Reynolds numbers is from 10^5 up to 6.7×10^6, the Mach number is 0.75. At the leading edge the minimum grid spacing normal to the surface was set to 0.1/Re. The minimum spacing at the trailing edge is two times larger. The CFL numbers were suppressed to about 40 in order to obtain better accuracy for the unsteady computation. The CPU time for 321x80 grid points was about one hour per thousand steps on FUJITSU scalar computer M380. It took a total of 20 hours for the unsteady computation in the case of Re = 6.7×10^6.

The unsteady vortex separation was observed in every case. The coefficient of pressure obtained numerically for the case of R = 6.7×10^6 is compared with the experimental data[13] (Fig.13). In this case the grid still needs refinement in order to capture turbulent phenomena.

Flow around an Airfoil at High Angle of Attack

Since the flow is highly unsteady in this case, the most time-accurate pentadiagonal scheme is employed with a 320x80 grid[14]. The Reynolds number is 10^6 and the Mach number is 0.4. The CPU time is 2 hours on S810. The time dependence of the density contours and the pressure coefficient curves for the case of an angle of attack of 15 degrees are presented in Fig.14. Small separation bubbles stick to the leading edge and this leads to the strong nearly steady suction peak there which agrees with experimental observation. The computation with a coarser grid of 160x40 could not capture this phenomenon well.

Flow around an Oscillating Airfoil

The flow field around an oscillating NACA0012 airfoil in pitch at 0.25 chord is analyzed by the pentadiagonal scheme. The angle of attack is from 0° to 20°. Even in the case of 161x40 mesh, the lift stall is clearly captured. Moreover in the case of 321x80 mesh, the restoration process of lift coefficient in the downstroke is clearly captured (Fig.15). In the fine mesh case, the process of the beginning of separation at stall stage is elucidated by computation for the first time (Fig.16).

Conclusions

From these computations, it has become clear that the high-Reynolds-number flows can be simulated by directly integrating the Navier-Stokes equations. The numerical diffusion plays a very important role in getting reasonable results. Numerical diffusion of second-order-derivative type which appears in the first-order upwind scheme or as an implicit diffusion in the Beam-Warming-Steger method is similar to the molecular diffusion and conceals the dependence of the flow on the Reynolds number and is not suitable for high-Reynolds-number-flow computation. On the other hand, the numerical diffusion of fourth-order-derivative type is of short range and does not conceal the effect of molecular diffusion and stabilizes the computation very well. At the present stage, this may be the best way to overcome the numerical instability in high-Reynolds-number-flow computation.

Even simulation of unsteady compressible flows at high Reynolds numbers is feasible. The numerical simulation of high-Reynolds-number flow is much simpler than it was previously believed.

Acknowledgements

This work has been done in cooperation with Dr. Tetuya Kawamura, Dr. Katsuya Ishii, Mr. Susumu Shirayama, Mr. Shigeru Obayashi and Mr. Yoshifumi Shida of the University of Tokyo and Dr. Satoru Ogawa of the National Aerospace Laboratory and Mr. Ryutaro Himeno of Nissan Motor Co. Ltd. and Dr. Wei J. Chyu of NASA Ames Research Center.

References

1) M. Kawaguti; 1953 Numerical Solution of the Navier-Stokes Equations for the Flow around a Circular Cylinder at Reynolds Number 40, J. Phys. Soc. Japan Vol.8, No.6, pp.747-757.
2) T. Kawamura and K. Kuwahara; 1984 Computation of High Reynolds Number Flow around a Circular Cylinder with Surface Roughness, AIAA paper 84-0340.
3) M. Beem and R. F. Warming; 1976 An Implicit Finite-Differnce Algorithm for Hyperbolic Systems in Conservation-Law Form, J. Comput. Phys. vol.22, pp.87-110.
4) S. Obayashi and K. Kuwahara; 1984 LU Factorization of an Implicit Scheme for the Compressible Navier-Stokes Equations, AIAA Paper 84-1670.
5) K. Ishii and K. Kuwahara; 1984 Computation of Compressible Flow aruond a Circular Cylinder, AIAA paper 84-1631.
6) Y. Shida and K. Kuwahara; 1985 Computational Study of Unsteady Compressible Flow around an Airfoil by a Block Pentadiagonal Matrix Scheme, AIAA paper 85-1692.
7) J. L. Steger; 1979 Implicit Finite-Difference Simulation of Flow about Arbitrary Two-Dimensional Geometries, AIAA Journal, Vol.16, No.7, pp.679-686.
8) K. Ishii, K. Kuwahara, S. Ogawa, W. J. Chyu and T. Kawamura; 1985 Computation of Flow aound a circular Cylinder in a Supercritical

Regime, AIAA paper 85-1660.
9) T. Kawamura and K. Kuwahara; 1985 Direct Simulation of a Turbulent Inner Flow by Finite-Difference Method, AIAA paper 85-0376.
10) J. W. Deardorff; 1970 A numerical study of three-dimensional turbulent channel flow at large Reynolds numbers. J. Fluid Mech. vol.41, pp.453-480.
11) P. Moin and J. Kim; 1982 Numerical investigation of turbulent channel flow. J. Fluid Mech. vol.118, pp.341-377.
12) S. Obayashi, H. Kubota and K. Kuwahara; 1985 Computation of Unsteady Shock-Induced Vortex Separation, AIAA paper 85-0183.
13) K. Takashima; to appear in Technical Memorandum of National Aerospace Laboratory, Japan.
14) Y. Shida, H. Takami, K. Kuwahara and K. Ono; 1986 Computation of Dynamic Stall of NACA0012 Airfoil by Block Pentadiagonal Matrix Scheme, AIAA Paper 86-0116.

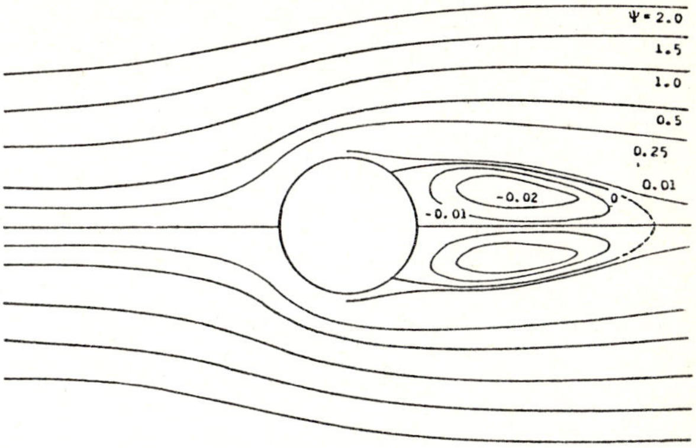

Fig.1 Streamlines around a circular cylinder at Re=40, by Kawaguti[1].

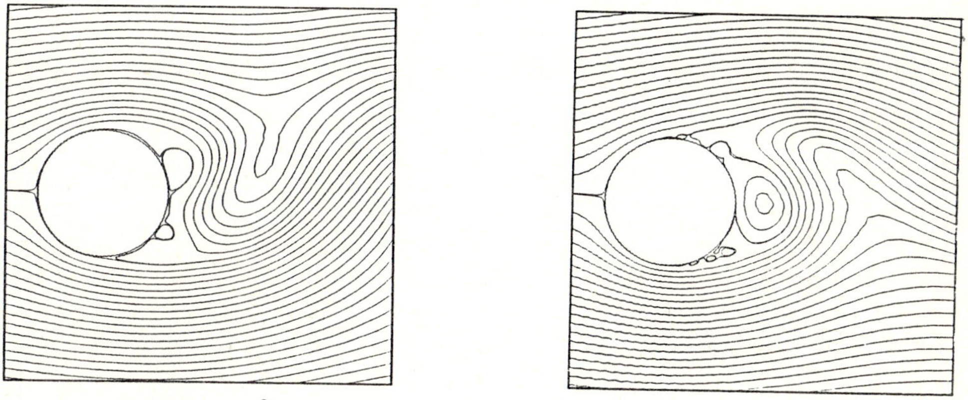

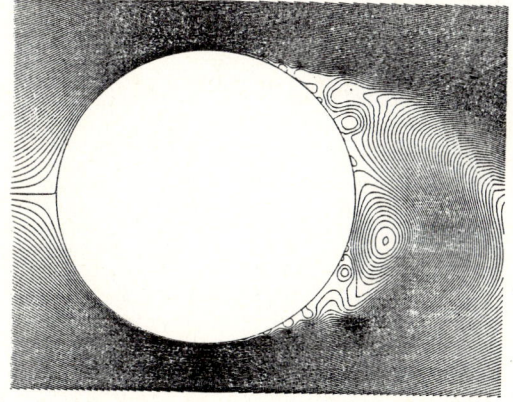

(a) Re=2.0x10^3 (b) Re=6.0x10^4

Fig.2 Streamlines around a circular cylinder with surface roughness.

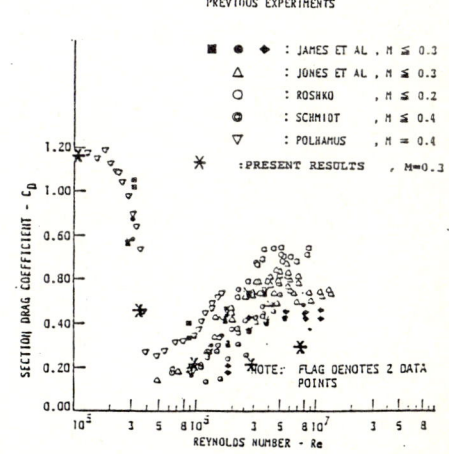

Fig.3 Streamlines around a smooth circular cylinder at Re=6.7x10^5.

Fig.4 The drag coefficients of the present computation with experimental data.

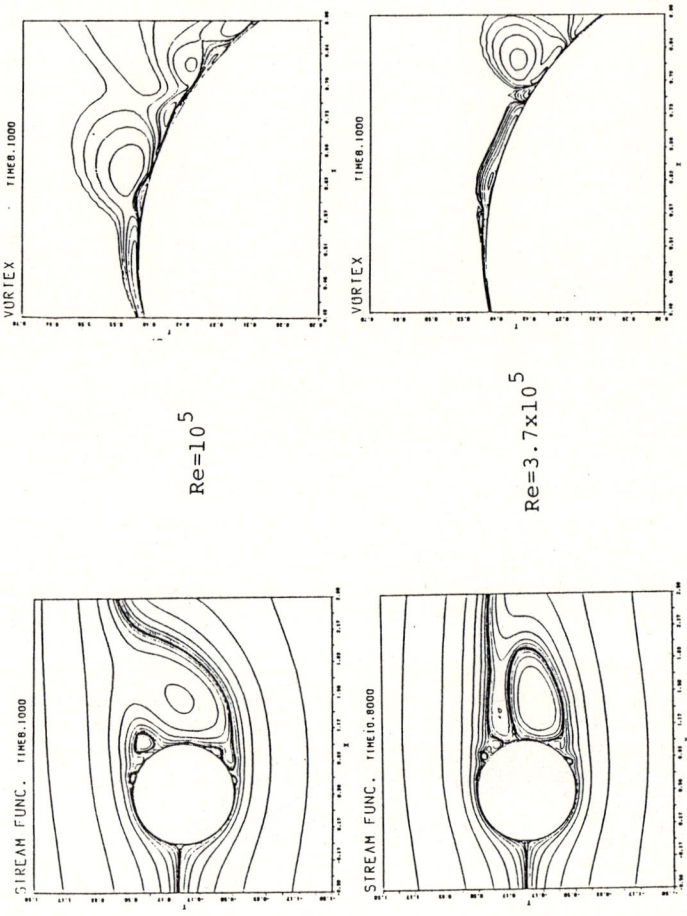

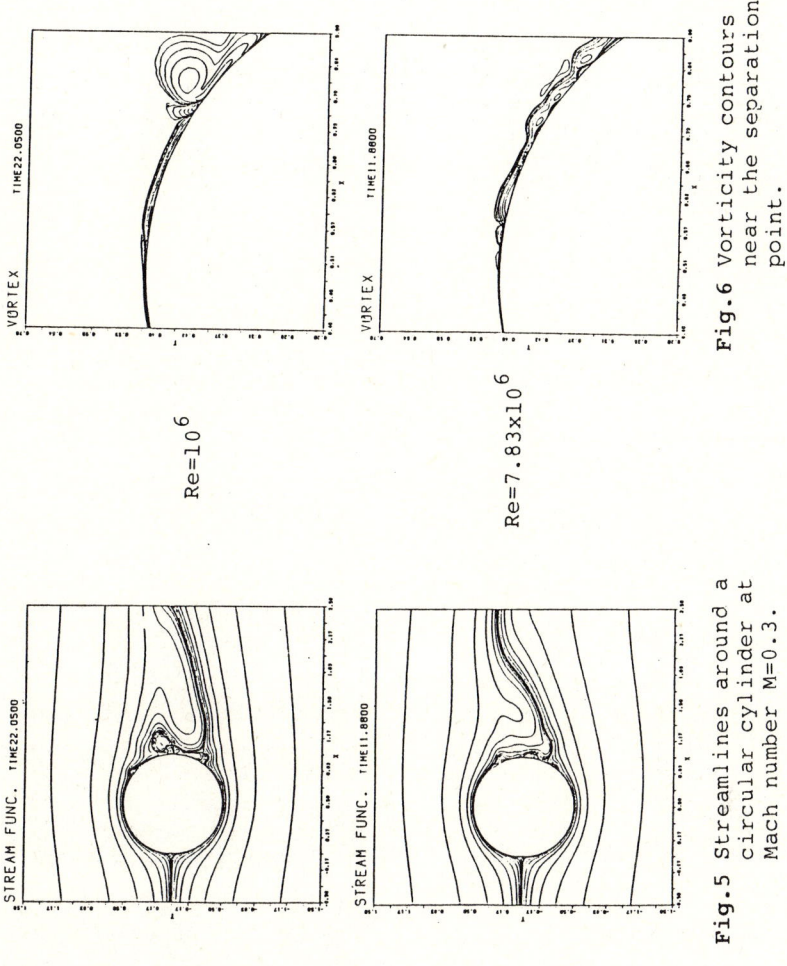

Fig.6 Vorticity contours near the separation point.

Fig.5 Streamlines around a circular cylinder at Mach number M=0.3.

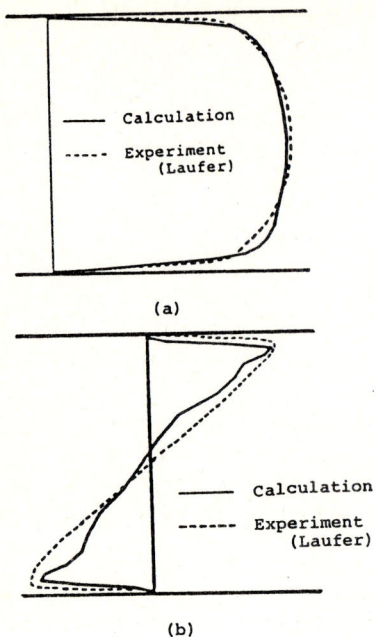

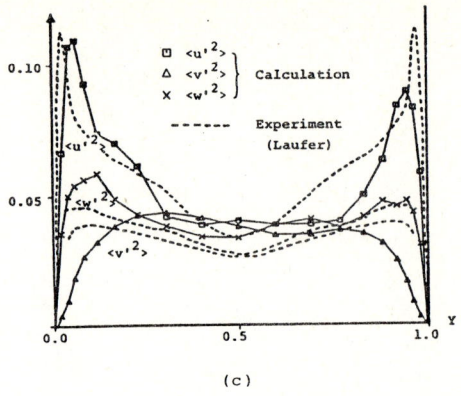

Fig.7 (a) Mean velocity profile.
(b) Reynolds stress $u'v'$.
(c) Turblence intensities for each direction.

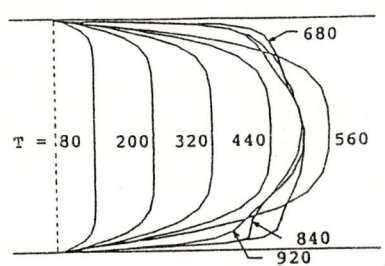

Fig.8 Horizontally averaged velocity profiles.

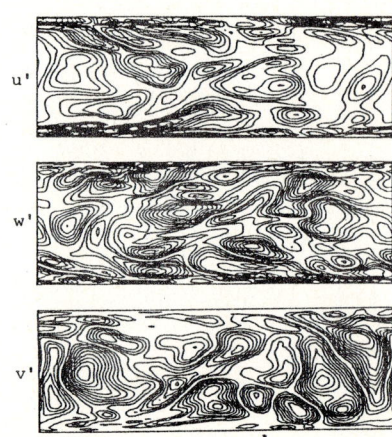

Fig.9 Velocity fluctuation.

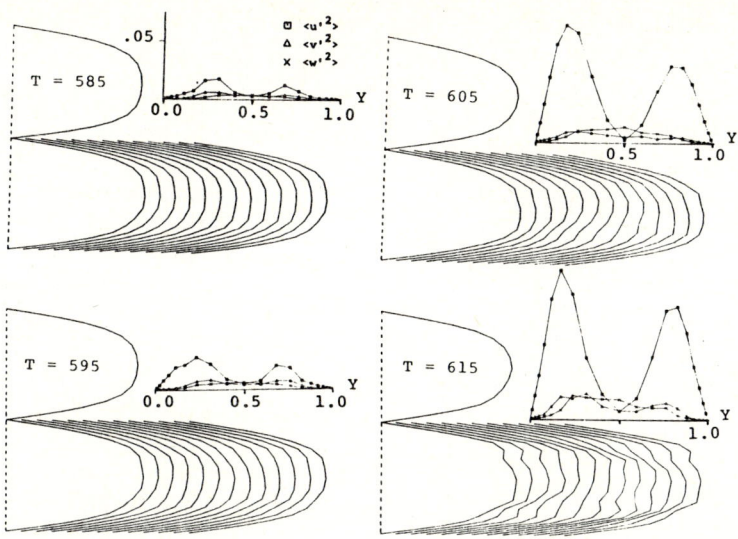

Fig.10 Mean velocity profiles, instantaneous velocity profiles in the center plane and turbulence intensities at various times at Re=5000.

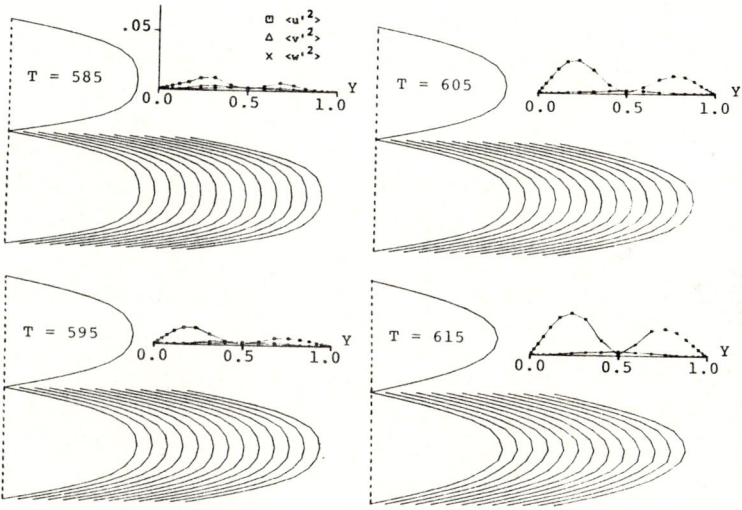

Fig.11 Mean velocity profiles, instantaneous velocity profiles in the center plane and turbulence intensities at various times at Re=2000.

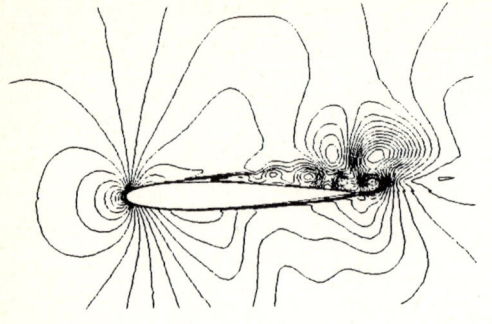

(a) $Re=10^5$

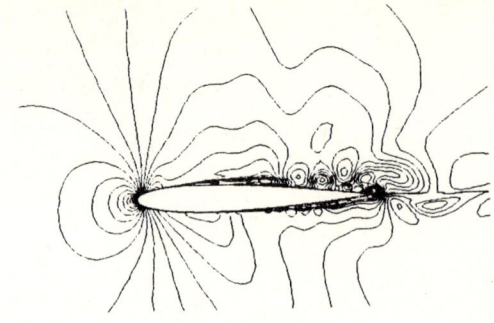

(d) $Re=5\times10^5$

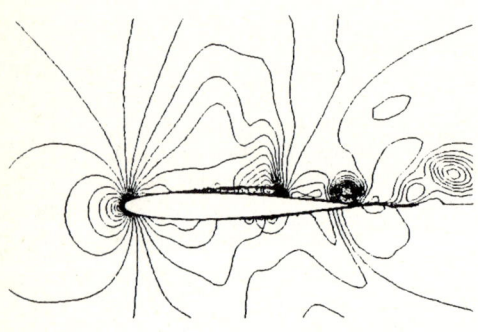

(b) $Re=10^6$

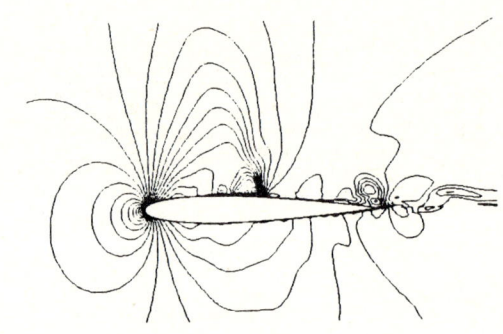

(e) $Re=3\times10^6$

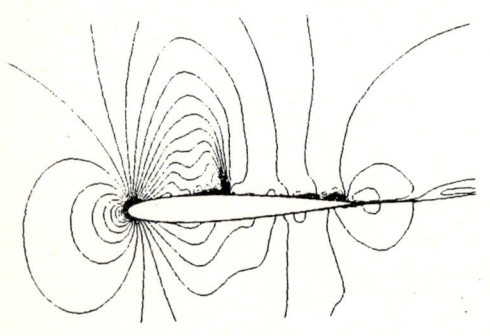

(c) $Re=6.7\times10^6$

Fig.12 Density contours around NACA0012.

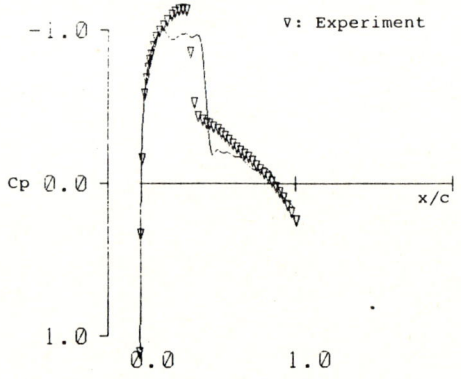

Fig.13 Upper surface pressure coefficient distributions averaged in time: $T=18-24$, $Re=6.7\times10^6$, $M=0.75$, $\alpha=2^0$.

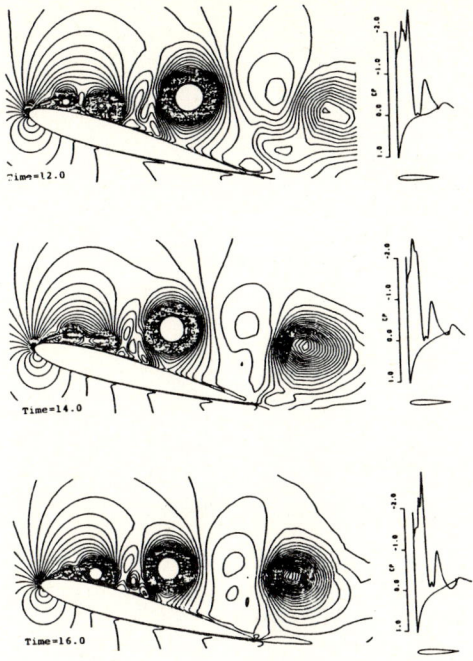

Fig.14 Density contours around NACA0012 at angle of attack of 15^0, $Re=10^6$.

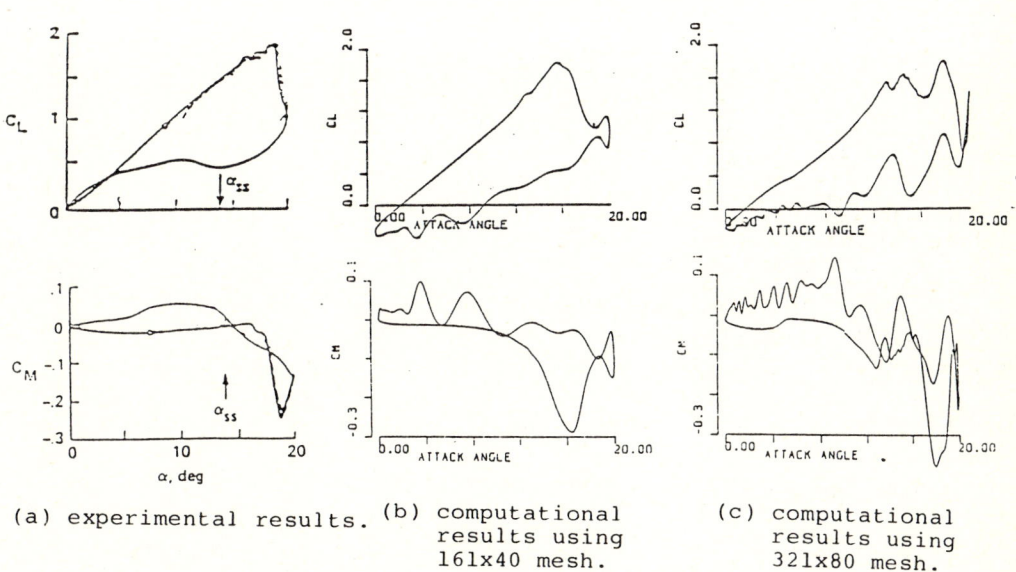

(a) experimental results.
(b) computational results using 161x40 mesh.
(c) computational results using 321x80 mesh.

Fig.15 Lift and angular momentum hysteresis curves versus angle of attack.

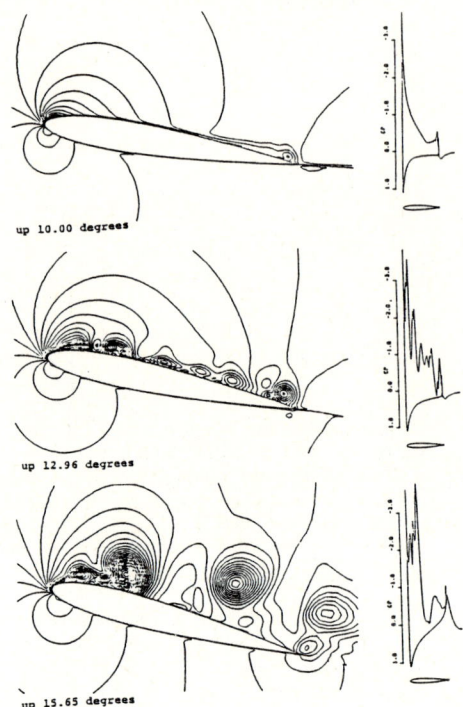

Fig.16 Density contours around NACA0012 in the dynamic stall process.

SPECTRAL ELEMENT SIMULATION OF FLOW IN GROOVED CHANNELS: COOLING CHIPS WITH TOLLMIEN-SCHLICHTING WAVES

A.T. Patera
Department of Mechanical Engineering
Massachusetts Institute of Technology
Cambridge, MA 02139

Abstract

The spectral element method is a high-order (p-type) finite element technique for the Navier-Stokes equations that combines the geometric flexibility of the finite element method with the rapid convergence and efficiency of spectral schemes. The method is applied here to steady and unsteady moderate Reynolds number flow and heat transfer in grooved channels. It is shown by direct numerical simulation that the least stable linear modes of the steady grooved-channel flow closely resemble Tollmien-Schlichting channel waves, forced by Kelvin-Helmholtz shear layer instability at the groove edge. For Reynolds numbers greater than a critical value, these modes become unstable and the flow takes the form of self-sustained oscillations. For Reynolds numbers less than this critical value, it is shown that oscillatory perturbation of the flow at the frequency of the least stable mode of the linearized system results in subcritical resonant excitation as the critical Reynolds number is approached. Application of this subcritical flow excitation to heat transfer enhancement and the cooling of chips (electronic components) is described.

1. Introduction

Flow over grooves and in grooved channels arises in a large number of practical applications, from the design of effective cooling systems for electronic devices [1], to the analysis of buffeting due to flow over airframe cutouts [2]. Flow in grooved channels can also be interpreted as a model for the more general class of problems involving flow over rough walls. In addition to any direct practical import, flow in grooved channels serves as a simple, yet rich, example of internal separated flow, in which a thorough numerical study of the stability properties of a strongly non-parallel flow in complex geometry can be performed.

In this paper, we investigate by direct numerical simulation the hydrodynamics and heat transfer of unsteady incompressible flow in two-dimensional periodically-grooved channels. In Section 2, we describe the spectral element numerical technique used for the solution of the Navier-Stokes and energy equations. In Section 3, the results of the grooved channel flow simulations are presented, and simple physical explanations are given for the complex flow behavior found. The dramatic effect of forced oscillations on heat transfer is demonstrated, and the relevance of this phenomena to the cooling of electronic chips is indicated.

2. The Spectral Element Method

To illustrate the spectral element method, we consider forced convection heat transfer in a domain D,

$$T_t + \nabla \cdot (\vec{v}T) = \alpha \nabla^2 T \qquad \text{in D}, \qquad (1)$$

where $T(\vec{x},t)$ is the temperature, $\vec{x}$ and t are space and time respectively, $\vec{v}$ is the velocity, and α is the (assumed constant) thermal diffusivity of the fluid. Boundary conditions on the temperature can be either temperature, flux, or mixed (heat transfer coefficient). Although we assume here that the velocity field is given, in an actual calculation it is determined simultaneously by solution of the Navier-Stokes equations using a procedure similar to that described here for the energy equation [3-6].

For the temporal discretization, a semi-implicit scheme is used, with the third-order (explicit) Adams-Bashforth method for the convection terms,

$$\hat{T}^{n+1} - T^n = -\Delta t \sum_{q=0}^{2} \beta_q \nabla \cdot (\vec{v}T)^{n-q} \qquad \text{in D} \qquad (2)$$

($\beta_0 = 23/12$, $\beta_1 = -16/12$, $\beta_2 = 5/12$), and the (implicit) Crank-Nicolson scheme for the conduction contributions

$$T^{n+1} - \hat{T}^{n+1} = \Delta t/2 \, \alpha \nabla^2 (T^{n+1} + T^n) \qquad \text{in D.} \qquad (3)$$

Boundary conditions are imposed on the conduction step, (3).

The motivation behind the semi-implicit time-stepping scheme is the observation that not only is the diffusion stability restriction significantly more severe than that due to the convective step, but that the (positive-definite symmetric) conduction operator is also more "easy" to invert. Recent developments indicate that balancing tensor diffusivity techniques [7,8] can be used to construct *full implicit* unconditionally-stable time-stepping schemes that require only marginally more work than the semi-implicit (conditionally stable) scheme given in (2-3).

We now turn to the spatial discretization. The isoparametric spectral element discretization proceeds by first breaking up the computational domain into general (curvilinear) brick elements, and expanding the geometry, velocity, and temperature in tensor product bases in terms of the local coordinates, $\vec{r}$ ($= rr + ss + tt$). In element k ([-1,1]x[-1,1]x[-1,1]), the variables are represented as

$$[\vec{x},\vec{v},T]_N^k(\vec{r}) = \sum_{i=0}^{N} \sum_{j=0}^{N} \sum_{m=0}^{N} [\vec{x},\vec{v},T]_{ijm}^k h_i(r) h_j(s) h_m(t)$$
$$= \sum_i [\vec{x},\vec{v},T]_i^k g_i(\vec{r}) \quad , \qquad (4)$$

where the $h_i(z)$ are Nth-order Lagrangian interpolants through the Gauss-Lobatto Chebyshev collocation points [3]. Local variables are related to the global decomposition so as to insure C^0-continuity of the approximation space, as required for the weak formulation to be presented below.

The interpolation (4) can be easily shown to result in exponential convergence for infinitely smooth functions as $N \Rightarrow \infty$ [9]; the choice of collocation points is important as regards the accuracy of the numerical quadratures, the interpolation of boundary data, and the collocation approximations. Although Chebyshev interpolants are convenient from the point of view of evaluation, Legendre (Lobatto) representation leads to more accurate and efficient quadratures for variable coefficient equations, as well as sparser matrix structure [8].

It is clear from the semi-discrete equations in (2,3) that to solve the energy (and Navier-Stokes) equations we must be able to accurately represent and invert both (nonlinear) hyperbolic and elliptic operators. Considering first the convective (hyperbolic) contributions, (2), a mixed collocation / Galerkin approach is used,

$$\nabla \cdot (\vec{v}T) \Rightarrow \Sigma_k' \iiint g_i g_j \nabla_{jp} \cdot (\vec{v}_p^k T_p^k) |J^k| d\vec{r} \quad , \quad (5)$$

(summation over repeated indices assumed), where Σ_k' denotes direct stiffness summation, ∇_{jp} is the discrete gradient operator (i.e., the gradient at point j due to node p), and J is the Jacobian of the global to local transformation defined by (4). In some sense, (5) corresponds to collocation of the derivative terms, followed by a Galerkin approximation for the resulting convective flux. This maintains many of the desirable features of a full Galerkin formulation (e.g., conservation [5]), while eliminating the triple products which can be prohibitively expensive for high-order methods [9]. Although for some problems the conservative form of the convective terms is necessary (e.g., Section 3 below), in other instances other forms are more desirable (e.g., skew-symmetric representation for temporal stability [8]).

For the diffusion contributions, (3), we use the standard (symmetric, negative-definite) variational formulation for second-order elliptic equations,

$$\nabla^2 T - \gamma^2 T \Rightarrow \Sigma_k' \iiint \{-\nabla_{pi} g_p g_q \nabla_{qj} - \gamma^2 g_i g_j\} T_j |J^k| d\vec{r}, \quad (6)$$

where ∇_{ij} and J are defined as for (5). Solution of general Helmholtz equations using (6) has been demonstrated numerically to give exponential convergence to smooth solutions as $N \Rightarrow \infty$ (despite a space which is only C^0), even for general geometries with relatively deformed macro-elements. The proof of such a result follows from classical Rayleigh-Ritz arguments, which in turn reduce the problem to one of standard approximation theory.

The key to the computational efficiency of both the hyperbolic and elliptic contributions, (5) and (6), respectively, is the sum factorization that follows from the tensor product bases, (4). For example, to perform sums of the form $\iiint g_i g_p T_p d\vec{r}$ in three space dimensions, we write

$$\iiint g_i g_p T_p d\vec{r} = (\int h_i h_p dz (\int h_j h_q dz (\int h_k h_r dz \; T_{pqr}))), \quad (7)$$

which gives an operation count of $O(N^4)$ per element, rather than the more obvious (and prohibitive) $O(N^6)$. As regards the (implicit) diffusion terms, we must not only evaluate, but also invert, operators of the form (6). In two space dimensions, a direct static condensation solver is used, as discussed in detail in [4]. In three space dimensions, static condensation is no longer a viable approach due to the relatively larger number of elemental boundary points, and we use instead a conjugate gradient iterative technique [10], guaranteed to converge given the symmetric negative-definite form of the elliptic discretizations.

Armed with the hyperbolic and elliptic discrete operators and associated inversion procedures described above, solution of the time-discretized energy equation (2,3) readily follows. The resulting method is well suited for problems in complex geometry at moderate Reynolds/Peclet number due to the minimal numerical dispersion and diffusion of the scheme [11], and the good resolution properties (e.g., for thermal boundary layers) of the elemental Chebyshev point distribution.

3. Flow in Grooved Channels

We consider here steady and resonantly forced flow and heat transfer in the periodically-grooved two-dimensional channel shown in Fig. 1. As regards the application of cooling of chips, the grooved bottom wall of the channel, ∂D_B, represents a regular array of electronic components (e.g., a memory board), while the flat top wall, ∂D_T, correponds to a chassis or rack for an adjacent board. The bottom wall is treated as a uniform surface heat source (flux q"), while the top (flat) wall is taken to be adiabatic. In addition to the chip cooling problem, grooved channel flows are relevant in other applications such as understanding the effect of roughness on transition and receptivity in laminar flow control devices.

Non-dimensionalizing distance by h (the channel half-width), velocity by 3V/2 (V the cross-channel and time-averaged velocity), and time by (2h)/(3V), the governing equations for the grooved channel flow can be written as,

$$\vec{v}_t + (\vec{v}\cdot\nabla)\vec{v} = -\nabla p + R^{-1}\nabla^2\vec{v} \qquad \text{in D}, \qquad (8a)$$

$$\nabla\cdot\vec{v} = 0 \qquad \text{in D}, \qquad (8b)$$

$$\theta_t + \nabla\cdot(\vec{v}\theta) = (RPr)^{-1}\nabla^2\theta \qquad \text{in D}, \qquad (8c)$$

where D is the domain corresponding to one periodicity unit of the grooved channel shown in Fig. 1. Here R is the Reynolds number, $R = 3Vh/2\nu$, Pr is the Prandtl number, $Pr = \nu/\alpha$, and θ is the non-dimensional temperature, $\theta = (T-T_b)k/q"h$, where T is the dimensional temperature, and T_b is the mixed-mean temperature. The kinematic viscosity, thermal diffusivity, and conductivity of the fluid are given by ν, α, and k, respectively. Natural convection and spanwise variation of the flow are assumed to be negligible, and physical properties are taken to be constant.

There is ample theoretical and experimental [1] evidence that after relatively few (identical, regularly-spaced) grooves, the flow in grooved-channel geometries can be treated as fully-developed in a periodic sense. As this reduction in domain leads to significant computational economies, it is important to develop proper boundary conditions for treatment of the fully-developed problem. For the velocity, the appropriate boundary conditions for fully-developed flow in a periodic geometry can be shown to be,

$$\vec{v} = 0 \qquad \text{on } \partial D_B, \partial D_T, \qquad (9a)$$

$$\vec{v}(x+L,y,t) = \vec{v}(x,y,t), \qquad (9b)$$

where L is the periodicity length between grooves. For the pressure we require not simple periodicity, but rather,

$$p(\vec{x},t) = -f(t)x + \tilde{p}(\vec{x},t) \qquad (10a)$$

$$\tilde{p}(x+L,y,t) = \tilde{p}(x,y,t), \qquad (10b)$$

where the term f(t) is the driving force for the flow, and is determined (indirectly) by the imposed flowrate condition,

$$Q = \int_{-1}^{1} u(x=0,y,t)dy = 4/3(1 + \eta\sin 2\pi\Omega_F t). \qquad (11)$$

Here η is the amplitude of the modulatory component of the flow ($\eta = 0$ corresponds to steady flow), while Ω_F is the Strouhal number (reduced frequency) of the forced oscillations. Note the linear-in-x term in p is consistent with periodicity for $\vec{v}$, as only ∇p enters into the Navier-Stokes equations.

Turning now to the temperature boundary conditions, we have

$$\nabla \theta \cdot \hat{n} = 1 \quad \text{on } \partial D_B, \quad (12a)$$

$$\nabla \theta \cdot \hat{n} = 0 \quad \text{on } \partial D_T, \quad (12b)$$

corresponding to uniform flux and insulation on the bottom and top walls, respectively. As regards the condition of fully-developedness, it is not possible to simply impose periodicity of $\theta(\vec{x},t)$, as this is inconsistent with the boundary conditions (12) if steady or steady-periodic (in time) solutions are sought. Rather, we must first subtract off a linear term to compensate for the rise in mixed-mean temperature along the channel due to the net flux input (12), giving as the appropriate periodicity condition,

$$\theta(\vec{x},t) = \tilde{\theta}(\vec{x},t) + {}^3/_4(1+2^a/_L)x/RPr , \quad (13a)$$

$$\tilde{\theta}(x+L,y,t) = \tilde{\theta}(x,y,t) , \quad (13b)$$

where a is the groove depth. These boundary conditions can be shown to result in a consistent (solvable) set of equations for determination of the temperature in steady or steady-(time) periodic fully-developed flows in periodic geometries. A complete derivation and mathematical and physical justification for the boundary conditions (9-13) is given in [5], along with the numerical requirements (e.g., conservation) that they imply.

In Figs. 2a and 2b we plot the (steady) streamlines and isotherms, respectively, for non-oscillatory flow ($\eta = 0$) at R = 525 in the "base" geometry, L = 6.666, l = 2.222, a = 1.111 (all results quoted here are for Pr = 1 and this base geometry). It is seen that, with the exception of the groove region of the flow, the thermal solution is essentially one of conduction, or, more precisely, fully-developed internal flow. The worst heat transfer in the system (maximum temperature) occurs at the groove upstream lower corner, as this point both has the largest "conduction length" and receives the least benefit of the re-circulating vortex boundary layer.

To investigate the linear stability of the flow presented in Fig. 2a, we solve as an initial value problem the Navier-Stokes equations linearized about the numerically-obtained steady state. We plot in Fig. 3 the perturbation (instantaneous less time-asymptotic steady) velocity as a function of time at a typical point in the flow domain for R = 525 ($\eta = 0$), obtained by direct numerical simulation. The least stable mode (i.e., the natural response) of the steady flow at this Reynolds number is seen to correspond to a damped oscillation, with a natural frequency of $\Omega = .142$.

As might be expected, the damping of these oscillatory modes decreases with increasing Reynolds number, and for Reynolds numbers greater than a critical value, $R_c = 975$, the stable flow is no longer steady, but rather takes the form of self-sustained oscillations [12]. This oscillatory flow is shown in Figs. 4 and 5 for R = 1200 in the form of unsteady streamlines and isobars during the course of one flow cycle. From these visualizations, it is clear that the oscillatory flow is a result of a Kelvin-Helmholtz shear layer instability at the groove lip.

In what follows, we shall be concerned with oscillatory perturbation of (subcritical) grooved channel flow, and it is therefore of interest to determine how the frequencies of the grooved-channel modes are selected. Inspection of the perturbation streamlines of the subcritical linear modes [12] (as well as the isobars of the supercritical flow shown in Fig. 5) reveal that the instability modes in the channel part of the grooved-channel closely resemble *straight-channel* Tollmien-Schlichting waves. (Note we restrict ourselves here to open cavities, in which the flow in the channel part of the domain is approximately parallel.) If this be the case, it seems plausible that the unstable, "massless" part of the flow, the shear layer, would allow the stable, "massive", part of the flow, the channel Orr-Sommerfeld mode, to dictate the frequency of their coherent oscillations. Numerical tests indicate that this is, indeed, the case, namely that that the grooved-channel and straight channel dispersion relations are approximately the same [12].

We now consider the possibility of extracting transport augmentation from decaying oscillations at subcritical Reynolds numbers by oscillatory modulation of the flow at the frequency of the least stable linear mode of the system, $\Omega_F = \Omega$. We expect that such forcing will result in resonant excitation and transport enhancement as $R \Rightarrow R_c$, with significant flow modification even for Reynolds numbers well below critical. To demonstrate that this is, in fact, the case, we plot in Fig. 6 the heat transfer enhancement parameter, E, as a function of driving frequency, Ω_F, for R = 525, η = .2, Pr = 1. Here E is defined as the the ratio of the average (in space and time) Nusselt number (non-dimensional heat flux) with oscillation to the corresponding quantity with no oscillation (η =0). The resonant nature of the system response is clearly seen, and even at this significantly subcritical Reynolds number a twenty percent modulation results in a doubling (halving) of the average heat transfer coefficient (maximum temperature) along the bottom device wall.

Although it may appear obvious that appropriately-tuned oscillatory modulation of a flow should result in resonance and transport augmentation, this phenomenon does not occur in all flow geometries. In particular, it can be shown that resonance does not obtain for plane Poiseuille flow in a straight channel [13], thus demonstrating the (empirically well-known) importance of rough-wall geometry on flow response and momentum and heat transport. The lack of resonance in plane Poiseuille flow can be understood as resulting from the translation invariance of this flow, a symmetry which is broken by the grooved-channel geometry. Paradoxically, it is precisely at the frequencies of the *straight-channel* instability modes that resonance occurs in grooved channels.

In order to better see the effect of oscillation on excitation of natural modes and associated convective mixing, we plot in Fig. 7 the instantaneous isotherms during the course of one cycle ($0 < t < \Omega_F^{-1}$) for R = 525, $\Omega_F = \Omega$, η = .2. The Tollmien-Schlichting structure of the travelling waves in the channel part of the domain can be clearly seen. The effect of these channel waves (which recall would not be excited in a flat channel) on the transport process is also readily observed in Fig. 7; the troughs of the waves act to force "cold" fluid from the channel into the groove, while the crests serve to subsequently accept "hot" fluid from the groove back into the channel. This very effective material exchange between groove and channel, as well as the significant vertical (i.e., normal to heat exchange surface) velocities generated in the channel itself, contribute to the great reduction in wall temperatures demonstrated in Fig. 7.

More details of the calculations presented above may be found in references [12] and [13], the former discussing a general theory for frequency prediction in grooved channel flows, the latter addressing the issues of resonance, and the effect of geometry, Reynolds number, flow amplitude, and Prandtl number on resonant transport enhancement. Comparison of the numerical results with a companion experimental program indicate qualitative and quantitative agreement as regards resonance, flow structure, and the magnitude of heat transfer augmentation [14].

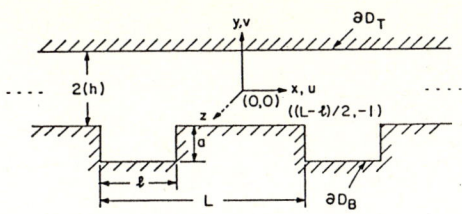

Fig. 1. The geometry of the periodically-grooved channel is described by the groove depth, a, groove length, l, and the separation distance between grooves, L. The bottom wall of the channel, ∂D_B, can be thought of as representing a regular array of electronic chips.

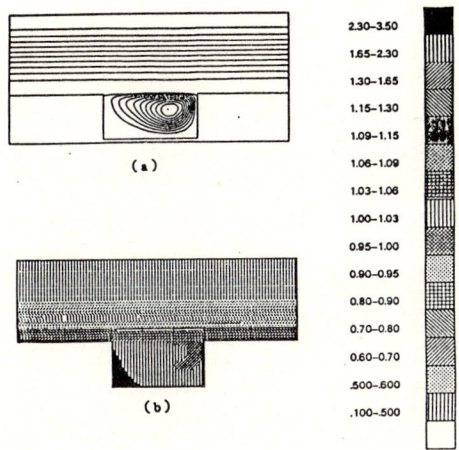

Fig. 2a. A plot of the steady streamlines at R = 525, η = 0. There is virtually no material exchange between the channel and groove regions of the flow.

Fig. 2b. A plot of the isotherms (temperature fills) for R = 525, η = 0, Pr = 1 (the temperature level has been arbitrarily set so that the minimum temperature is zero). The hottest point in the system is seen to be the upstream lower groove corner.

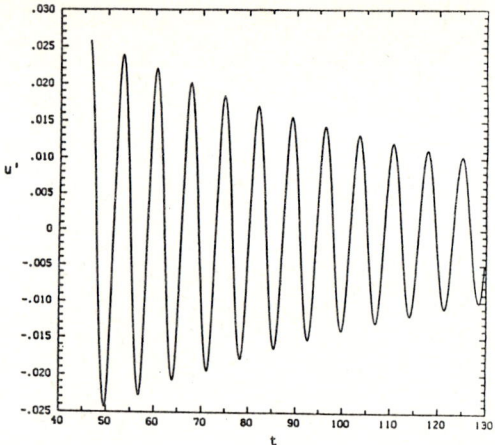

Fig. 3. A plot of the perturbation velocity, u', as a function of time at a typical point in the grooved channel shown in Fig. 1, obtained by direct simulation of the Navier-Stokes equations at R = 525. The least stable mode of the system corresponds to a decaying oscillation.

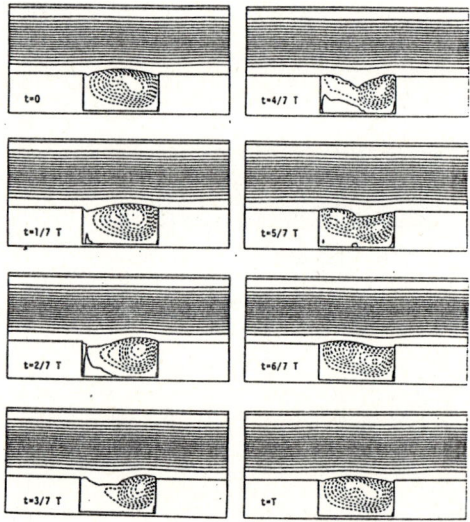

Fig. 4. A plot of the streamlines of the self-sustained flow oscillation at R = 1200 for various times during the flow cycle. Note the wavy structure at the groove lip, indicating a Kelvin-Helmholtz instability of the groove shear layer. (Here T is the period of the flow.)

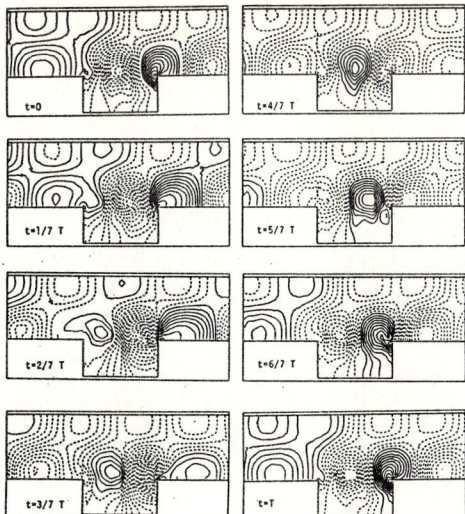

Fig. 5. A plot of the pressure contours of the self-sustained oscillations at R = 1200 at various times during the flow cycle. Not the propagating pressure pulse across the cavity shear layer (correlated with the streamline patterns in Fig. 4), suggestive of vortex sheet instability. Note also the regular pressure pattern (travelling wave) in the channel portion of the flow; this is, in fact, the pressure signature of Tollmien-Schlichting waves.

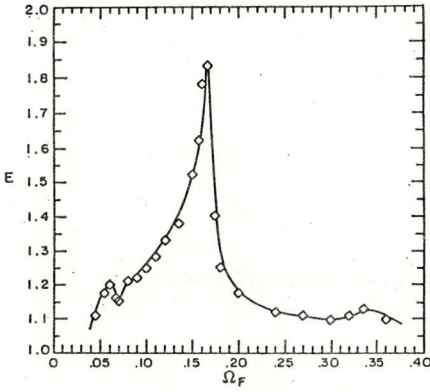

Fig. 6. A plot of the transport enhancement, E, as a function of forcing frequency, Ω_F, at R = 525, η = .2, Pr = 1 (base geometry). The response of the system is seen to be strongly peaked at the natural frequency of the flow, Ω = .142.

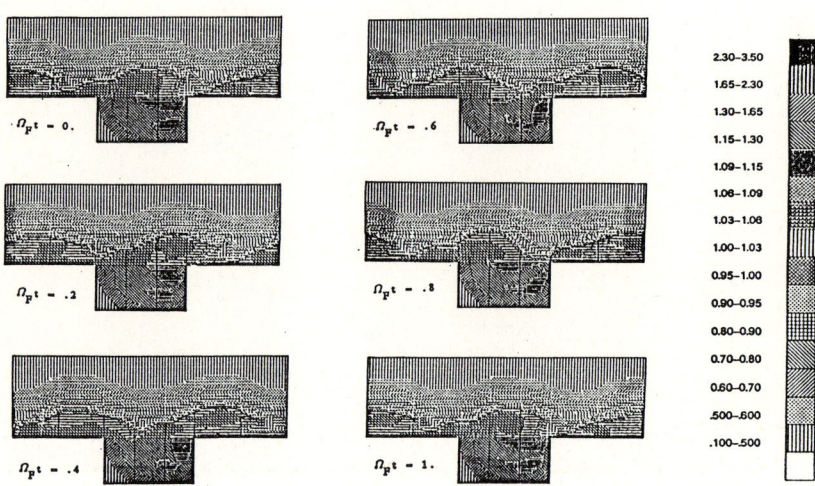

Fig. 7. A plot of the instantaneous isotherms during the course of one flow cycle at R = 525, η = .2, Ω_F = Ω (natural frequency), Pr = 1. Excitation of the least stable mode of the system results in a wavy channel motion (a Tollmien-Schlichting wave) that acts to effectively exchange material between the channel and groove parts of the domain.

Acknowledgements

This work was supported by the NSF under Grant MEA-8212469, and by a Rockwell Assistant Professorship.

References

1. Ashiwake, N., Nakayama, W., Daikoku, T., and Kobayashi, F., in "Heat Transfer in Electronic Equipment - 1983" (eds. S. Oktay and A. Bar-Cohen), HTD - Vol. **28**, ASME, New York, New York, 1983, 35.

2. Karachmeti, K., Sound radiated from surface cutouts in high-speed flows. Ph.D Thesis, California Institute of Technology, Pasadena, California, 1956.

3. Patera, A.T., J. Comput. Phys., **54** (1984), 468.

4. Korczak, K.Z. and Patera, A.T., J. Comput. Phys., **62** (1986).

5. Ghaddar, N.K., Karniadakis, G.E., and Patera, A.T., Numerical Heat Transfer, **9** (1986).

6. Karniadakis, G.E., Bullister, E.T., and Patera, A.T., in Proc. Europe-U.S. Conf. on Finite Element Methods for Nonlinear Problems, Trondheim, Norway, 1985, Springer.

7. Gresho, P. and Chan, S., in Proc. Fourth Int. Conf. Num. Methods in Laminar and Turbulent Flow, Wales, 1985, to appear.

8. Bullister, E.T., Karniadakis, G.E., Ronquist, E.M., and Patera, A.T., in Proc. Sixth Int. Symp. on Finite Element Methods in Flow Problems, Antibes, 1986, to appear.

9. Gottlieb, D.O. & Orszag, S.A., "Numerical Analysis of Spectral Methods," SIAM, Philadelphia, 1977.

10. Golub, G.H. and Van Loan, C.F., "Matrix Computations," Johns Hopkins University Press, Baltimore, 1983.

11. Basdevant, C., Deville, M., Haldenwang, P., Lacroix, J.M., Orlandi, P., Ouazzini, J., Patera, A.T. and Peyret, R., Computers and Fluids, **14**, (1986), 23.

12. Ghaddar, N.K., Korczak, K.Z., Mikic, B.B., and Patera, A.T., J. Fluid Mech., **163** (1986), 99.

13. Ghaddar, N.K., Magen, M., Mikic, B.B., and Patera, A.T., J. Fluid Mech., to appear.

14. Greiner, M., Ghaddar, N.K., Mikic, B.B., and Patera, A.T., in Proc. Eighth International Heat Transfer Conference, San Francisco, 1986, to appear.

A VORTEX RING INTERACTING WITH A VORTEX FILAMENT AND ITS DEFORMATION NEAR THE TWO-DIMENSIONAL STAGNATION POINT

M. Kiya and T. Sato
Department of Mechanical Engineering,
Faculty of Engineering, Hokkaido University,
Sapporo, 060, Japan

1. Introduction

In this paper the interaction between vortex filaments and vortex rings and the deformation of vortex rings near the two-dimensional stagnation point are simulated by a three-dimensional vortex method (Shirayama et al. 1985, Leonard 1985). The two problems are respectively concerned with the effect of free-stream turbulence on turbulent plane mixing layers (Pui & Gartshore 1979) and the production of turbulence by the vortex stretching near saddles associated with large-scale coherent structures (Cantwell & Coles 1983, Kiya & Matsumura 1985). We assume that the first step to understand the free-stream turbulence effects is to study the interaction between a vortex ring and a vortex filament and that the process of deformation of a vortex ring gives us a clue to understand physical processes occurring near the saddles.

2. Numerical method

A vortex stick is represented by the position of its centre $\underline{x}(\underline{\ell}, t)$, where $\underline{\ell}$ is a material coordinate and t is the time, and by its vorticity $\underline{\omega}(\underline{\ell}, t)$. A vortex stick has also its own radius and length. The velocity $\underline{v}(\underline{\ell}, t)$ induced at the centre of a vortex stick $\underline{\ell}$ can be obtained by the Biot-Savart law

$$\underline{v}(\underline{\ell}, t) = \frac{1}{4\pi} \sum_{\underline{\ell}'} \underline{\omega}(\underline{\ell}', t) \times \frac{\underline{r}(\underline{\ell}, \underline{\ell}', t)}{r^3} \, dV(\underline{\ell}') \qquad (1)$$

where $\underline{\ell}'$ is the material coordinate of other vortex sticks in the flow field, $\underline{r} = \underline{x}(\underline{\ell}, t) - \underline{x}(\underline{\ell}', t)$ is the position vector of the vortex stick $\underline{\ell}$ relative to the vortex stick $\underline{\ell}'$, and $dV(\underline{\ell}')$ is the volume of the vortex stick $\underline{\ell}'$. We assume an incompressible fluid, so that the volume $dV(\underline{\ell}')$ is constant in time. The summation of (1) is taken over all the vortex sticks except the vortex stick $\underline{\ell}$. The motion of the vortex stick $\underline{\ell}$ is given by

$$\frac{D\underline{x}(\underline{\ell}, t)}{Dt} = \underline{v}(\underline{\ell}, t) \tag{2}$$

The vorticity $\underline{\omega}(\underline{\ell}, t)$ of (1) is calculated from the vorticity equation

$$\frac{D\underline{\omega}(\underline{\ell}, t)}{Dt} = [\underline{\omega}(\underline{\ell}, t) \cdot \nabla]\underline{v}(\underline{\ell}, t) + \nu\Delta\underline{\omega}(\underline{\ell}, t) \tag{3}$$

where the first term on the right-hand side describes the change of vorticity due to the stretching and rotation of the vortex sticks and the second term represents that due to the viscous diffusion. At first we delete the viscous term from (3). Substituting (1) into (3) and performing the differentiation, we have

$$\frac{D\underline{\omega}(\underline{\ell}, t)}{Dt} = \frac{1}{4\pi}\sum_{\underline{\ell}'} \underline{\omega}(\underline{\ell}, t) \times \left(\frac{1}{r^3}\underline{r}(\underline{\ell}, \underline{\ell}', t)\right.$$
$$\left. - \frac{3}{r^5}[\underline{\omega}(\underline{\ell}, t) \cdot \underline{r}(\underline{\ell}, \underline{\ell}', t)]\underline{r}(\underline{\ell}, \underline{\ell}', t)\right)dV(\underline{\ell}') \tag{4}$$

The velocity induced by a vortex stick is proportional to the radial distance from the centre inside the core and governed by the Biot-Savart law outside the core. The radius of the vortex stick, say σ_s, is related to its circulation Γ by

$$\Gamma = \pi\sigma_s^2\omega \tag{5}$$

where ω implies $|\underline{\omega}|$. The radius σ_s is also related to the mass, say m, by $m = \rho dV(\underline{\ell}, t) = \rho\pi\sigma_s^2 L$, where L is the length of the stick. Since the circulation Γ and the mass m are invariants of the vortex stick, we can calculate the evolution of σ_s and L in time if the vorticity $\underline{\omega}$ has been determined from the vorticity equation. When the length of a vortex stick reached a cut-off value, which was taken as twice the original length in this calculation, it was subdivided into two smaller sticks.

We approximately incorporated the viscous diffusion of vorticity into the evolution of the core. The radius of the core increases in proportion to $(\nu t)^{1/2}$, ν being the kinematic viscosity, owing to the viscosity. Accordingly the viscous core can be described by the equation $D\sigma/Dt = c^2\nu/(2\sigma)$, where c is a numerical constant, which was chosen as 2.245 in this study on the the basis of the solution for a rectilinear viscous vortex. σ on the right-hand side of this equation is replaced by the inviscid core radius σ_s, i.e. $D\sigma/Dt = c^2\nu/(2\sigma_s)$ (Shirayama et al. 1985), where σ_s is calculated from (5). Then the total (inviscid plus viscous) radius σ of the core was calculated from $\sigma = \sigma_s + (D\sigma/Dt)dt = \sigma_s + c^2\nu/(2\sigma_s)$.

3. Results

3.1 Interaction between a vortex filament and a vortex ring

The configuration of a vortex ring and a vortex filament is depicted in figure 1. The vortex filament lies on the y-axis, the x- and z-axes are taken so as to form a right-handed Cartesian coordinate. Without any loss of generality, the configuration of the vortex ring can be described by the coordinate (ξ, 0, ζ) of its centre and the angle α between the plane of the vortex ring and the xy-plane. In this calculation the vortex filament had a finite length of 8.4 times the diameter R of the vortex ring, its centre being at the origin of the xyz-coordinate. The vortex ring was initially subdivided into 30 vortex sticks; the vortex filament was also subdivided into vortex sticks of the same length.

The circulation of the vortex filament is denoted by Γ_f and that of the vortex ring by Γ_r. The ratio $\Gamma_f/\Gamma_r = \lambda$ defines the relative strength of the vortex filament and the vortex ring. Reynolds number Γ_r/ν was chosen as 1500 and the kinematic viscosity as 1.512×10^{-5} m^2/s (air). This led to the circulation $\Gamma_r = 0.0227$ m^2/s. The time step dt of the computation was chosen as $0.00147R/U_c$, where U_c is the undisturbed translation velocity of the vortex ring. The numerical calculations were performed for the following values of the parameters

λ = 1.0 and 2.0,

ξ/R = -2.0, -1.0, 0, 1.0 and 2.0,

α = 0° and 30°.

The distance ζ/R was chosen as 1.0 for all the calculations.

The coherent vortices formed in the plane mixing layers between a uniform flow and a still fluid are the strongest appearing in the uniform flow, so that the ratio λ should be greater than unity because the vortex ring is a model of the free-stream turbulent eddies. This is the reason why the values λ = 1.0 and 2.0 were employed in the calculations. The results are shown in figure 1, which suggests following patterns of the interaction.

(i) Exchange mode (figure 1a; $\lambda = 1.0$, $\xi/R = 0$, $\alpha = 0°$). A part of the vortex filament is replaced by a part of the vortex ring. The former part forms a new vortex ring togeher with the remaining part of the vortex ring. This is well represented by the velocity-vector fields in the mid section, see figure 2. At junctions we observe a region of diffused and random distribution of the vortex sticks.

(ii) Coalescence mode (figure 1b; $\lambda = 1.0$, $\xi/R = -1.0$, $\alpha = 30°$). The vortex ring and the vortex filament coalesce to form a single highly-deformed vortex filament. Again we observe a region of diffused and random distribution of the vortex sticks in the region where they come into contact.

(iii) Coalescence mode (figure 1c; $\lambda = 1.0$, $\xi/R = -2.0$, $\alpha = 0°$ and figure 1d; $\lambda = 1.0$, $\xi/R = -1.0$, $\alpha = 0°$). These are other patterns of coalescence of the vortex filament and the vortex ring. It is interesting to note that a part of them forms a vortex-pair-like structure during the process of the coalescence. These parts eventually mingle to form a region of diffused and random distribution of the vortex sticks. Since the vortex sticks which come from the vortex filament and the vortex ring have opposite signs of rotation, they are probably cancelled out owing to the viscous diffusion. Eventually a single deformed vortex filament will emerge.

(iv) Capture mode (figure 1e; $\lambda = 2.0$, $\xi/R = -1.0$, $\alpha = 0°$). The initial configuration of the vortex ring and the vortex filament is the same to that of figure 1d except that the circualtion of the former is a half of the circulation of the latter. Again in this case we observe the formation of a vortex-pair-like structure but this structure does not merge as in the case of figures 1c and 1d. The vortex ring is rotated by the velocity field induced by the vortex filament. This mode can be termed as the capture of the vortex ring by the vortex filament. The absence of merging is owing to the fact that the circulation of the filament and the ring is not the same.

(v) Weak-interaction mode (figure 1f; $\lambda = 1.0$, $\xi/R = 1.0$, $\alpha = 0°$). In this configuration the initial position of the vortex ring is the mirror reflection of figure 1d with respect to the yz-plane, other parameters being exactly the same. The vortex filament and the ring experience only a slight deformation. In this sense this pattern represents a weak-interaction mode.

Other calculations were made for various combinations of the parameters; the patterns (i)-(v) were found to be typical.

3.2 Deformation of a vortex ring in the stagnation-point flow

The velocity field in the two-dimensional stagnation-point flow is given by $\underline{u} = (ax, 0, -az)$ where a (> 0) is a constant which represents the rate of strain. The coordinate system xyz is given in figure 3. The circulation Γ_r and the diameter R of the vortex ring can be described in relation to the rate of strain by a non-dimensional parameter $k = R^2 a/\Gamma_r$.

The numerical calculations were performed for k = 0.1, 0.5 and 1.0. The centre of the vortex ring was initially located on the z-axis at a distance 1.0R above the xy-plane. The sense of rotation of the vortex ring is such that it approaches to the stagnation point by its own velocity of induction. The vortex ring was initially divided into 50 vortex sticks. The time interval of advancing the vortex sticks was the same to that in §§3.1.

Results are shown in figure 3, which shows the process of the deformation of the vortex ring. It is interesting to note that a strong vortex ring (k = 0.1, figure 3a) experiences a small deformation and develops an instability. On the other hand, for weak vortex rings (figures 3b and c), we observe a great deformation of the vortex rings, which develop no instability. This suggests that the stretching prohibits for such an instability to occur. Moreover, the ends of the stretched vortex rings are seen to be bent downwards; this is caused by the velocity induced by the stretched part of the vortex rings.

It is interesting to see how the circumferential velocity at the radius of the core increases as the vortex ring approaches to the saddle since the vortex rings are a model of turbulent eddies near the saddles. This is shown in figure 4, which is given at the bottom of next page. The greater the rate of strain, the greater is the amplification of the circumferential velocity (or turbulent velocity).

This calculation suggests that, if the rate of strain is weak, vortex rings experience no significant stretching so that the production of turbulent energy will be insignificant at saddles. On the other hand, even if a strong saddle exists in the flow field, the absence of suitable turbulennt eddies near the saddle will also produce no turbulent energy. Such a case is found by Suzuki et al. (1986).

4. Conclusion

Three-dimensional discrete-vortex method has demonstrated several typical patterns of the interaction between a vortex ring and a vortex filament, i.e. exchange mode, coalescence mode, capture mode and weak-interaction mode, depending on their circulation and configuration. The deformation of a vortex ring near a two-dimensional saddle has shown the formation of a pair of counter-rotating vortices elongated in the direction of out-going separatrices; the amplification of the circumferential velocity at the edge of vortex rings has also been demonstrated. The present results may give a clue to understand the free-stream turbulence effects on shear layers and the production of turbulence at saddles due to the vortex stretching.

REFERENCES

Cantwell, B. & Coles, D. 1983 J. Fluid Mech. 136, 321.
Kiya, M. & Matsumura, M. 1985 Bull. JSME, 28, 1054.
Leonard, A. 1985 Ann. Rev. Fluid Mech. 17, 523.
Pui, N. K. & Gartshore, I. S. 1979 J. Fluid Mech. 91, 111.
Shirayama, S., Kuwahara, K. & Mendez, R. 1985 AIAA Paper 85-1488.
Suzuki, Y., Kiya, M. & Takahashi, T. 1986 The 3rd Asian Cong. Fluid Mech., Tokyo (to be presented).

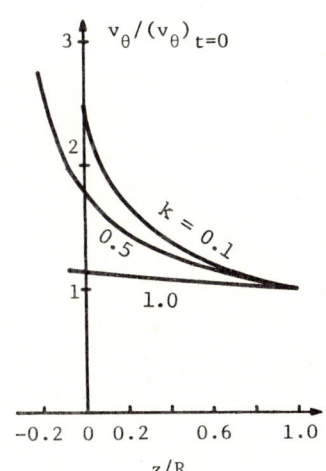

Figure 4. Amplification of circumferential velocity at the mid section of a vortex ring during its stretching near a saddle. v_θ is the circumferential velocity and $(v_\theta)_{t=0}$ is its initial value.

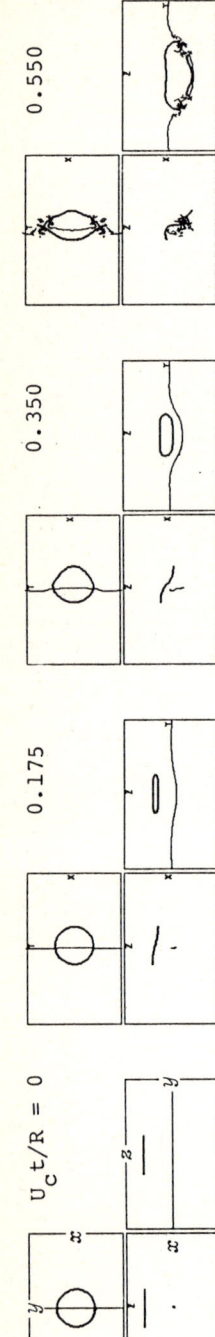

(a) Exchange mode ($\lambda = 1.0$, $\zeta/R = 0$, $\alpha = 0°$)

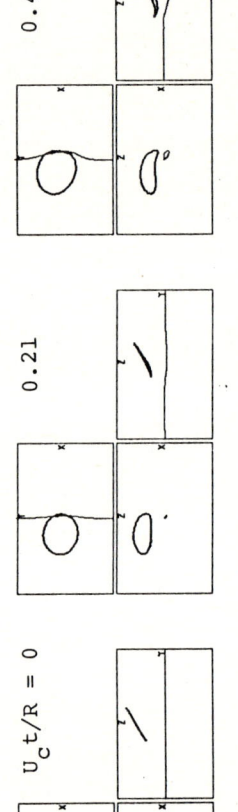

(b) Coalescence mode ($\lambda = 1.0$, $\zeta/R = -1.0$, $\alpha = 30°$)

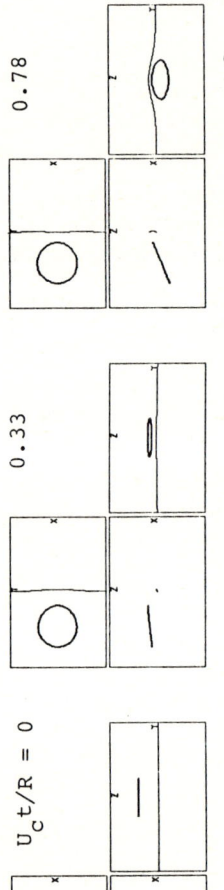

(c) Coalescence mode ($\lambda = 1.0$, $\zeta/R = -2.0$, $\alpha = 0°$)

Figure 1. Interaction between a vortex ring and a vortex filament. The initial z-coordinate of the centre of the vortex ring is located at $\zeta/R = 1.0$.

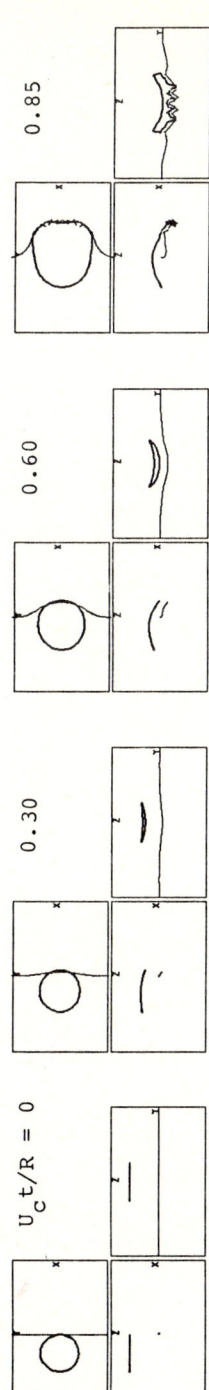
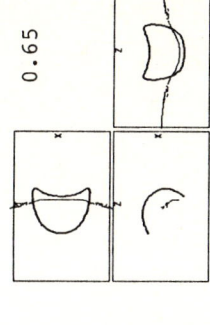
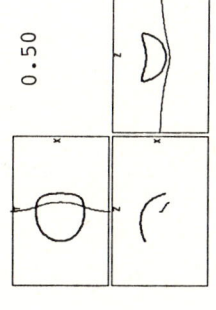
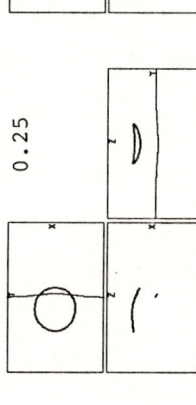
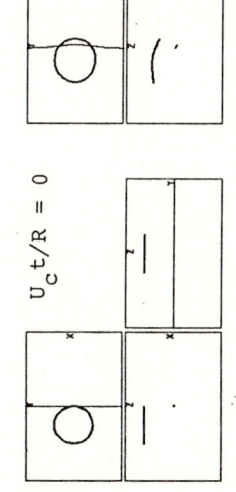

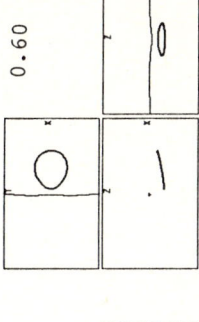
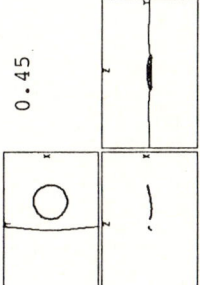
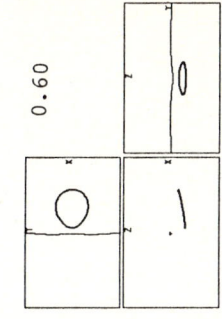

(d) Coalescence mode ($\lambda = -1.0$, $\xi/R = -1.0$, $\alpha = 0°$)

(e) Capture mode ($\lambda = 2.0$, $\xi/R = -1.0$, $\alpha = 0°$)

(f) Weak-interaction mode ($\lambda = 1.0$, $\xi/R = 1.0$, $\alpha = 0°$)

Figure 1. Interaction between a vortex ring and a vortex filament. The initial z-coordinate of the centre of the vortex ring is located at $\zeta/R = 1.0$. (Continued)

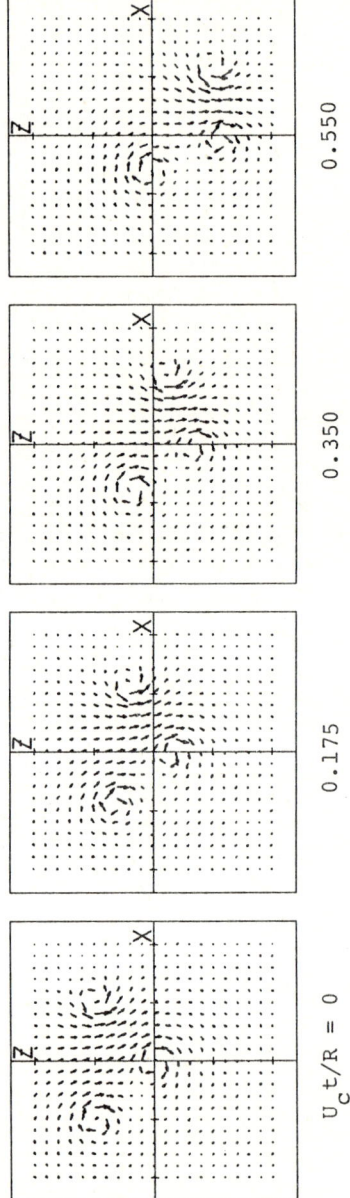

Figure 2. Velocity-vector fields induced by a vortex filament and a vortex ring during the interaction of exchange mode.

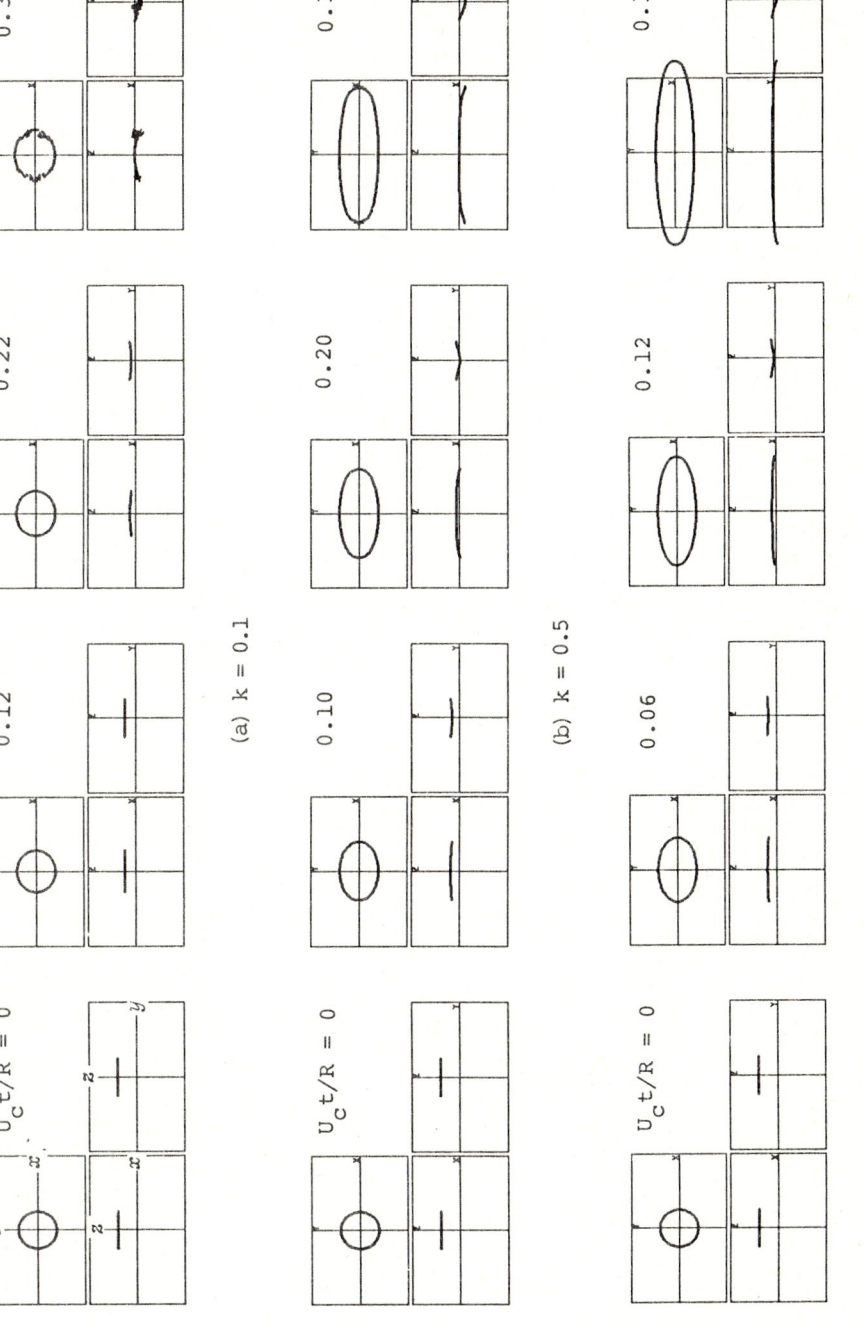

Figure 3. Deformation of a vortex ring in the two-dimensional stagnation-point flow. The centre of the vortex ring was initially located on the z-axis at $\zeta/R = 1.0$.

A New Three-Dimensional Vortex Method

S.Shirayama and K.Kuwahara[*]

[*]Department of Aeronautics, University of Tokyo,
The Institute of space and Astronautical Science,
4-6-1 Komaba, Meguroku, Tokyo, 153 JAPAN

Abstract

A new vortex method based on the vorticity equation is introduced to simulate incompressible vorticity-dominated flows. This method is based on Lagrangian way of tracking vortices a three-dimensional flow where the vortices are replaced by a number of disconnected vortex sticks. The interaction of vortex rings and three-dimensional flow past a parachute are simulated by this method. In the problems of flow past a parachute, a simplified vortex-lattice method is combined with this method and a potential theory is applied to introduce, an effect of porosity. The cross-linking of vortex rings and spiral structure of the wake behind the parachute were well simulated. Also the effect of the porosity and shape of the parachute can be estimated.

Introduction

Many vortex methods have been studied to simulate incompressible vorticity dominated flows/1/. In two dimensions some of these methods have been quite successful. In three dimensions vortex strecthing introduces formidable difficulties for numerical methods. Ordinary methods are based on representing numerically each continuous vortex filament by discrete vortex segments, and as the vortex filament stretches, increase in the number of computational elements quickly make the calculation impractical.

Recently, several vortex methods based on the vorticity equation have been proposed. Chorin introduced a stick method/2/. Beale and Majda have proved the convergence to Euler equations of their own schemes but have not implemented them numerically/3/. Anderson and Greengard proposed two algorithms, and they have shown many vortex methods are classified into their two algorithms. Also they have proved the convergence to Euler equations of their own schemes and simulated the interaction of two vortex rings/4,5/. However, it is difficult to apply these methods to complicated problems.

The method introduced in this paper does not attempt to track the dynamics of each vortex filament but instead follows a collection of fluid particles with vorticity which are used to represent the vorticity-concentrated fluid. Each fluid particle is represented by a cylinder called a vortex stick whose dimensions change in time according to the vorticity equation; the sticks need not be connected with each other but when their strength reaches a given cutoff they are subdivided as in Chorin's work.

Two problems are solved by this method; one is interraction of vortex rings and the other is simulation of flow past a body. In latter problem, a simplified vortex lattice method is introduced to represent a immersed body. Also, by introducing a grid system a velocity distribution and pressure fields are obtained.

These results suggest that this method is well suited for representing the reconnection between vortex filaments and for resolving the qualitative features of the flows. Additionally, computer cost in a vector processor as a function of the number of vortex elements appears to be closer to linear than to quadratic.

Computational Method

The present method consists of two parts. One is solving the flow equations. The other is the representation of an immerced body.

a) Solving the flow equations

In two dimensions, a point vortex has been exclusively used as a computational element. In three dimensions, several different types can be taken as an element. The present method employs a vortex stick as the basic computational element. The stick named as Λ_i is defined by the following eight quantities (Fig.1(b)): the coordinates $\mathbf{r}=(x_1,x_2,x_3)$ of the center of the sticks, its vorticity $\omega=(\omega_1,\omega_2,\omega_3)$ its length δl, and its core radius σ . The vorticity field is replaced by that induced by a number of vortex sticks (Fig.1(a)). The trajectory $\mathbf{r}_i$ of the i-th stick is determined by ,

$$\frac{D\mathbf{r}_i}{Dt} = \mathbf{u}_i, \qquad \mathbf{u}_i = \sum_j \mathbf{u}_{ij} , \qquad (1)$$

where $\mathbf{u}_{ij}$ is the velocity induced by j-th stick and is determined by using Biot-Savart law :

$$\mathbf{u}_{ij} = \frac{1}{4\pi} \int \frac{\omega_j(\mathbf{r}_j') \times (\mathbf{r}_i - \mathbf{r}_j')}{|\mathbf{r}_i - \mathbf{r}_j|^3} d\mathbf{r}_j' . \qquad (2)$$

This can be integrated, and we can get the following algebraic expression (see Fig.2 for notations) :

if $h \geq \sigma_j$:
$$\mathbf{u}_{ij} = \frac{k_j}{4\pi} \left(\frac{1}{f} + \frac{1}{g}\right) \cdot \left(\frac{1}{f+g-\delta l_j} - \frac{1}{f+g+\delta l_j}\right) \cdot \frac{\omega_j}{|\omega_j|} \times f_j , \qquad (3)$$

if $h < \sigma_j$:
$$\mathbf{u}_{ij} = \frac{k_j}{8\pi \sigma_j^2 \delta l_j} \cdot \left(\frac{1}{f} + \frac{1}{g}\right) \cdot (\delta l_j - f + g)(\delta l_j + f - g) \cdot \frac{\omega_j}{|\omega_j|} \times f_j . \qquad (4)$$

The vorticity is determined by the following vorticity equations:

$$\frac{D\omega_i}{Dt} = \omega_i \nabla \mathbf{u}_i + \nu \Delta \omega_i . \qquad (5)$$

Since we shall consider an invisid flow, Eq.(5) becomes

$$\frac{D\omega_i}{Dt} = \omega_i \nabla \mathbf{u}_i = \omega_i \sum_j \nabla \mathbf{u}_{i,j} \qquad (6)$$

As the velocity $\mathbf{u}_{i,j}$ is the function of $\mathbf{r}_i$, $\nabla \mathbf{u}_{i,j}$ can be calculated analytically. For example,

If $h \geq \sigma_j$:
$$\frac{\partial u_{i,j,1}}{\partial x_{i,1}} = \frac{k_j}{4\pi} (G (x_{i,1} - x_{p,j,1}) + H (x_{i,1} - x_{q,j,1}))$$

$$((x_{i,3} - x_{p,j,3}) (x_{q,j,2} - x_{p,j,2})$$

$$- (x_{i,2} - x_{p,j,2}) (x_{q,j,3} - x_{p,j,3}))/\delta l_j$$

$$G = -\frac{1}{f^3} \cdot \left(\frac{1}{f+g-\delta l_j} - \frac{1}{f+g+\delta l_j}\right) + \frac{1}{f}\left(\frac{1}{f}+\frac{1}{g}\right) \cdot \left(\frac{-1}{(f+g-\delta l_j)^2} + \frac{1}{(f+g+\delta l_j)^2}\right)$$

$$H = -\frac{1}{g^3} \cdot \left(\frac{1}{f+g-\delta l_j} - \frac{1}{f+g+\delta l_j}\right) + \frac{1}{2}\left(\frac{1}{g}+\frac{1}{f}\right) \cdot \left(\frac{-1}{(f+g-\delta l_j)^2} + \frac{1}{(f+g+\delta l_j)^2}\right) \quad (7)$$

The position and vorticity of the next step are determined by solving Eqs.(1) and (6). The radius σ_i is determined by Kelvin's theorem on vortex:

$$\pi(\sigma_i^n)^2 |\omega_i^n| = \pi(\sigma_i^{n+1})^2 |\omega_i^{n+1}| . \quad (8)$$

The length δl_i is determined by the continuity equation:

$$\pi(\sigma_i^n)^2 \delta l_i^n = \pi(\sigma_i^{n+1})^2 \delta l_i^{n+1} . \quad (9)$$

Thus, the eight quantities of the stick at the next time step are determined. This procedure is illustrated in Fig.3. That for the ordinary vortex filament method is illustrated in Fig.4 for comparison.

The viscous effect is estimated by the following conception. Eq.(5) is splitted into the vorticity stretching equations (Eq.(6)') and the vorticity diffusion equation.

$$\frac{D\omega_i}{Dt} = \nu \Delta \omega_i \quad (10)$$

The solution of this equation is used to implement the viscous effect. It is approximated via a viscous vortex core:

$$\sigma = \alpha \sqrt{\nu t} . \quad (11)$$

To add the strong effect that viscosity has when the vortex-core size is small, Eq.(11) is differentiated. Then,

$$\frac{D\sigma}{Dt} = \frac{\alpha^2 \nu}{2\sigma_s} \quad (12)$$

where σ_s is vortex-core size of inviscid flow. This makes the computation more stable. The theoretical work of Greengard suggests that this numerical implementation may not represent a real viscous effect/4/ but it is effective at least for stabilization of the computation.

b) Representation of an immerced body

A body in the flow field is expressed by means of a vortex lattice. The lattice is composed of a number of vortex sticks, each of which induces the velocity field same as the previous procedure. This makes the computation very simple. As an example, we consider a flow past a circular disk(Fig.5). The disk composed of rectangular vortex lattices which are the basic elements (Fig.6). The strength of the lattice is determined by the following boundary condition.

$$v_{ni} = 0 \quad (i=1,\ldots m) \quad (13)$$

where v_{ni} is the velocity in the nomal direction at the i-th control point, and m is the number of the lattice or control points. In the case of axisymmetric body, the configuration of the lattice is simplified. If the flow in front of the body is approximately axisymmetric, the strength of the side of the lattice in the radial direction is nearly zero (Fig.7).   As a result, the vortex lattice system can be symplified as shown in Fig.8.   The strength of the lattice have to be determined at each time step to satisfy the boundary condition.

A separation model is explained by the following conception. This method aims to simulate a high-Reynolds-number flow.   In this range of Reynolds number, the viscosity acts only in the boundary layer of the body and vortices are generated only in this region. They roll up and separate from the edge.   The separation model is considered to follow this mechanism.   Firstly the strengths of vortex sticks at the edge are determined to satisfy the boundary condition at the control points (Fig.9) and those at the edge are separated from the body and these nascent vortices become free vortices.   Shown in Fig.10 is the flow fields simulated by this model.

The effect of the porosity is introduced by imposing the uniform flow; as mentioned previously the Reynolds number is high and the effect of the viscosity is restricted only in the boundary layer, so potential theory can be applied to this method.   Firstly flow fields without porosity is calculated and velocity potential ϕ_1 is obtained. Here we impose that of uniform flow (ϕ_2), then potential in this flow fields is obtained as a linear combination.

$$\phi = (1-\beta)\phi_1 + \beta\phi_2$$

$$u = \text{grad } \phi \qquad (14)$$

where β is porosity.

Results

a) The interaction of vortex rings

Firstly, the problem of interaction of two vortex rings was computed: each rings is replaced by 36 vortex sticks and the time step is taken to 0.005.   The cross-linking of two rings was well simulated in Fig.12.   In these figures and in the next figure, the upper left part is the top view, the lower right part is the side view and lower left part is the front view.   In the case of high Reynolds number, turbulent diffusion of vorticity propagates from the closer part of the two rings to other parts (Fig.13); in this case each ring consists of 50 sticks.   The passage of the two vortex rings is simulated in Fig.14. In this case, each physical vortex ring is replaced by four mathematical rings, each of which consists of 50 sticks.   After the merging, a distore ring diffuse rapidly with a deformation which is observed in the experiment.   In every case, turbulent diffusion is qualitatively simulated.

b) A flow past a parachute

The parachute is modeled by a rigid circular disk or a part of sphere.   A configulation parameter θ is defined in Fig.11.   (for example, if θ takes 0 degree, the configuration is a circular disk). In this paper , three cases is computed(θ = 0, 45 , 90 degrees), and in each case porosity takes 0 or 0.25.   The body is replaced by 14x15 vortex sticks and nascent vortices are consisted of fifteen vortex sticks.   The body starts impulsively with velocity U.   At every three time steps, nascent vortices separate from the edge of the body. The non-dimensional time step is taken to be 0.0025.   As shown in Figs.15 to 17, the flow pattern is divided into four stages.
1) The starting vortex separates behind the body.   The flow field is axisymmetric.
2) The flow begins to be disturbed ans the disturbance grows where the vortices are rolled in.   Then the vortices stretch perpendicularly to

the disk, and the axisymmetry of the flow is destroyed.
3) The big turbulent vortices separates suddenly into the flow, and the spiral structure of the wake vortices is observed.
4) As the wake vortices with the spiral structure flows out, the near wake becomes rather stable.

In each case, as the porosity becomes larger, the flow becomes more stable and width of wake narrower. This means that the drag of the body decreases. Also it is found that, if the parameter θ is large, the width of wake is broad near the edge of the body. Especially in the case which the parameter θ is 90 degrees and porosity is 0 (Fig.17(a)), two vortex tubes interact with around the body surface and are distinguished from each other clearly.

In this way, the effect of porosity and configuration was simulated well.

This method is based on the Lagrangian way of tracking vortices and the result is represented by vorticity vectors. The qualitative validity of this method is easily seen by the interaction of vortices and vortex structure in three-dimensional wake. However, to analyze a flow field quantitatively, it is necessary to compare with a experimental results and other numerical methods. To facilitate this comparison, a grid system is constructed (Fig.18) and velocity components are calculated at each grid points by the Biot-Savart law(Fig.19). If velocity field can be obtained, the pressure is computed by the following poisson equation.

$$\Delta p = - \text{div}(u \cdot \text{grad } u) \tag{15}$$

This equation is obtained by taking the divergence of the Navier-Stokes equations with the relation of div u =0.

This is transformed to genarated curvelinear coordinates and solved by S.O.R. Fig.20 shows the pressure contours and velocity distribution in the initial stage of the flow past a circular disk without the porosity. Shown in Figs.21,22 are pressure contours and velocity distribution, corresponding to Fig.15(a),(b). The history of the drag coefficients is shown in Fig.23. The time averaged coefficients are 0.95 without porosity and 0.67 with porosity 0.25. Thus effect of the porosity is clearly obtained by the present method. Finally the computation with a fine lattice system (16x24) is done in the case of a circular disk without porosity. Fig.24 shows the pressure contours and vorticity vectors. Fig.25 shows the flow structure at t=12.85, seen from various view points. The contour surface of an absolute value of the vorticity at the same time is shown in Fig.26. The history of drag coefficients is shown in Fig.27. Compared to the previous case(Fig.23), the drag in the first stage is different. The drag of the fine case agree with the experimental result better but after the separation of starting vortex, the one of both cases takes almost same values.

The computational code for this method is easily vectorized and runs on HITACHI super computer S810/20 about fifty times as fast as the original scalar speed, thus a speed of about 400 MFLOPS was obtained. The computation of this case is three minutes by S810, or two hours on Fujitsu M380. The computation time of most of vortex methds on a scalar machine is proportional to the square of the elements, but it was found that, on S810, CPU cost is almost propotional to the number of elements itself. This is because S810 becomes much more effective as vector length increase.

Conclusion

It was found that the present vortex method is capable to treat the vortex reconnection as well as the flow past a body, giving a three-dimensional wake structure clearly and some properties (pressure distribution, drag coefficient , etc.) can be obtained by using finite difference type grid system. Also the porosity can be easily included. This method is natural extension of two-dimensional vortex methods and the vectorization for supercomputers is easy and very effective.

Acknowledgements

I would like to thank Professor Alexandre Chorin for his advice during my stay at U.C Berkeley.

References

1) Leonard,A. : Computing Three-Dimensional Incompressible Flows with Vortex Elements, Annual Review of Fluid Mech.,17(1985)
2) Chorin,A.J. : Vortex Models and Boundary Layer Instability, SIAM J.Sci.Stat.Comput.,1(1980) pp.1-21
3) Beale,J.T. & Majda,A. : Vortex Methods I:Convergence in Three-Dimensions, Math.Comput.,39(1982) pp.1-27
4) Greengard,C. : Three-Dimensinal Vortex Methods, Ph.D.Thesis, Department of Mathematics,U.C.Berkeley(1984)
5) Anderson,C. & Greengard,C. : On Vortex Methods, SIAM J.Numer.Anal. 22(1985) pp.413-440

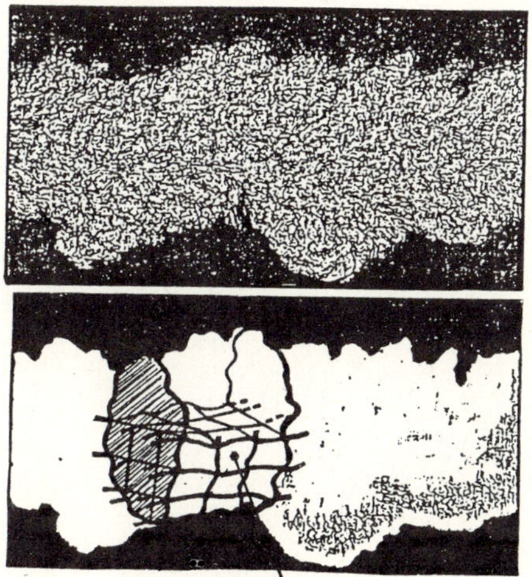

Fig.1(a)

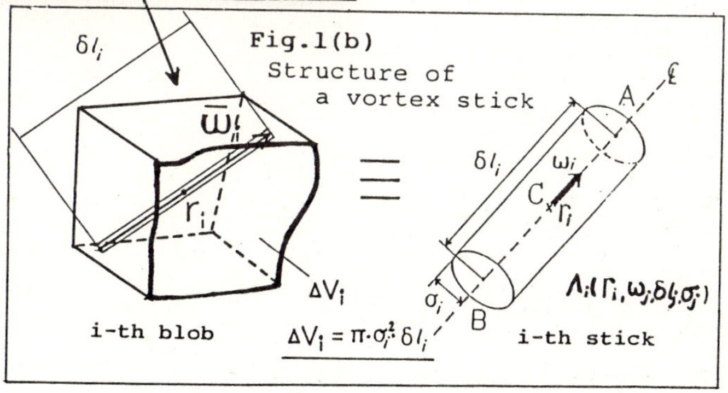

Fig.1(b) Structure of a vortex stick

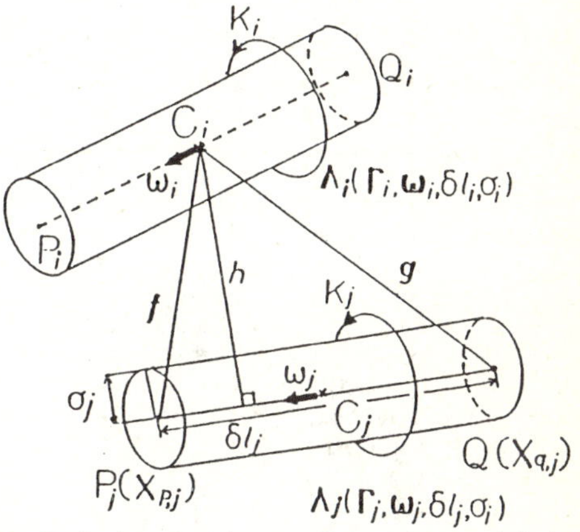

Fig.2 Interaction of vortex sticks

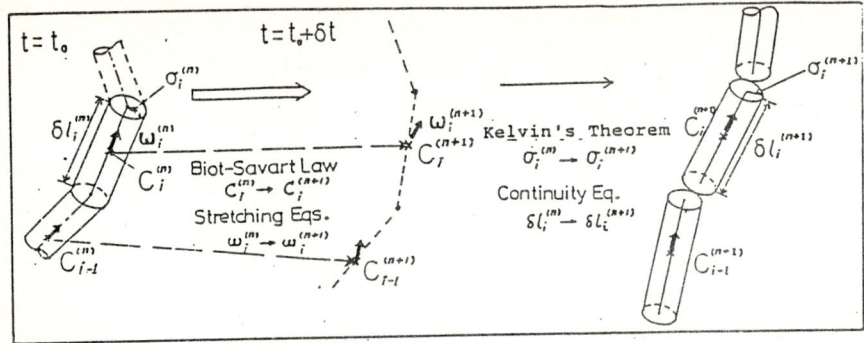

Fig.3 Present method

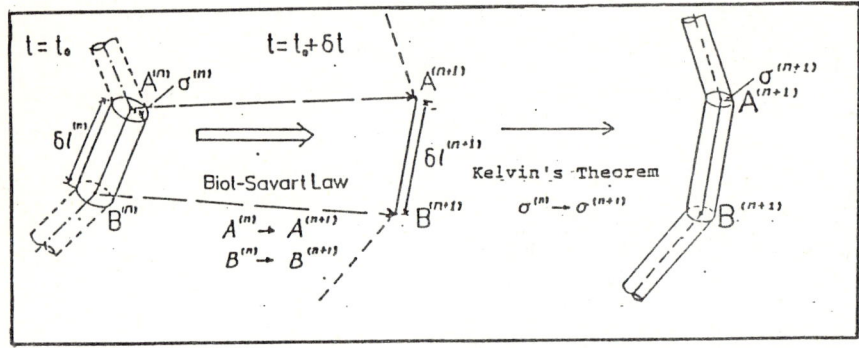

Fig.4 Ordinary method

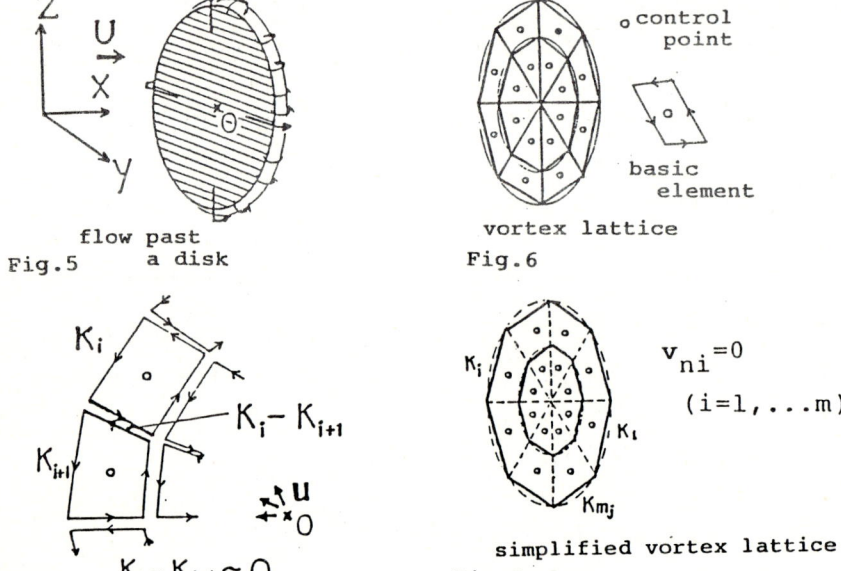

Fig.5 flow past a disk

Fig.6 vortex lattice

Fig.7 $K_i - K_{i+1} \approx 0$

Fig.8 simplified vortex lattice
$v_{ni} = 0$ $(i=1,\ldots m)$

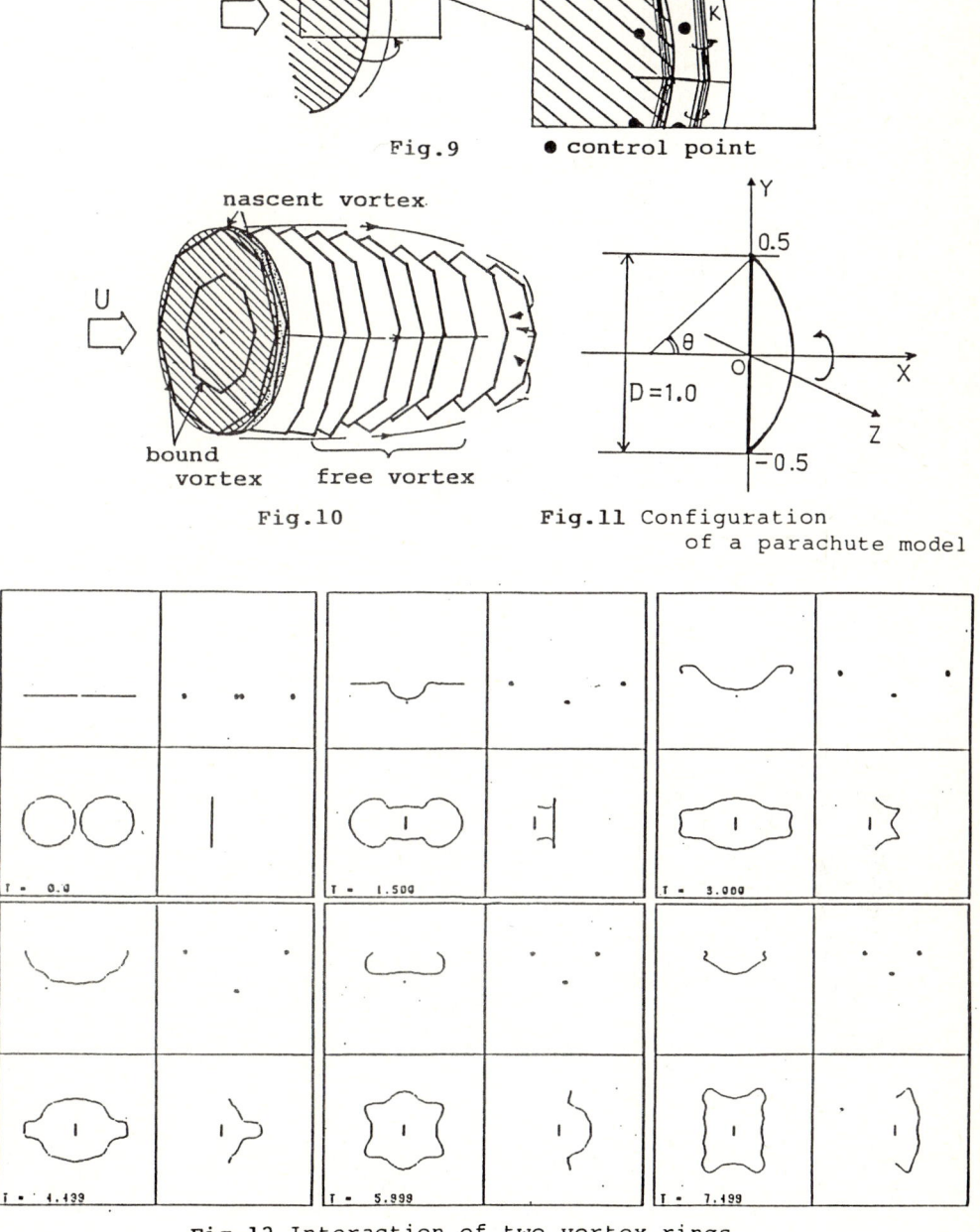

Fig.9 ● control point

Fig.10

Fig.11 Configuration of a parachute model

Fig.12 Interaction of two vortex rings

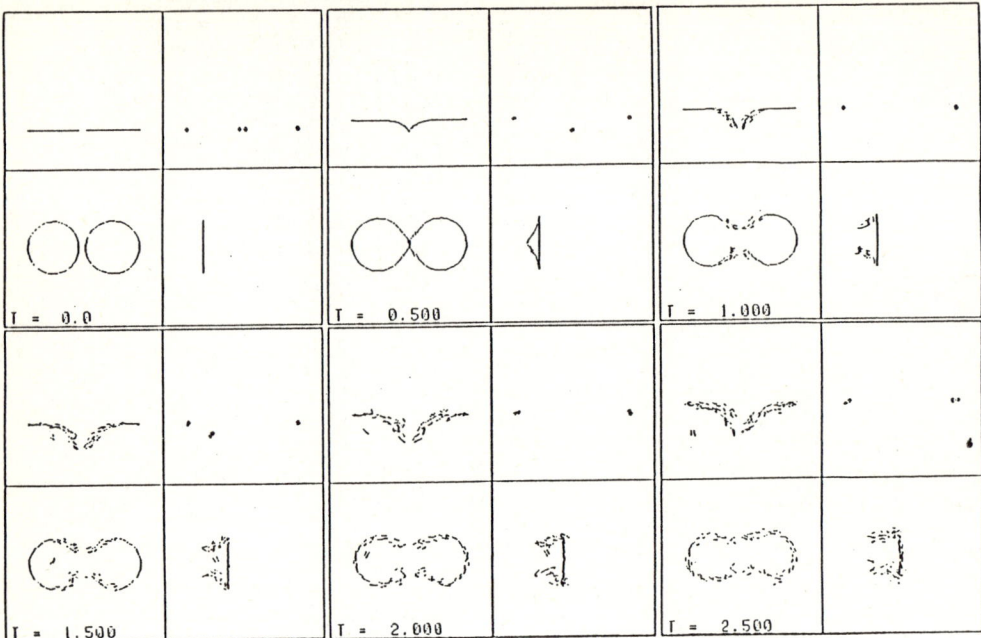

Fig.13 Interaction of two vortex rings (high Reynolds number)

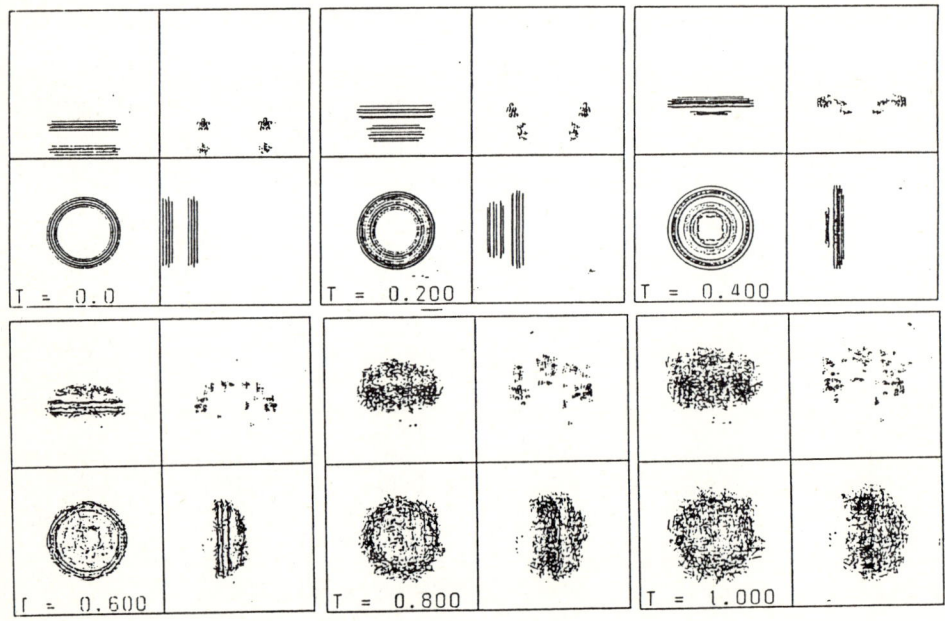

Fig.14 Passing of two vortex rings

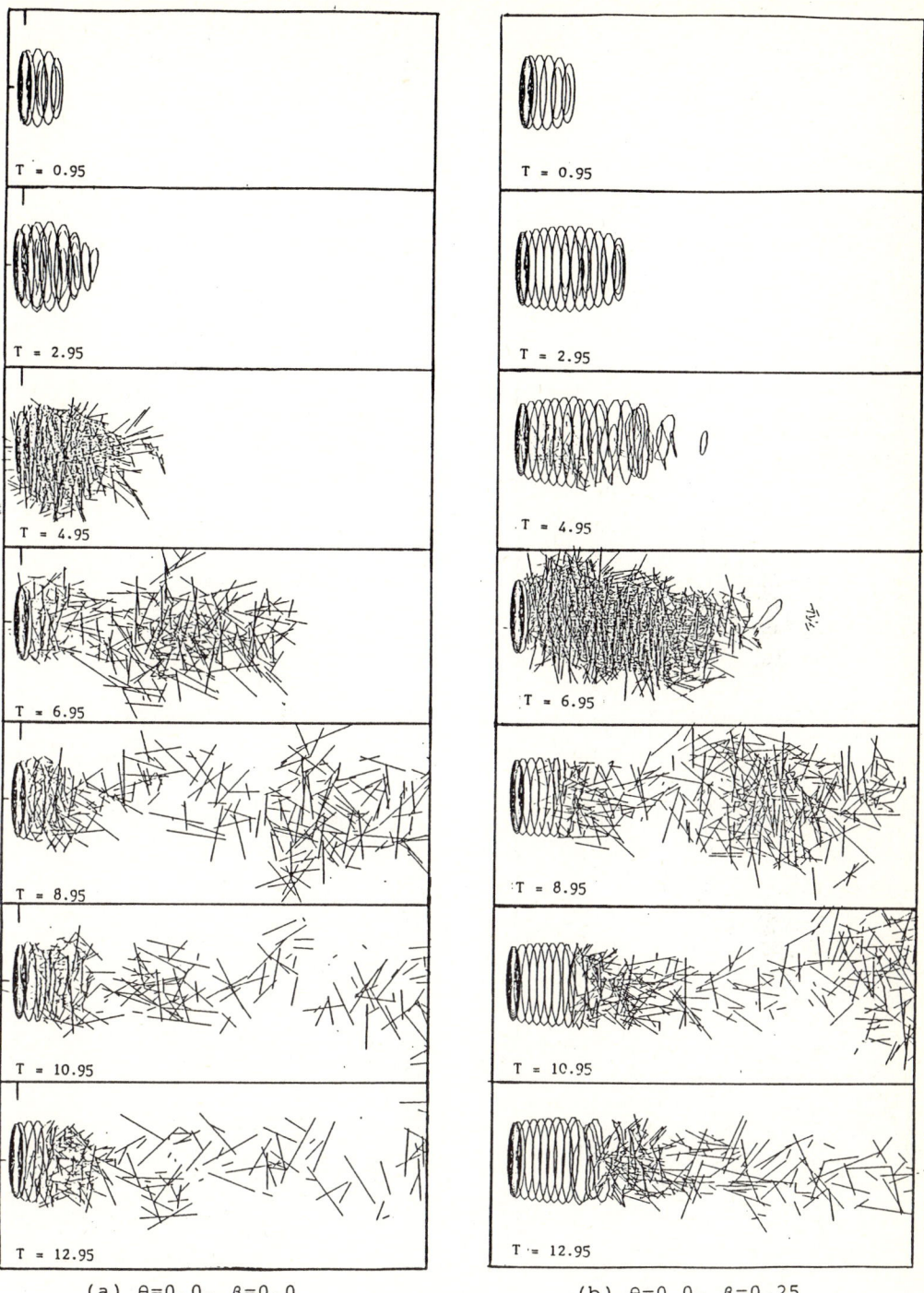

(a) θ=0.0, β=0.0   (b) θ=0.0, β=0.25

Fig.15 Development of vortex pattern

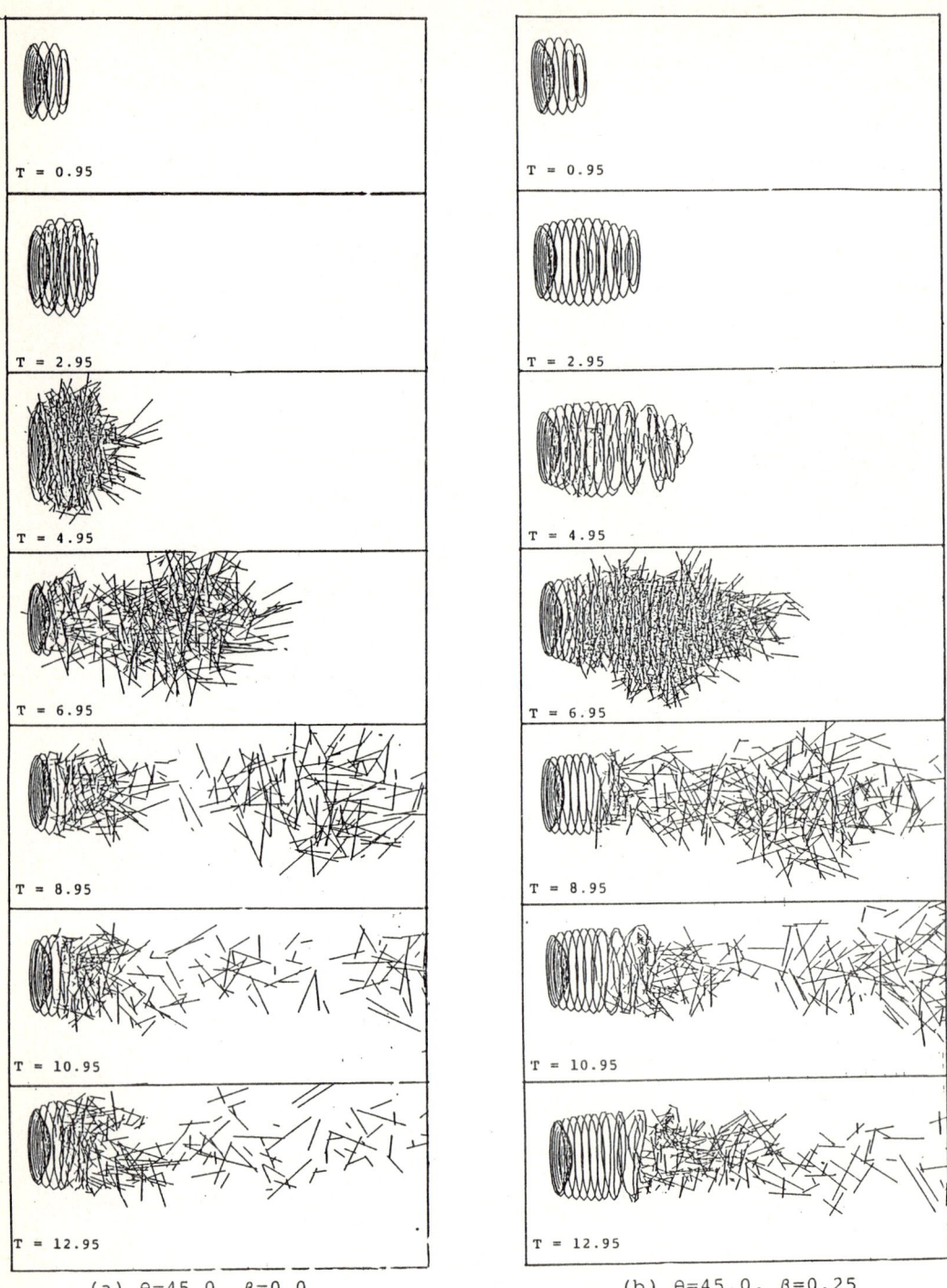

(a) θ=45.0, β=0.0 (b) θ=45.0, β=0.25
Fig.16 Development of vortex pattern

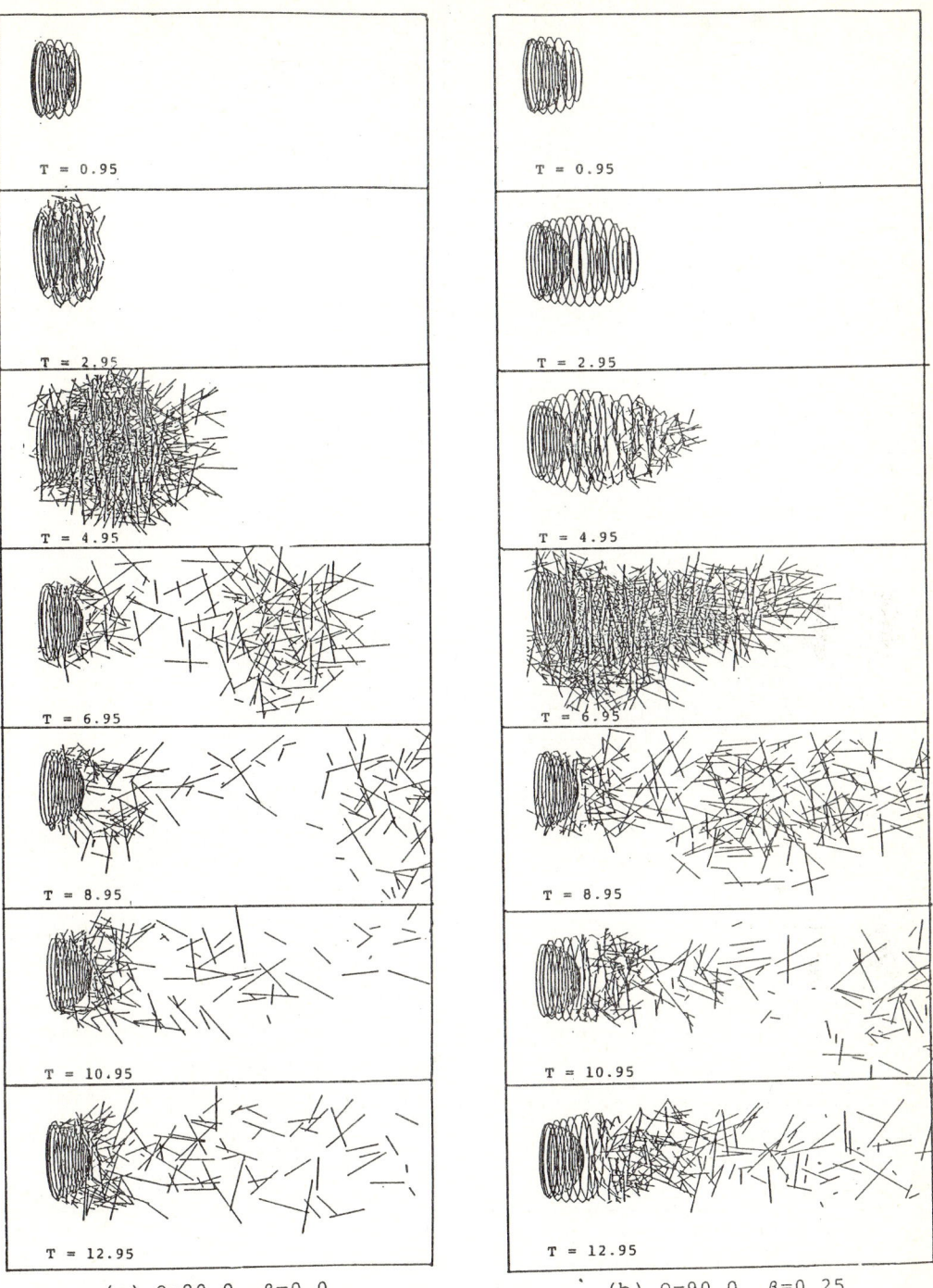

(a) θ=90.0, β=0.0   (b) θ=90.0, β=0.25
Fig.17 Development of vortex pattern

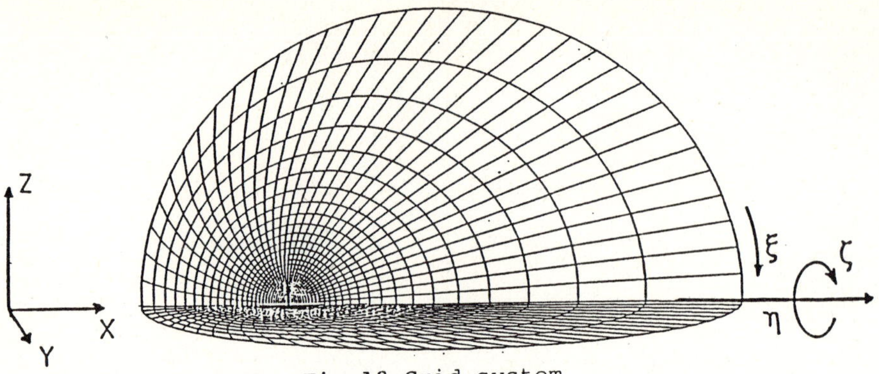

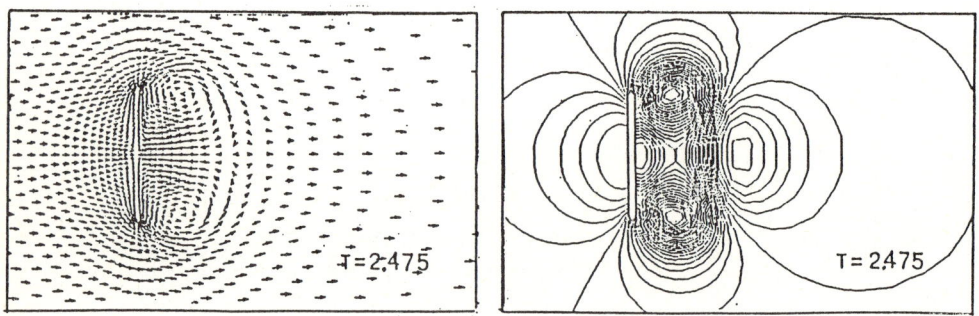

Fig.18 Grid system

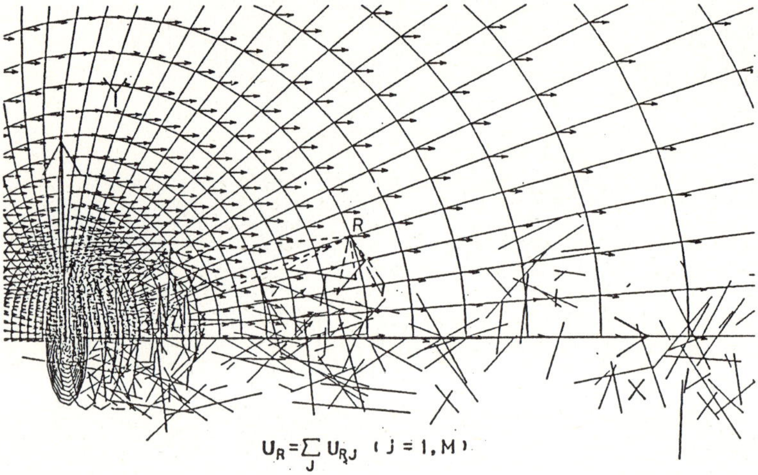

Fig.19 Procedure of computation of velocity field
$$U_R = \sum_J U_{R,J} \quad (J = 1, M)$$

Fig.20 Pressure contours and velocity vectors in the initial stage

T = 2.475

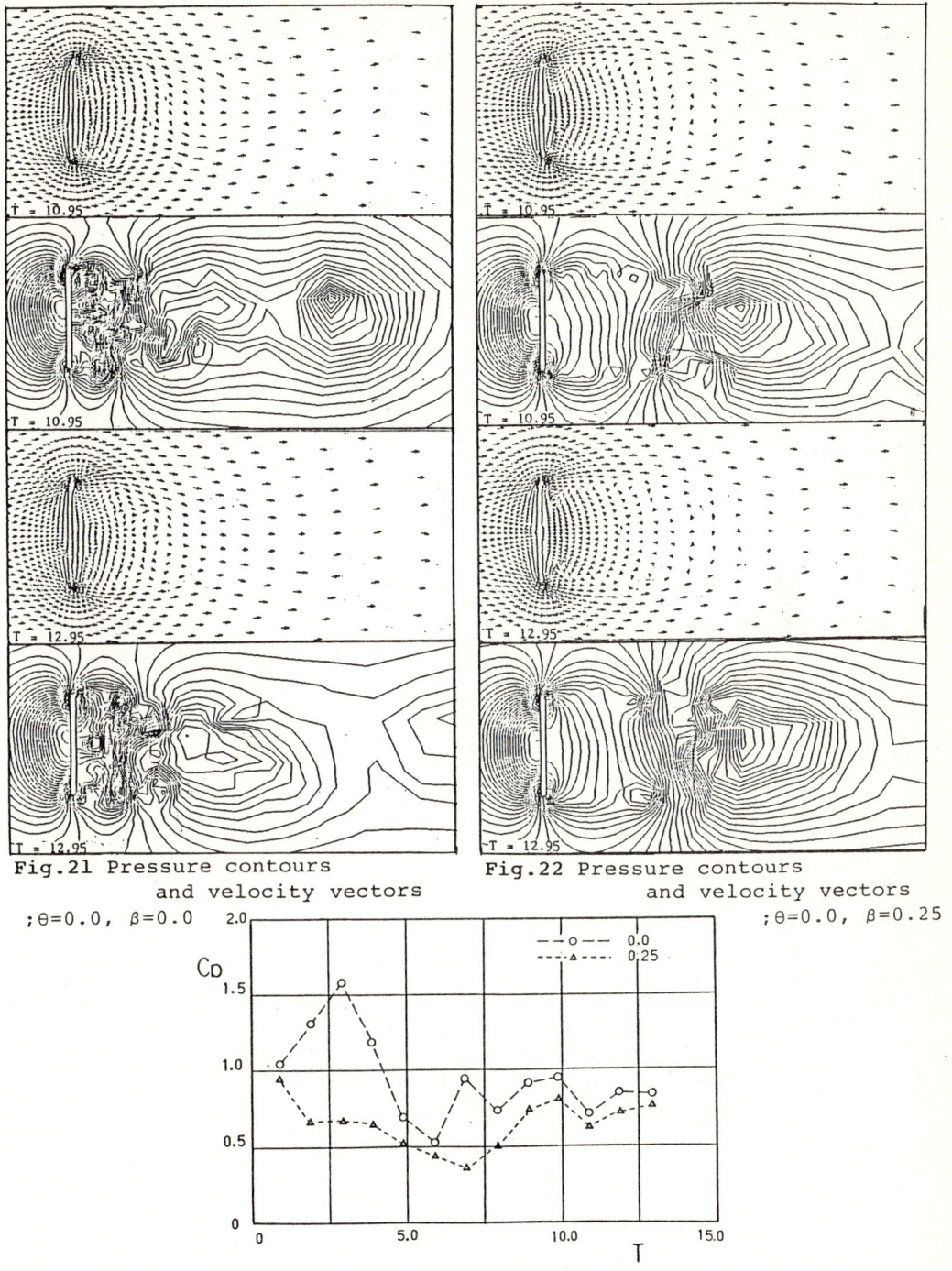

Fig.21 Pressure contours and velocity vectors ; θ=0.0, β=0.0

Fig.22 Pressure contours and velocity vectors ; θ=0.0, β=0.25

Fig.23 The history of drag coefficients

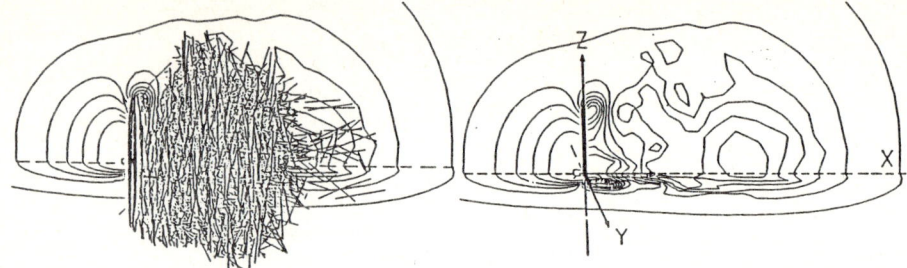

Fig.24 Pressure contours at the second stage (t=4.95)

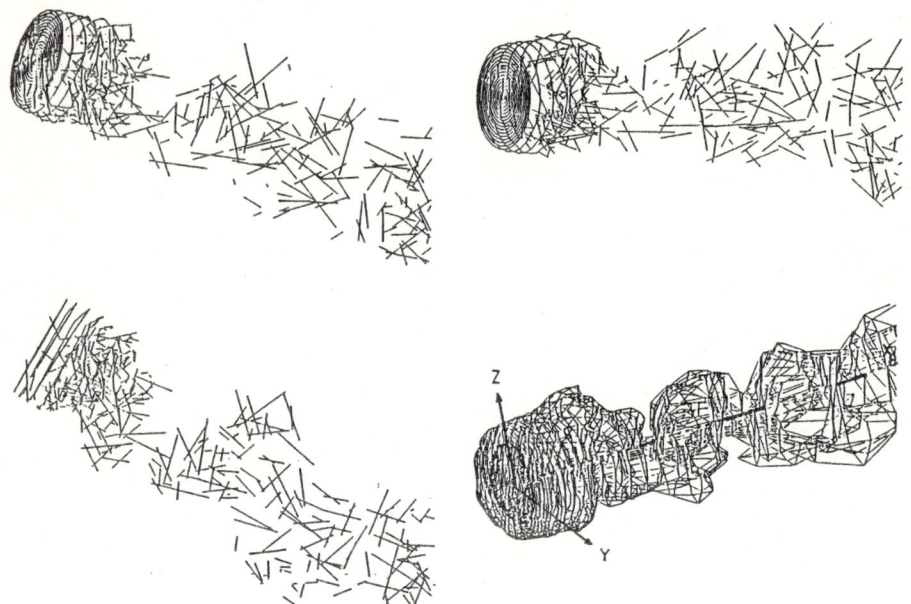

Fig.25 Representation of vortex sticks at t=12.85

Fig.26 Equi-vorticity surface

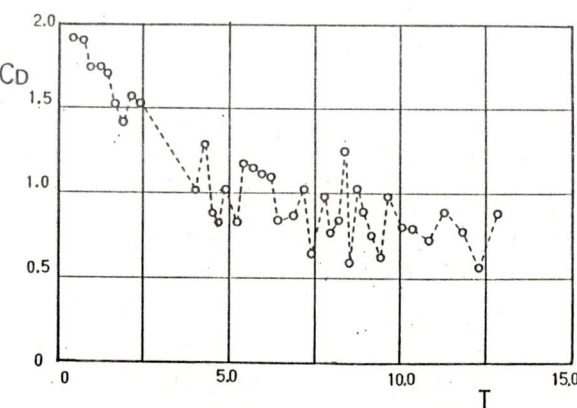

Fig.27 The history of drag coefficients by a vortex stick

MULTI-CELL VORTICES OBSERVED IN FINE-MESH SOLUTIONS TO THE INCOMPRESSIBLE EULER EQUATIONS

Arthur Rizzi[*]

FFA The Aeronautical Research Institute of Sweden,
S-161 11 BROMMA, Sweden

ABSTRACT

Results are presented for a three dimensional flow, containing a vortex sheet shed from a delta wing. The numerical solution indicates that the shearing caused by the trailing edge of the wing sets up a torsional wave on the vortex core and produces a structure with multiple cells of vorticity. Although observed in coarse grid solutions too, this effect becomes better resolved with mesh refinement to 614 000 grid volumes. In comparison with a potential solution in which the vortex sheet is fitted as a discontinuity, the results are analyzed for the position of the vortex features captured in the Euler flow field, the accuracy of the pressure field, and for the diffusion of the vortex sheets.

INTRODUCTION

Consider incompressible flow past a flat delta wing in which a stable vortex sheet is shed from the leading edge and then coils up into a steady vortex over the wing (Fig. 1). We have investigated the qualitative as well as quantitative aspects of this flow, computed by artificial compressibility, in comparison to the results of a 3D panel method that fits the vortex sheet to the surrounding potential flowfield[1]. The comparison between these two was quite favorable, but the Euler solution indicated a peculiar structure within the vortex core that was not seen in the potential results. There are, however, grounds to believe that such azimuthal components on an otherwise conical vorticity field may in fact be physically realistic. At the trailing edge the flow experiences a substantial upwash (Fig. 2),

---

[*] also Adjunct Professor, Royal Institute of Technology, Stockholm

which lifts the vortex core, giving it curvature and therefore torsion[2]. The induced torsional force then gives rise to helical wave motions throughout the region of vorticity, and, it is conjectured here, this leads to a multiple-vortex phenomenon[3].

This paper attempts to test this hypothesis, namely that the torsional structure is real rather than numerical, by the method of grid refinement in order to see if the sequence of finer and finer grids approaches some limit. Our previous solution was obtained on a medium-sized grid of 80×24×40 cells[4]. The fine-mesh solution presented here using 160× 48×80 cells confirms, but in greater detail, the presence in the medium-mesh calculation of an azimuthal disturbance superposed upon the vortex core as it approaches the trailing edge of the wing. It seems likely that the shearing of the flow by the trailing edge causes this wave-like disturbance and the occurrence of the multicelled vortex core.

FINITE-VOLUME METHOD USING ARTIFICIAL COMPRESSIBILITY

The equations of the artificial compressibility concept are solved using a spatially centered Runge-Kutta method in finite-volume form

$$\frac{\partial}{\partial t} \int q \, dvol + M \cdot \iint \underline{H} \cdot \underline{n} \, ds = T \qquad M = \begin{bmatrix} c^2 & 0 & 0 & 0 \\ 0 & 1 & 0 & 0 \\ 0 & 0 & 1 & 0 \\ 0 & 0 & 0 & 1 \end{bmatrix} \qquad (1)$$

where $q=[p/\rho_o, u, v, w]$ and $\underline{H} \cdot \underline{n} = [\underline{V} \cdot \underline{n}, u\underline{V} \cdot \underline{n} + p/\rho_o \, \underline{n} \cdot \underline{e}_x, v\underline{V} \cdot \underline{n} + p/\rho_o \, \underline{n} \cdot \underline{e}_y, w\underline{V} \cdot \underline{n} + p/\rho_o \, \underline{n} \cdot \underline{e}_z]$ is the vector flux of q across the surrounding faces of the hexahedronal cells. The term T is a fourth-difference artificial-viscosity model. It has the property of an energy sink, i.e. $(d/dt)q^2 < 0$ summed over all the cells including those at the boundaries. The finite-volume method then discretizes (1) by assuming that q is a cell-averaged quantity located in the center of the cell, and the flux term $\underline{H}(q) \cdot \underline{n}$ is defined only at the cell faces by averaging the values on each side. With these definitions and calling the cell surfaces in the three coordinate directions of the mesh $\underline{S}_I$, $\underline{S}_J$, and $\underline{S}_K$, we obtain the semi-discrete finite-volume form for cell ijk

$$\frac{d}{dt} q_{ijk} = -[\delta_I(\underline{H} \cdot \underline{S}_I) + \delta_J(\underline{H} \cdot \underline{S}_J) + \delta_K(\underline{H} \cdot \underline{S}_K)]_{ijk} - (\delta_I^4 + \delta_J^4 + \delta_K^4) q_{ijk} = FD(q_{ijk}) \qquad (2)$$

where $\delta_I(\underset{\sim}{H}\cdot\underset{\sim}{S}_I) \equiv (\underset{\sim}{H}\cdot\underset{\sim}{S}_I)_{i+1/2} - (\underset{\sim}{H}\cdot\underset{\sim}{S}_I)_{i-1/2}$ is the centered difference operator. A more detailed description of the method is given in Ref. 5. With the appropriate boundary conditions we integrate this last equation with the two-level three-stage scheme

$$\begin{aligned}
q_o &:= q \\
q &:= q_o + \Delta t\; FD(q_o) \\
q &:= q_o + \Delta t[1/2\; FD(q_o) + 1/2\; FD(q)] \\
q &:= q_o + \Delta t[1/2\; FD(q_o) + 1/2\; FD(q)]
\end{aligned}$$

that steps the solution forward in time.

COMPARISON OF COMPUTED VORTEX FLOWS

The mesh around the 70 deg. swept flat-plate delta wing is an O-O type constructed by Eriksson's interpolation method[6] that places a polar singular line at the apex and a parabolic singular line at the tip of the trailing edge (Fig. 3). Hoeijmakers and Rizzi[1] demonstrated that a stable vortex sheet can be captured in a numerical solution to Eq.(1) which does agree well with the fitted potential one. The Euler solution, however, indicates a wave-like structure superposed upon the vortex core as it nears the trailing edge. A further question then arises, does the stability of the captured sheet, its close agreement in size and position with the fitted one, and the observed wave structure all change as the mesh size is refined?

Hoeijmakers's potential boundary-integral (panel) method inserts a vortex sheet, adjusts it to the surrounding irrotational flowfield, and allows it to rollup under its own influence for several turns, and then models the remaining core by an isolated line vortex[7]. The position and strength of the vortex sheet and isolated vortex are determined as part of the solution, sometimes termed "fitting" the rotational flow features. They are true discontinuities, infinitesimally thin, and for this reason a very good choice for comparison with a sheet and vortex smeared or "captured" over a number of computational cells. The comparison therefore offers a good check on the position of the computed vortex and the diffusion of the sheet as well as how these change with mesh size. Furthermore such panel-method results have been found to agree reasonably well with measurements made in turbulent flow[8].

The thickness of the rotational flow features captured in the solution to the Euler equations varies directly with the size of the mesh cells. The simplest way, therefore, to minimize the diffusion of vorticity and to confirm the accuracy of the solution is to use as dense a mesh as possible. The fine mesh here consists of over 600 000 cells. The computations were carried out on the CYBER 205 vector computer in 32-bit precision at the rate of 6 microsec. per cell per iteration which translates to over 125 mflops. The medium-mesh solution was advanced an additional 2000 steps beyond the solution discussed by Rizzi and Eriksson[4] with no discernible change found with time. That medium-mesh solution, therefore, is steady. It was interpolated to the fine mesh and then iterated for 2500 steps.

The overall features of the flows in the medium and the fine mesh are compared in Fig. 4 by isograms, drawn in plane projection, of the computed solution in three nonplanar mesh surfaces x/c= 0.3, 0.6 and 0.9 over the wing, one surface in the wake at x/c= 1.15 and one cutting axially through the core of the vortex. The two solutions do agree and reveal qualitatively the leading-edge vortex over the wing, as well as the trailing-edge vortex that develops from the trailing-edge sheet. The comparison shows that the broad features of the flow are represented in both grids. The isograms viewed axially through the core indicate the approximately conical nature of the flow starting at the apex. In both solutions at about the 80% chord position, however, the leading-edge vortex lifts up slightly and an abrupt change takes place which might be interrepted as a multi-celled vortex phenomenon. Although the cause of this feature may still be numerical, we should expect physically the core to undergo a helical disturbance that could excite an instability like the one discussed by Snow[3] which results in multiple vortices. In any event more of the details are brought out in the fine mesh. The computed total pressure losses in the core, however, are high, and can be attributed to the numerical effect of capturing the vortex sheet[9]. Theoretically the loss should be zero on each side of the sheet, even though the velocity is in shear. But the numerical solution has to support this shear with a continuous profile over several mesh cells through the sheet, and any sort of reasonable profile (say a linear one) connecting the velocity vector on one side with the one on the other side immediately implies a total pressure loss for the profile even if the velocities at both sides are correct. As the vortex sheet wraps up tighter and tighter there will be only one or two cells located between the coils, and ultimately it will disappear off the mesh completely. The amount of loss then is related directly to the strength of the sheet. The fine mesh supports more coils, but the sheet must eventually disappear in the same way off this mesh too, producing about the same loss at the center of a now smaller diameter core. It is the size therefore of the contour rings, but not their number, that varies with mesh spacing.

Figure 5 presents the shape of the fitted vortex sheet (dashed lines) from the potential method superimposed upon the vorticity magnitude contours of the Euler-equation solution in three cross-flow planes. We see that the vorticity captured in the field is diffused over 5 or 6 cells in both the medium and fine mesh solutions*, and that, in general, the vortical flow region occupies a larger volume than that enclosed by the vortex sheet fitted to the potential solution. But the positions of the vortex cores in the comparisons and even the curvature of the sheets agree remarkably well. The vorticity in the fitted sheet is largest near the leading edge where the curvature of the sheet is singular, and the Euler-equation solutions indicate the same trend. The sheet appears to depart tangentially from the lower surface of the leading edge. This comparison with mesh refinement confirms that a stable vortex sheet separating from a swept leading edge can be captured in the vorticity field of the Euler-equation solution with a reasonable degree of realism. The curious distortion of the contours in the $x/c= 0.9$ station and the associated cellular pattern of vorticity are another indication that a torsional wave may be standing on the core and giving rise to subsiderary vortices.

Figures 6(a-b) present isograms on the wing surface together with the more quantitative graphs of spanwise distributions at three $x/c=$ constant stations and compare them with the potential values. In the sets of computed isobars (Fig. 6a) the pressure trough under the leading-edge vortex has about the same shape, position, and width, and the three agree rather well. The peak level of the suction along the entire trough on the upper surface is somewhat lower in the medium-mesh Euler results, and shifted slightly inboard at $x/c= 0.3$, but the fine-mesh results show a trend toward the potential solution. The fine-mesh

---

* the increment between isovorticity contours is not the same for the medium and fine-mesh solutions.

results show a pronounced waviness that may be a reflection of the character of the vortex sheet as it approaches the trailing edge. A vortex core in helical motion might well produce such a pattern on the upper surface. This waviness, however, is not present in the circumferential $(v^2+w^2)^{1/2}/V_\infty$ velocity components on the upper surface (Fig. 6b).

CONCLUDING REMARKS

The artificial compressibility approach is an interesting one for solving the incompressible Euler equations because it is equally applicable in small as well as large-scale simulations, and the latter provide a lot of insight into the local details of the flow. As a demonstration of the method, and as an example of a vortex flow requiring further understanding, a steady 3D flowfield with a free-shear layer has been computed, and its features have been discussed under grid refinement. Comparison with an accepted solution is reasonable, even large (but local) errors in total pressure do not seriously degrade the global accuracy, and are shown to be an artifact of the numerical capturing of the vortex sheet. A curious cellular pattern of vorticity in the core, coupled to a wave structure in the flow properties, also is seen to develop just ahead of the trailing edge, and believed to be caused by a three-dimensional disturbance on the vortex core.

Acknowledgement

I wish to thank ETA Systems, Inc. for providing computer time for the further development of this method, and Charles Purcell for his ever-present help in the running of the program.

REFERENCES

1. Hoeijmakers, H.W.M. and Rizzi, A.: Vortex-Fitted Potential Solution Compared with Vortex-Captured Euler Solution for Delta Wing with Leading Edge Vortex Separation, AIAA Paper No. 84-2144, 1984.

2. Betchov, R.: On the Curvature and Torsion of an Isolated Vortex Filament, J. Fluid Mechanics, Vol. 22, 1965, pp. 471-479.

3. Snow, J.T.: On Inertial Stability as Related to the Multiple-Vortex Phenomenon, J. Atmos. Sci., Vol. 35, Sept 1978, pp. 1660-1677.

4. Rizzi, A. and Eriksson, L.E.: Computation of Inviscid Incompressible Flow with Rotation, J. Fluid Mechanics, Vol. 153, April 1985, pp. 275-312.

5. Rizzi, A., and Eriksson, L.E.: Computation of Flow Around Wings Based on the Euler Equations, J. Fluid Mech., Vol. 148 pp. 45-71, Nov. 1984.

6. Eriksson, L.-E.: Generation of Boundary-Conforming Grids Around Wing-Body Configurations Using Transfinite Interpolation, AIAA J., Vol. 20, pp. 1313-1320, Oct. 1982.

7. Hoeijmakers, H.W.M., and Vaatstra, W.: A Higher-Order Panel Method Applied to Vortex-Sheet Roll-Up. AIAA Journal, Vol. 21, April 1983, pp. 516-523.

8. Hoeijmakers, H.W.M., Vaatstra, W., and Verhaagen, N.G.: Vortex Flow Over Delta and Double-Delta Wings, J. Aircraft, Vol. 21, No. 9, Sept. 1983.

9. Powell, K., Murman, E., Perez, E., and Baron, J.: Total Pressure Loss in Vortical Solutions of the Conical Euler Equations, AIAA Paper No. 85-1701, 1985.

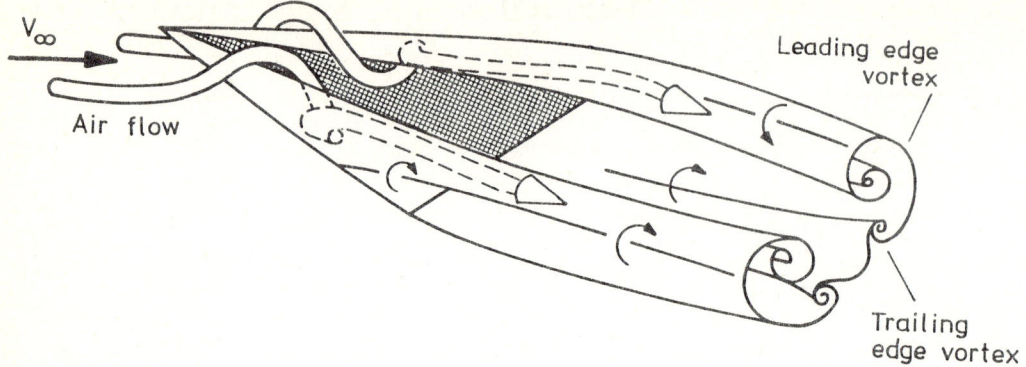

Fig. 1 Schematic of rolling up to shed vortex sheds into stable vortex structures.

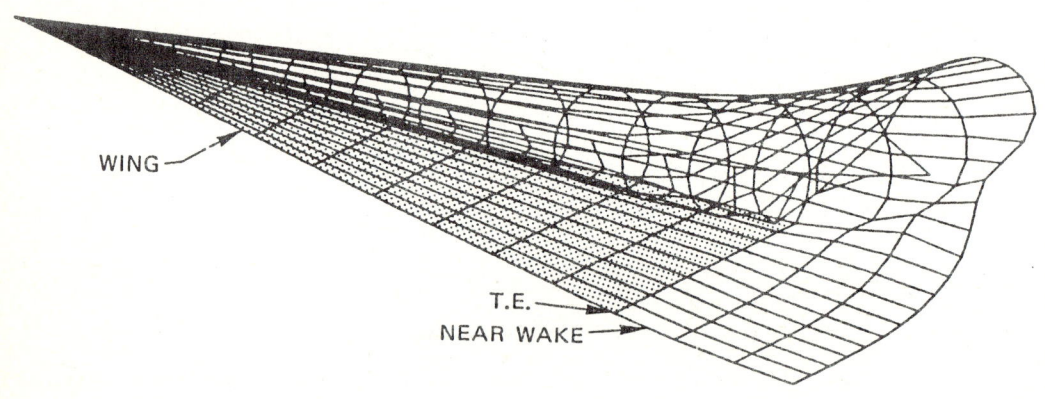

Fig. 2 The vortex sheet fitted as a discontinuity to the potential solution shows the curving of the vortex structure due to the upwash at the trailing edge.

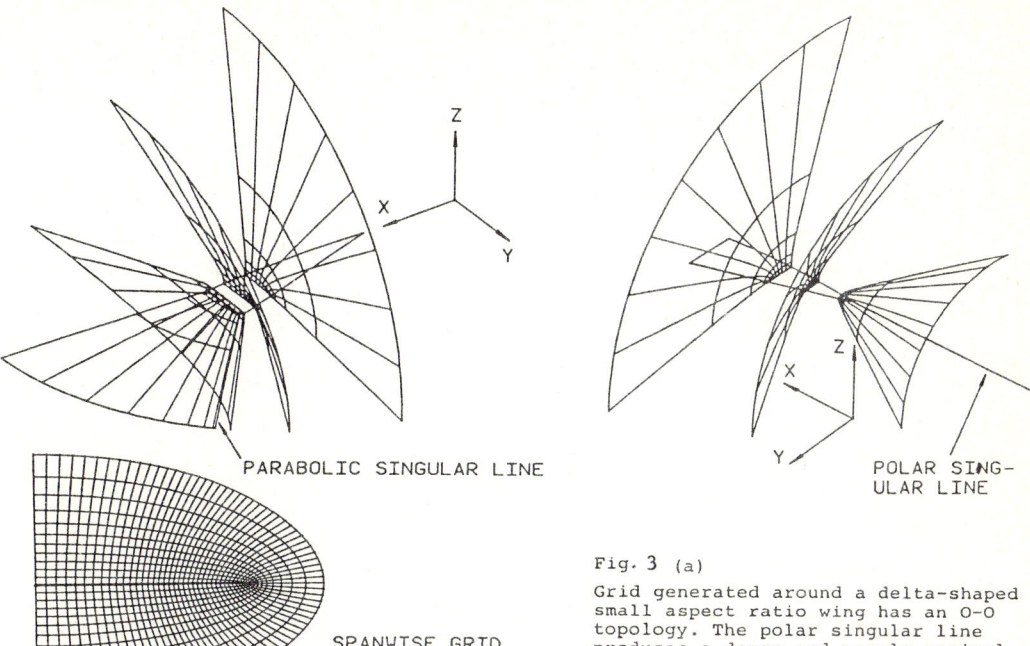

Fig. 3 (a)
Grid generated around a delta-shaped small aspect ratio wing has an O-O topology. The polar singular line produces a dense and nearly conical distribution of points at the apex which is needed to resolve the rapidly varying flow there. This mesh is well-suited for computing the flow around wings of combat aircraft.

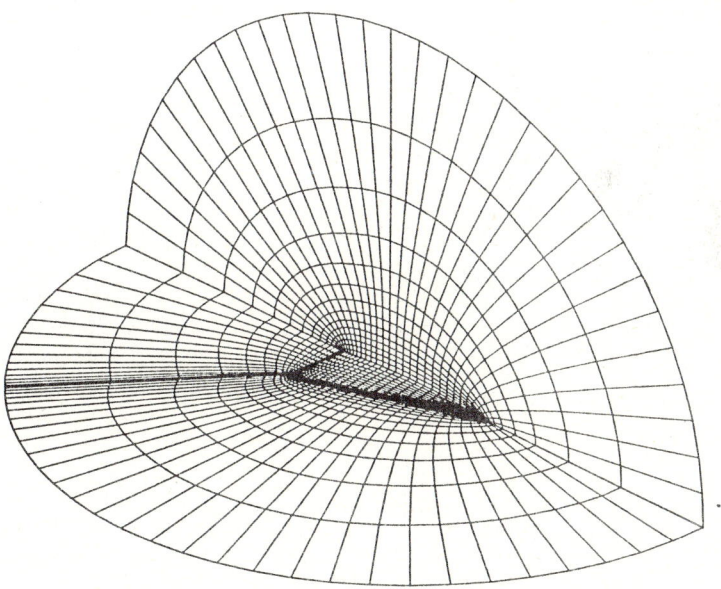

Fig. 3 (b)   three-dimensional view of the delta wing mesh

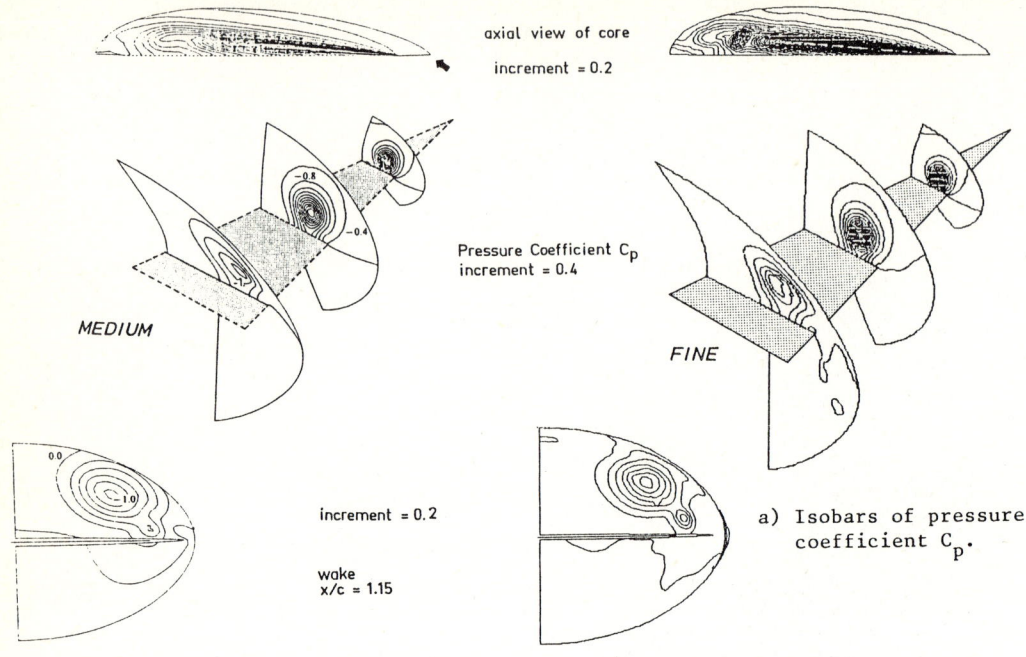

a) Isobars of pressure coefficient C_p.

Fig. 4 Comparison of contour maps of the medium-mesh (80x24x80) and fine-mesh (160x48x80) solutions to the Euler equations for flow past a 70 deg. swept flap plate delta wing. They are drawn in four non-planar mesh surfaces at the x/c=0.3, 0.6, 0.9 and 1.15 stations and in one mesh surface which passes approximately through the axial core of the vortex. $M_\infty = 0$, $\alpha = 20$ deg.

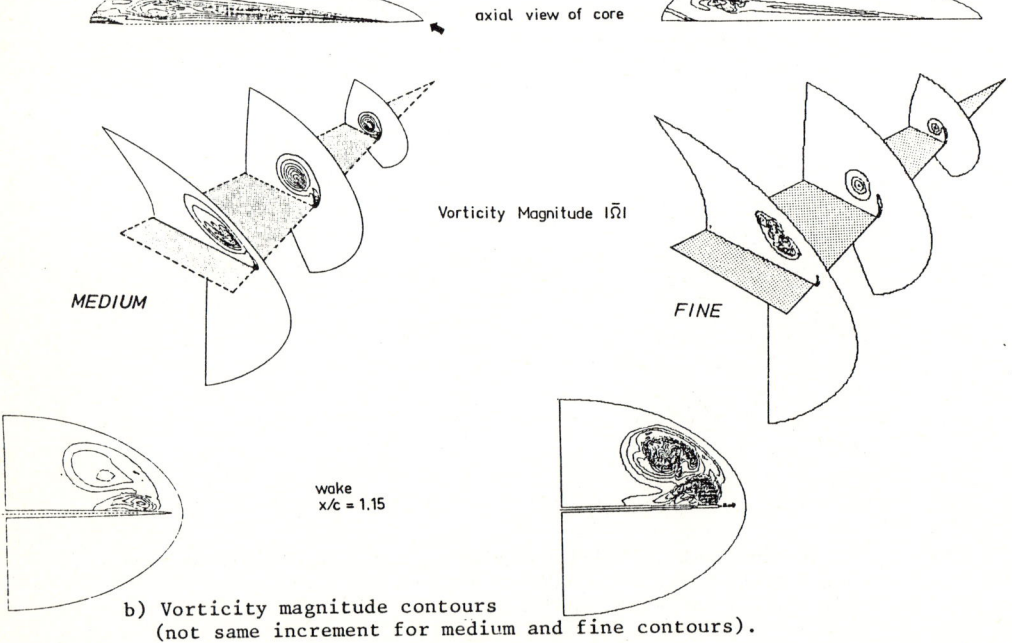

b) Vorticity magnitude contours (not same increment for medium and fine contours).

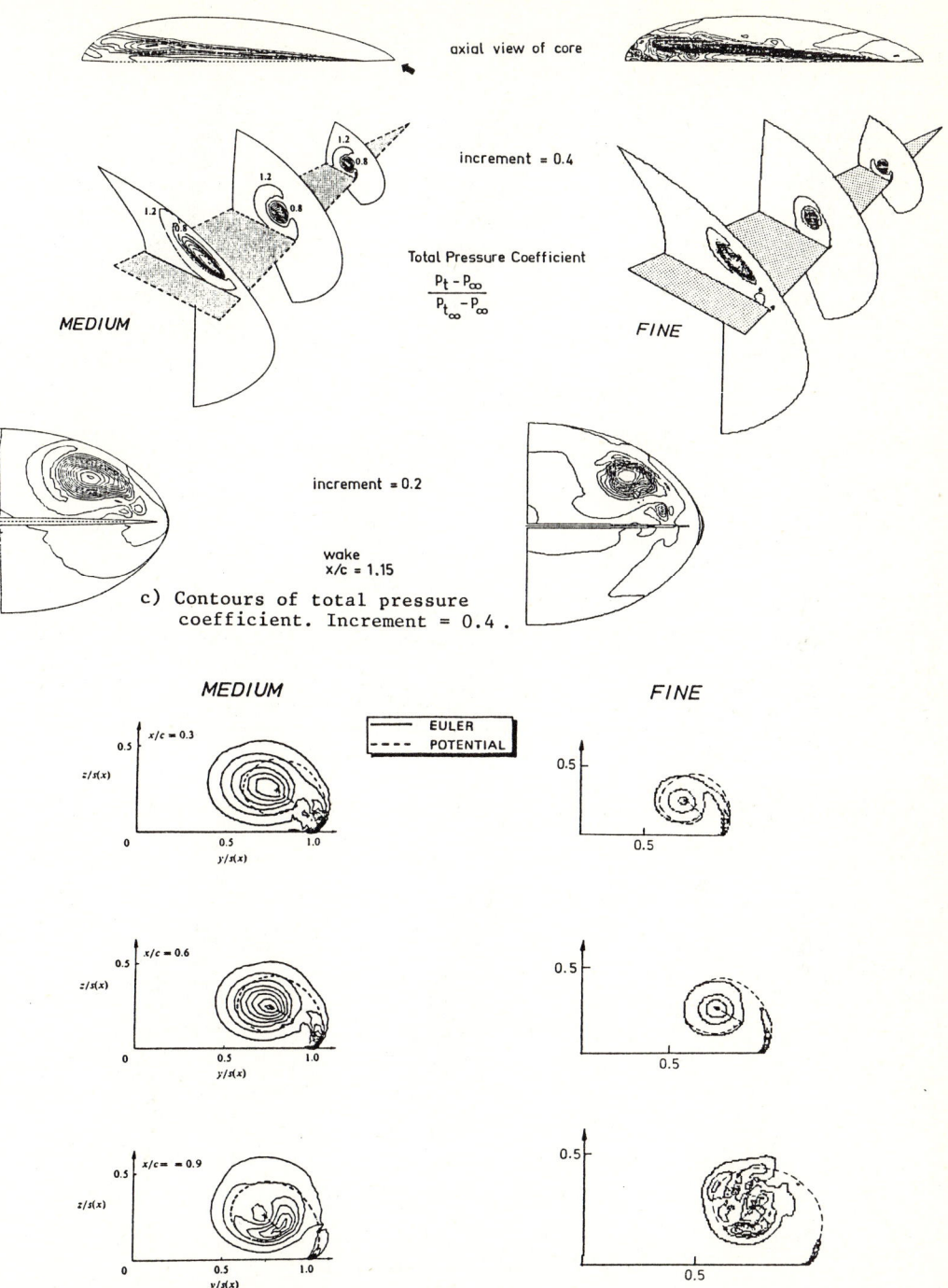

c) Contours of total pressure coefficient. Increment = 0.4.

Fig. 5 Comparison of the vorticity fields indicated by vorticity magnitude contours (solid lines) computed with the Euler equations, using the medium and fine meshes, and the shed vortex (dashed lines) that is fitted as a discontinuity to the surrounding potential solution.

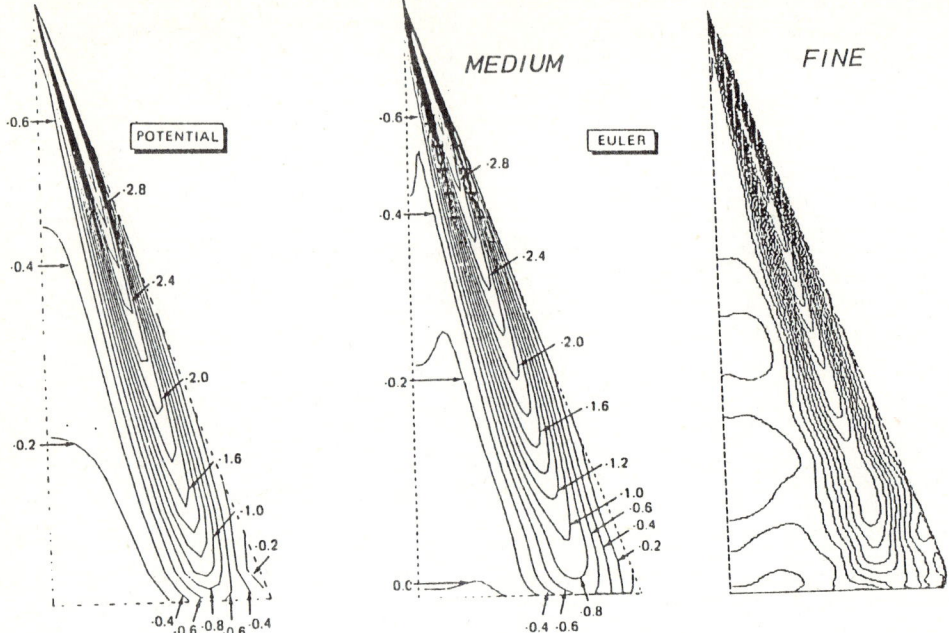

a) Isobars of pressure coefficient C_p compared with the potential solution together with three corresponding graphs versus local semispan at $x/c=0.3, 0.6$ and 0.9.

Fig. 6   Isograms of the computed medium-mesh and fine-mesh solutions on the upper surface of the wing.

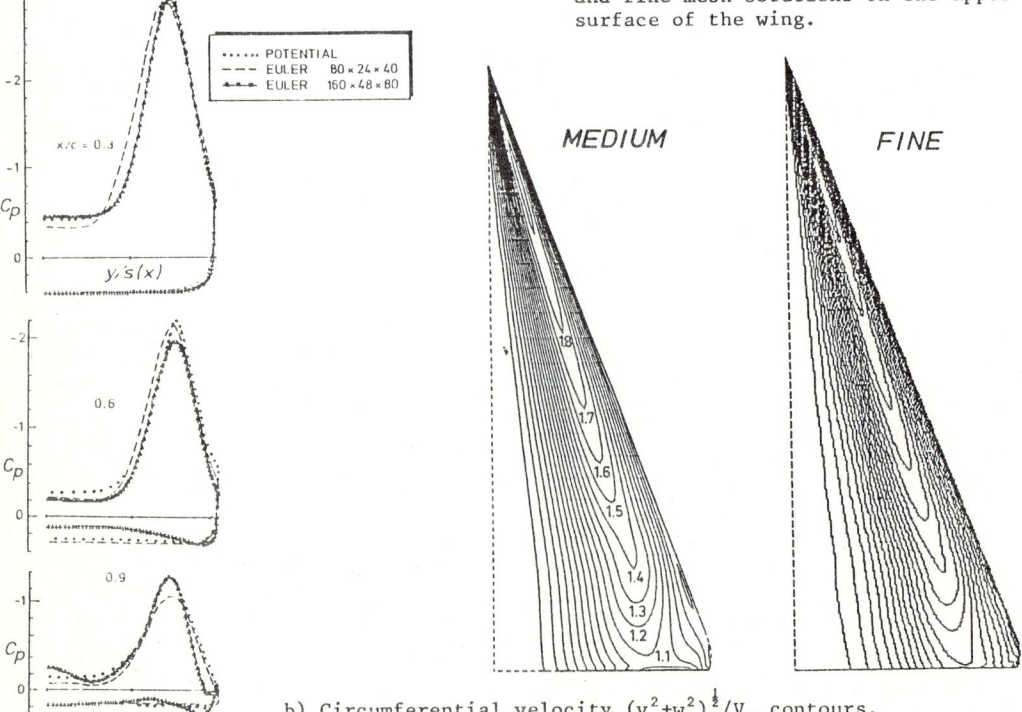

b) Circumferential velocity $(v^2+w^2)^{\frac{1}{2}}/V_\infty$ contours.

IMPLICIT BOUNDARY TREATMENT FOR JOINED AND DISJOINT PATCHED MESH SYSTEMS

C.K. Lombard and Ethiraj Venkatapathy
PEDA Corporation
Palo Alto, California

Abstract

The CSCM flux difference eigenvector split upwind scheme for the compressible Euler or Navier-Stokes equation is adapted to solve the problem of capturing embedded flow structures with high resolution on systems of aligned overset meshes.

Characteristics based upwind operationally explicit implicit difference relations with diagonally dominant approximate factorization are argued to be appropriate for compatibly and stably exchanging data in the vicinity of interior patch boundaries through simple interpolation of conservative variable data. Particular interpolation procedures are advocated that involve only positive weights and interpolant data with consistent upwind domain of dependence with respect to the receiving grid. A linearly equilvalent procedure involving interpolation of needed flux components is given and argued to be somewhat more accurate in the vicinity of discontinuities. With minimal overlap, sections on the coarse mesh that underly overset refinements are removed from the computation. The resulting segmented mesh data structure leads to interesting opportunities including nonaligned mesh-boundary intersections which we exploit for high resolution capture of shock reflections.

Factors in accuracy of the flow structure adaptive patching technique are demonstrated in an inviscid supersonic inlet problem involving weak shocks and an expansion fan. In the context of that two dimensional problem with shock aligned patched meshing, it is found that similar accuracy can be achieved with a savings of an order of magnitude in computed points relative to uniformly refined mesh.

Introduction

The challenge to utilize the maturing finite difference algorithms of computational fluid dynamics to accurately solve flow problems involving more complicated and realistic geometries has led to the exploration of patched mesh techniques. In these approaches the global mesh covering the computational domain is constructed in topologically quadrilateral patches whose boundaries align piecewise with sections of the domain boundary or internal flow structures of interest to capture with high numerical accuracy.

Two avenues of development may be generally distinguished in patched meshing depending on whether or not the interior boundary of one patch is the boundary of another, (usually) with geometric continuation of at least some of the other family of mesh lines across the common boundary. Without complete agreement of terminology in the literature, in the former case the resultant global mesh is referred to as joined, composite or zonal; and, in the latter, oversetting or (nodally) disjoint. Both strategies have been referred to as mesh embedding.

Thompson[1] has provided a survey of grid concepts, generation and related issues. Berger and Oliger[2] have described a strategy and data structure for auto-adaptive mesh refinement in overset patches. Lombard, et al.[3] demonstrated solution of the conservative compressible Navier-Stokes equations on a topologically singular patched composite mesh covering a complete bluff body flow. The now extensive literature in composite patched meshing is recognized in reference 4. Of direct interest here, Benek, et al.[5] and Eberhardt[6] have considered the solution of the conservative Euler equations with the Beam-Warming central difference algorithm on overset meshes.

The major subject of the present paper is numerical boundary approximations for the conservative system of equations (Euler), at interior patch interfaces. This subject has been attacked by

Berger[7,8] who, starting from Lax Wendroff theory, derives flux conservative interface boundary conditions that yield weak solutions (capture shocks) when (if) the associated finite difference procedure converges. Berger's results[8] which extend to overset meshes are developed in the finite volume conservative framework and embrace the method of Rai[9].

Benek, et al.[5] employed linear interpolation of the conservative variables from the interior solution of one mesh to give Dirichlet boundary data for the other. With several points of mesh overlap at the mesh boundaries, transonic solutions exhibited considerable oscillation in the vicinity of shocks propagating through the boundary region. Eberhardt[6] with the code of Benek, et al.[5] attempted to reduce the oscillation and attendant stability problems encountered in the vicinity of a bluff body shock intersecting an embedded patch boundary by introducing a characteristic computed boundary point approximation with scalar upwind difference equations in Riemann variables. In his procedure, interpolation was performed in only the variables whose characteristics ran to the patch boundary from outside the computational domain. Eberhardt based the decision about domain of dependence of the characteristics on eigenvalues computed within the patch domain. When this decision was compatible with the flow, then the characteristics boundary procedure gave markedly superior results compared to interpolation of conservative variable data, which leads to solution overspecification in subsonic zones. In other cases where incorrect domain of dependence was inferred, the characteristic boundary procedure was unstable.

The present paper describes a simple, robustly stable implicit approach to computing solutions of the conservative equations of gasdynamics on either composite or overset meshes. Without requiring special flux conservative operators, but rather, interpolating conservative variable data at mesh boundaries, the implicit upwind method is accurate and relatively free of oscillation where shocks intersect interior patch boundaries. In a supersonic inlet problem with expansion and reflected shocks, the paper demonstrates the capability to conveniently carry out with rapidly convergent implicit methods for systems of equations the adaptive refined meshing strategy in overset patches proposed by Berger and Oliger[2]. Further, the test case shows concretely in a realistic aerodynamic problem the savings in mesh points (about an order of magnitude here in two dimensions) for similar accuracy that flow structure aligned adaptive patched meshing affords compared to uniform grid refinement.

The factors in our approach are supported by previous research by ourselves and generically by others cited above and are proven in numerical experiments reported here and elsewhere[4,10]. We employ an implicit conservative upwind scheme CSCM[11] with which in the present work we can solve to either first or second order spatial accuracy the Euler or compressible Navier-Stokes equations in two-dimensional planar or axisymmetric flows. The flux difference split upwind schemes of generalized Roe form such as CSCM have a number of qualities that make them ideal for the purpose of solving on discontinuous patched mesh systems.

First, conservative schemes in the Roe form satisfy Roe's property U that guarantees the correct speed for captured shocks. The CSCM scheme has been tested in a wide variety of internal and external transonic and hypersonic flows[11,14] and has been found to capture strong and weak shocks accurately in location and with little oscillation. The shock transition is particularly sharp, about two mesh cells wide, on an aligned grid; and this factor will be accommodated as much as possible in our adaptive patched mesh strategy.

Second, in the Roe form the difference operators on conservative variable data represent the effects of differencing to characteristic data only for disturbances propagating toward the given node and reject the mathematically unstable contribution from disturbances that may be propagating downwind of the node. The one sided upwind difference operation represents identically[13] the (split) conservative partial flux difference between the nodes. To the extent that the data from an adjacent mesh is consistent with the solution, then the associated upwind partial flux difference to that data will serve to provide at convergence consistency of the partial flux convective into the given mesh from its neighbor, and vice versa for signals of the other eigenvalue sign. Thus the method acts within truncation error to provide the similar continuity of the flux tensor among patched grids that exists in the physical solution across shocks and would obtain on a single grid alone. The correct domain of dependence coupled with the well posed characteristic boundary point approximations[11] tend not to support oscillatory disturbances but convect them out of the flow domain.

Third, one sided difference interval averaged eigenvalues let majority rule determine the direction of local signal propagation. When applied, as we do, to a difference operator between boundary data obtained from an adjacent mesh and the local mesh solution point, the data of both meshes participate in making the decision as to whether an incoming signal is being sent. Both in concept and our experience, this factor seems to overcome the inter mesh communication difficulty experienced by Eberhardt[6] with his characteristic boundary procedure.

Lastly, with the CSCM difference equations, with diagonally dominant approximate factorization[11,14] that retains on the diagonal the contributions from both sets of eigenvalues in what is effectively an absolute value Jacobian matrix, we can solve the equations either with two data level linearized block implicit methods[11] or with a single data level relaxation technique[14] that is substantially more rapidly convergent than the linearized implicit procedures. As can be inferred from the theory and numerical experiments of reference 14, the use of DDADI on the solution point while differencing effectively explicitly to data obtained from an adjoining mesh (which may be at either the old (n) or new (n+1) level) is unconditionally stable. When the solutions on the patched meshes are alternately updated using either the linearized implicit or relaxation methods the global procedure is implicit. As will be shown here, the robust stability of the global procedure has been confirmed to approximately coarse mesh CFL 100.

One point that has not been touched on is the form of interpolation that we use. Differencing to interpolated data is equivalent to a weighted sum of differences operating on the interpolants. It is intuitive that for robust stability each of these assumed upwind differences ought to be well posed. This implies that the interpolation weights should all be positive and the domains of dependence of all the interpolants should be outside (i.e. on the assumed side) of the solution point with respect to its mesh interior. Neither of these properties was shared by the data interpolation schemes used by Benek, et al.[5] or Eberhardt[6].

Finally, extending a direction of Benek, et al.[5], we do not compute on sections of coarser meshes underlying patches of overset refinement. Our data structure and automated procedures for the consequent partitioning of meshes are described in reference 15. The partitioning concept in which coordinate lines of a patch have differing (index) lengths in computational space also leads to useful possibilities including as will be shown here, fitting mesh patches obliquely to boundaries, e.g. to sharply capture reflecting shocks.

Formulation

We sketch here the first order scheme for one space dimension. More details of the CSCM formulation can be found in the references, particularly 11 and 14. The two level time dependent interior point implicit difference equation is

$$(I + \widetilde{A}^+ \nabla + \widetilde{A}^- \Delta)\delta q_j = -\widetilde{A}^+ \Delta q)_{j-1} - \widetilde{A}^- \Delta q)_j \tag{1}$$

with $q^{n+1} = q^n + \delta q$. For notation, the right paranthesis with subscript j means quantities to the left are evaluated over the difference interval $j, j+1$. In the equation the CSCM flux difference splitting is

$$(\widetilde{A}^+ + \widetilde{A}^-)\Delta q \equiv \Delta F^+ + \Delta F^- = \Delta F$$

with

$$\widetilde{A}^\pm = (\overline{MT}I^\pm \overline{T}^{-1}\overline{M}^{-1})\widetilde{A} \equiv \hat{A}^\pm \widetilde{A} \tag{2}$$

and

$$I^\pm = \frac{1}{2}(I \pm \operatorname{sgn}(\overline{\Lambda}))$$

exhibiting the similarity transformation that diagonalizes the constructed flux difference Jacobian $\tilde{A}$. Here $\bar{\Lambda}$ is a diagonal matrix of the interval averaged eigenvalues that through the truth function diagonal matrices $I^{\pm}$ make the decisions about directions of characteristic wave propagation and whether or not to send signal to the solution point. Thus in the equation, $\tilde{A}^{+}\Delta q)_{j-1}$ represents the convection of characteristic wave contributions in the positive coordinate direction from grid point $j-1$ to solution point j and $\tilde{A}^{-}$, in the negative direction from $j+1$ to j. As the result of incorporating multiplicatively the (local) time step (for pseudo time relaxation) and the spatial (divided) differences in the matrices, the numerical eigenvalues are Courant numbers for the characteristic waves whose speeds are u, $u+c$ and $u-c$, with c the sound speed.

For exterior boundaries of the computational domain, at a right boundary point we retain only the right running positive eigenvalue contributions and, negative at left. At such boundary points the identity matrix on the left hand side of the equation (1) is replaced by a matrix[11] that contains the time linearized conservative variable representations of the computed characteristic variable fluctuations at the boundary and also imposed boundary condition relations.

Of more interest here is what we do at an interior patch boundary. The left hand side of equation (1) has the tridiagonal structure

$$\tilde{A}^{+} \quad , \quad I + \tilde{A}^{+} - \tilde{A}^{-} \quad , \quad \tilde{A}^{-} \qquad (3)$$

In relation (3), the central block which we call D can be seen to contain the absolute values of the eigenvalues for signals propagating to the solution point from either left or right. Indeed, the simplified approximation to equation (1)

$$D\delta q_j = \tilde{A}^{+} q_{j-1}^{n,n+1} - (\tilde{A}^{+} - \tilde{A}^{-})q_j^n - \tilde{A}^{-} q_{j+1}^{n,n+1} \qquad (4)$$

leads to an operationally explicit implicit relaxation procedure[14] that is unconditionally stable either as a computed interior patch boundary point or general interior point relation. Here $n, n+1$ means data from either time level. If the interior point implicit solution procedure is two level, then, the term of equation (3) at the interior point $j-1$ or $j+1$ will be linearized (assumed at the $n+1$ level) as in equation (1).

For left or right boundary points, the frozen (i.e. not computed on the patch) data at $j-1$ or $j+1$ in equation (4) is gotten from adjacent patch mesh data. If the mesh system is composite and mesh lines cross the boundary to the solution point, then, the frozen boundary data is the solution point data of the adjoining mesh. For the case of nodes on lines ending at the patch boundary, which case relates equally to composite mesh with lines of either patch ending at the boundary or to overset meshes, the frozen data is got by interpolation of adjacent mesh patch data to the boundary point location.

Linear interpolation to an included point on a coordinate line or within a polygonal cell involve only positive weights on the interpolant data. In most of the numerical experiments made to date with overset grids we have employed a bilinear interpolation[15] based on the four corner points of the overlapping mesh cell enclosing the frozen boundary point. However, with less data processing a linear interpolation involving the three corner points on the including triangle (Figure 1a) generalizes to the use of the four corner points of the enclosing tetrahedron in three dimensions.

In the composite mesh case, Figure 1b, interpolation is naturally along an interior coordinate line paralleling the zonal boundary. Such interpolation is one-dimensional for a two-dimensional problem and two-dimensional for a three-dimensional problem. The generic composite grid problem just described and which we have tested among the numerical experiments to be reported in the next section also serves as a *gedanken* model problem for the overset mesh case. Possible solutions that come to mind by analogy are shown in Figure 1c and Figure 1d. In both figures the interpolation is along two point coordinate lines segments (or three point triangular surfaces in 3-D) of the adjacent mesh and thus is a direct analog with the attendant data requirements of the composite mesh case.

We use stable and consistent first order differencing and interpolation at the boundaries regardless of the order of accuracy of the difference approximation in the patch interiors. Since the divided differences of the computed boundary point approximation are of the same accuracy as the interpolation, the approaches sketched in Figures 1c and 1d may be regarded as letting the difference operator perform the interpolation (to uniformly spaced data Figure 1a) in the direction away from the computed boundary. Thus, to the extent that the solution is locally well represented by a linear function the approaches sketched in Figures 1a and 1c and 1d are equivalent. The treatment shown in Figure 1a, however, requires the same dimensionality of the (triangular) interpolation procedure as that of the problem and one higher than for the (linear) treatment of Figures 1c and 1d.

As a final theoretical point regarding data exchange at patch mesh boundaries, we note here that equations (2) imply[13]

$$\Delta F^{\pm} = \hat{A}^{\pm} \Delta F \tag{5}$$

Hence we may equivalently write the right hand side difference operators of equation (4) directly in terms of flux components. An advantage of this approach is that the flux components normal to the shock discontinuity are continuous across the discontinuity. Thus interpolating flux data from one grid to serve as needed boundary data of another can be a smoother more accurate procedure than interpolating conservative variable data.

We close this section by noting that, consistent with the 2-D interior point schemes,[11,14] we difference along the computed boundary coordinate line with operators written for the boundary aligned coordinate. In the diagonally dominant approximate factorizations that we employ in multidimensions, the convective matrices with absolute values of the eigenvalues for both coordinate directions are retained in the diagonal block.

Numerical Experiments

To achieve both accuracy and robust stability in this difficult problem area, particularly with overset meshes, theory can provide insight into what to attempt but the acid test of numerical methods is performance in relevant numerical experiments.

We present here some sample results with major findings from a substantial number of experiments[4] designed to test various aspects of the accuracy and stability question for the conservative system of equations for gasdynamics solved on patched meshes.

The numerical experiments to be discussed here involve solution of an inviscid flow in a Mach 5 inlet with 10deg compression ramp that we have employed in previous experiments with first and second order upwind methods on uniform meshes[11]. The problem involves two of the generic kinds of flow structure, shock and expansion fan, which are not possible to resolve both efficiently and to the extent desired on uniform mesh. As the result of interaction of the expansion fan with the compression corner and reflected shocks, they curve in non simple regions for which the exact solution is not known analytically. The coarse base level grid of the experiments has 26×26 points.

Composite Grid with Boundary Overlap

As a simple test of employing frozen interpolated boundary data, we show in Figure 2a and 2b the grid and density contours for a patched mesh with two full cell overlap and refinement with twice as many mesh points in the streamwise direction in the lower patch. Thus every other mesh point at the upper interior boundary of the lower patch is interpolated between computed conservative variable data of the upper patch along the common streamwise coordinate line. This test case solving sequentially on the patches with the first order method is numerically stable with local time steps based on CFL 100. There is no oscillation in the solution in the vicinity of the patch boundary (shown) and refinement in the lower patch has served to sharpen the solution in that region, though high gradient regions of the solution are very smeared on the coarse, nonaligned meshes.

Solutions on Uniformly Refined Mesh

As a standard for comparison with results from overset patched refinement, we show in Figures 3a and 3b pressure contours for first and second order upwind methods on 101×101 point uniform grids, i.e. 4 times refined in each coordinate direction.

Adaptive Refinement in Overset Grids

Based on a uniform coarse mesh solution similar to Figure 2b, the coarse mesh with overlaid with two refined mesh patches, Figure 4a, aligned with the compression corner and reflected shocks. Note in the reflection region, the two overset patches have been constructed to share the same coordinate lines for superior grid communication. The coarse grid is segmented (broken) under the overset patches and the refinement is segmented to terminate at the reflecting boundary (symmetry plane). In Figures 4b and 4c we show respectively pressure contours for the first and second order upwind methods on the overset grid.

Discussion

While the adaptive refinement about doubled the coarse mesh, the shock structures treated are better resolved than with the uniformly refined mesh in 16 times the points. Thus the results demonstrate an order of magnitude improvement in data efficiency to be gained by overset refinement. We sketch in Figure 4d a strategy of refinement for the as yet untreated expansions of the problem.

Acknowledgements

The authors acknowledge helpful discussions with Professor Joseph Oliger of Stanford University. This work was supported by AFOSR under contract F49620-83-C-0084.

References

1. Thompson, J.F.: "A Survey of Grid Generation Techniques in Computational Fluid Dynamics," AIAA 83-0447, Jan. 1983.
2. Berger, Marsha J. and Oliger, Joseph: "Adaptive Mesh Refinement for Hyperbolic Partial Differential Equations," *J. of Computational Physics*, Vol. 53, No. 3, March 1984, pp. 484-512.
3. Lombard, C.K., Davy, W.C., and Green, M.J.: "Forebody and Base Region Real-Gas Flow in Severe Planetary Entry by a Factored Implicit Numerical Method – Part 1 (Computational Fluid Dynamics)," AIAA 80-0065, Jan. 1980.
4. Lombard, C.K. and Venkatapathy, Ethiraj: "Implicit Boundary Treatment for Joined and Disjoint Patched Mesh Systems," AIAA-85-1503, 1985.
5. Benek, J.A., Steger, J.L., and Dougherty, F.C.: "A Flexible Grid Embedding Technique with Application to the Euler Equations," AIAA 83-1944, July 1983.
6. Eberhardt, David Scott: "A Study of Multiple Grid Problems on Concurrent Processing Computers," Ph.D. Dissertation, Stanford University, Sept. 1984.
7. Berger, Marsha J.: "Stability of Intefaces with Mesh Refinement," ICASE Report No. 83-42, Aug. 1983.
8. Berger, Marsha J.: On Conservation at Grid Interfaces," ICASE Report No. 84-43, Sept. 1984.
9. Rai, Man Mohan: "A Conservative Treatment of Zonal Boundaries for Euler Equation Calculations," AIAA 84-0164, Jan. 1984.

10. Venkatapathy, Ethiraj and Lombard, C.K.: "Application of Patched Meshes to Viscous and Inviscid Flows," presented at the Sixth GAMM Conference on Numerical Methods in Fluid Mechanics at Gottingen, West Germany, Sept. 1985.

11. Lombard, C.K., Bardina, J., Venkatapathy, E. and Oliger, J.: "Multi-Dimensional Formulation of CSCM - An Upwind Flux Difference Eigenvector Split Method for the Compressible Navier-Stokes Equations," AIAA-83-1895, July 1983.

12. Lombard, C.K., Bardina, Jorge and Venkatapathy, Ethiraj: "Forebody and Baseflow of a Dragbrake OTV by an Extremely Fast Single Level Implicit Algorithm," AIAA 84-1699, 1984.

13. Lombard, C.K., Oliger, J. and Yang, J.Y.: "A Natural Conservative Flux Difference Splitting for the Hyperbolic Systems of Gasdynamics," Presented at the Eighth International Conference on Numerical Methods in Fluid Dynamics, in Aachen, West Germany, 1982.

14. Lombard, C.K., Venkatapathy, E. and Bardina, J.: "Universal Single Level Implicit Algorithm for Gasdynamics," AIAA-84-1533, June 1984.

15. Venkatapathy, Ethiraj, and Lombard, C.K.: "Flow Structure Capturing on Overset Patched Meshes," AIAA-85-1690, 1985.

16. Yang, J.Y., Lombard, C.K. and Bardina, Jorge: "Implicit Upwind TVD Schemes for the Euler Equations with Bidiagonal Approximate Factorization," Presented at the International Symposium on Computational Fluid Dynamics - Tokyo, 1985.

Figure 1. Boundary condition interpolation procedures. Solution points O , interpolation points X , interpolant data points ☐ .

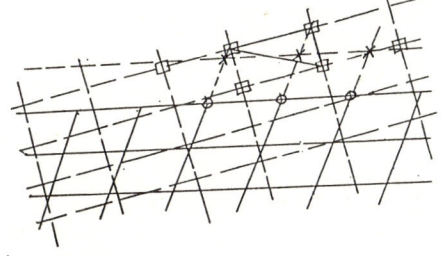
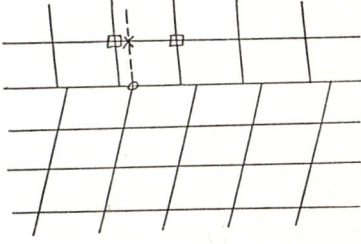

1a) Triangle interpolation for overset mesh.

1b) Line interpolation for composite mesh.

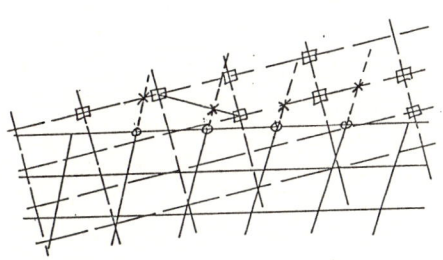
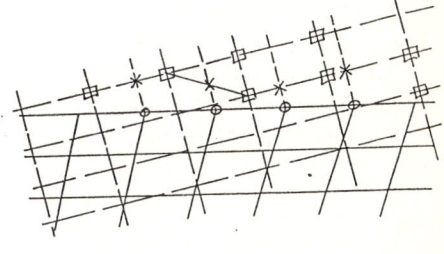

1c) Line interpolation for overset mesh. Straight line extrapolation.

1d) Line interpolation for overset mesh. Extrapolated lines turned in composite mesh analog.

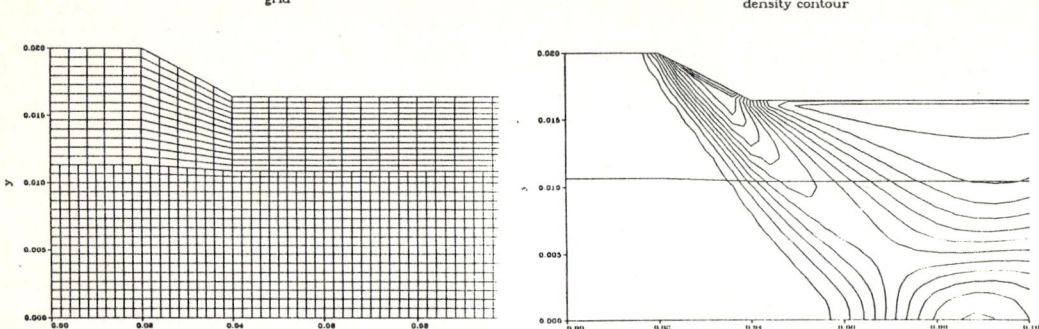

Figure 2. Test of stability of implicit numerical procedure exchanging frozen boundary point data between patched grids.
2a) Two patch computational mesh, line interpolation.   2b) Density contours for mesh 4a.

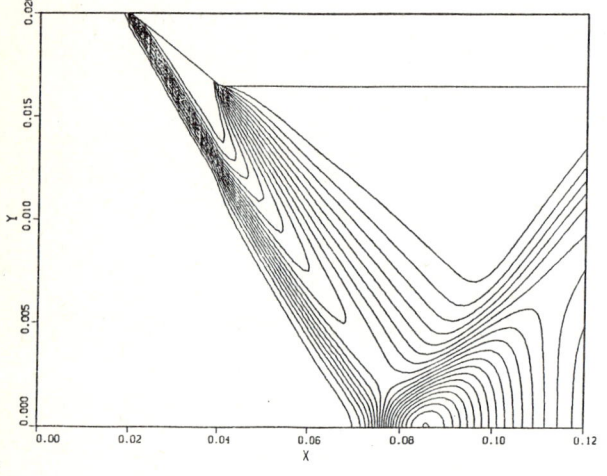

Figure 3. Pressure contours computed on 101 x 101 point uniform mesh.

3a) First order.

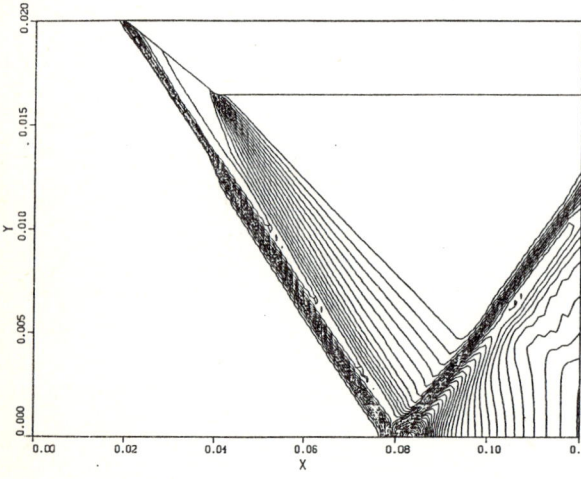

3b) Second order.

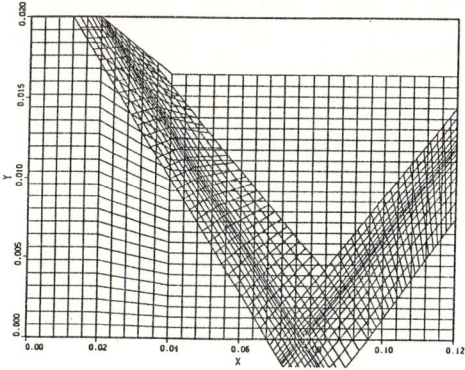

Figure 4a) Shock aligned patched grids for the inlet problem.

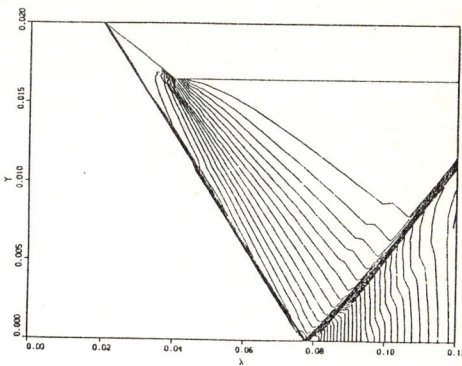

Figure 4b) Pressure contours from first order solution on patched grid.

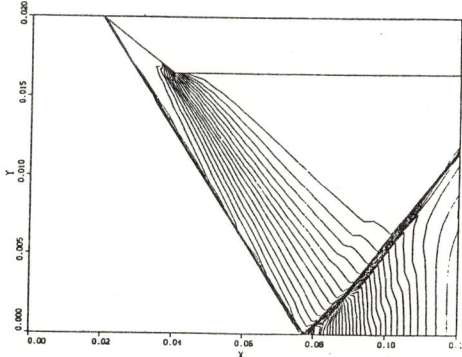

Figure 4c) Pressure contours from second order solution on patched grid.

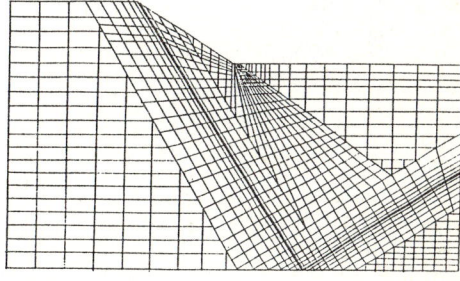

Figure 4d) Sketch of patched adaptive mesh topology concluded from present results to be effective for capture of flow structure of the inlet problem.

Computational Study of Three-Dimensional Wake Structure

Ryutaro Himeno
Central Engineering Laboratories, Nissan Motor Co., Ltd.
Yokosuka, Kanagawa, Japan

Susumu Shirayama, Keisuke Kamo
Department of Aeronautics, The University of Tokyo
Hongo, Bunkyo-ku, Tokyo, Japan

Kunio Kuwahara
The Institute of Space and Astronautical Science
Komaba, Meguro-ku, Tokyo, Japan

Abstract

Three-dimensional wake structure is studied by numerically solving the incompressible Navier-Stokes equations. Results are visualized by a three-dimensional color graphic system. It was found that a pair of vortex tubes separated from a body plays the most important role in the wake. Near the body vortex tubes are rather stable, however, they gradually become unsteady as they flow down.

Introduction

Two-dimensional wake structure past a bluff body is well understood and is characterized by a Karman vortex street (1). On the other hand, little is known about three-dimensional wake structure (2). This is probably because of the difficulty of the visualization and measurement of three-dimensional flow field are very difficult. In the present paper, three-dimensional wake structure is investigated computationally by solving the incompressible Navier-Stokes equations, and numerical results are visualized by using a three-dimensional color graphic system.

Four different types of flows are investigated here. The first is a flow around a cone on a flat plate. The second is a flow around a sphere. The third is a flow past a circular cylinder with a slanted base set parallel to the flow. The last is a flow around a rocket. The computational method is based on the third-order upwind scheme which was successfully applied to the flow around a circular cylinder at critical Reynolds number (3) and to a three-dimensional turbulent channel flow (4).

Computational Scheme

The incompressible Navier-Stokes equations are expressed as follows:

$$\mathbf{w} + \text{grad } p = \mathbf{F}, \quad \mathbf{w} = \frac{\partial \mathbf{v}}{\partial t} \tag{1}$$

$$\text{div } \mathbf{w} = 0 \tag{2}$$

where the vector $\mathbf{F}$ is

$$\mathbf{F} = -(\mathbf{v} \cdot \text{grad})\mathbf{v} + \frac{1}{\text{Re}} \Delta \mathbf{v} \tag{3}$$

The acceleration $\mathbf{w}$ and the pressure p are the solenoidal and irrotational part of the vector **F** respectively. Any vector can be decomposed into its solenoidal and irrotational parts and this decomposition is unique under certain boundary conditions. This is known as the Helmholtz decomposition. This decomposition can be completed by the following iteration (5):

$$\mathbf{w}^n = \mathbf{F} - \text{grad } p^n \qquad (4)$$

$$p^{n+1} = p^n - \varepsilon \text{ div } \mathbf{w}^n \qquad (5)$$

This iteration ends when the mean value of $|\text{div } \mathbf{w}|$ becomes smaller than some prescribed small positive constant δ. However, this makes div **v** grow linearly. To prevent this accumulation of the numerical error for div **v**, the above iteration is modified as follows (6):

$$\mathbf{w}^n = \mathbf{F} - \text{grad } p^n \qquad (6)$$

$$p^{n+1} = p^n - \varepsilon \text{ div}(\mathbf{w}^n + \frac{\alpha}{\Delta t}\mathbf{v}) \qquad (7)$$

This iteration ends when the following inequality is satisfied:

$$| \text{div}(\mathbf{w}^n + \frac{\alpha}{\Delta t}\mathbf{v}) | < \delta \qquad (8)$$

where α is an arbitary positive constant. If div **v** is set as D, the following equation can be derived.

$$\frac{\partial D}{\partial t} + \frac{\alpha D}{t} = \delta_0 \qquad (9)$$

where $-\delta < \delta_0 < \delta$. Solving this as an ordinary equation, the following equation is obtained.

$$D = (D_0 + \frac{\Delta t}{\alpha}\delta_0) \exp(- \frac{\alpha}{\Delta t}t) + \frac{\alpha}{\Delta t}\delta_0, \qquad (10)$$

where

$$D_0 = \text{div } \mathbf{v} |_{t=0}.$$

Apparently, $|\text{div } \mathbf{v}|$ decreases as time goes on.

The Euler implicit scheme is used for the time integration. All spatial derivatives except those of the nonlinear terms are approximated by the central difference. Nonlinear terms in **F** are approximated by the following third-order upwind scheme;

$$(u\frac{\partial u}{\partial x})_i =$$

$$u_i(- u_{i+2} + 8(u_{i+1} - u_{i-1}) + u_{i-2})/12h$$
$$+ |u_i|(u_{i+2} - 4u_{i+1} + 6u_i - 4u_{i-1} + u_{i-2})/4h \qquad (11)$$

Finite-difference equations are obtained by discretizing above equations written in a curvilinear coordinate system. Resulting equations are solved by SOR method. Computations were done on a Fujitsu M380 which is a scalar computer whose speed is about 9 MFLOPS.

Results

(i) Cone on a Flat Plate

The grid is generated by solving the Poisson equation in a two-dimensional plane through the axis and extended into three-dimensions by using axisymmetry. Along the symmetry axis, equations were solved in a Cartesian coordinate system. Figure 1(a) shows the velocity distribution on the surface at the Reynolds number 1000 by using a very coarse grid as 20x16x11; the apex angle α is 90°. The agreement with the expreimental observation (Fig.1(b)) (7) is reasonable. Figure 2 shows the comparison between the coarse and fine grids in the case of $\alpha=60^{\circ}$. The agreement is satisfactory; we can see a horse shoe vortex clearly in both cases and the size of the recirculating region is almost the same. Thus the grid need not be so fine at least to see a global structure of the wake. The computation time for the coarse grid calculation was 5 minutes, and that for the fine grid is one hour. Figure 3 shows the grid system. Figure 4 shows the time development of equi-pressure surfaces. Two equi-pressure surfaces in front of a cone indicate higher pressure regions and those in the wake indicate lower pressure regions. It can be clearly seen that a vortex tube shown by the contour surface of lower pressure is arched in the wake. Figure 5 shows velocity vectors and pressure contours on the central plane and velocity vectors on the surface of the body. Figure 6 shows pressure contours on the surface. Figure 7 shows pressure contours and velocity vectors on the surface. Figure 8 shows particle paths drawn under the condition that the flow field be frozen at non-dimensional time: $t=10.0$.

(ii) Sphere

An unsteady flow around a sphere which started impulsively was computed at the Reynolds number 10000. The grid was made following the same method as in the case of a cone on a flat plate. The number of grid points is 30x30x33. At the initial stage a ring type vortex develops. As time goes on, the ring type vortex inclines and the downstreamwise part of the ring is elongated. Finally it flows down making a pair of vortex tubes as seen in Fig.9 which shows equi-pressure surfaces at non-dimensional time $t = 35.04$. Figure 10 shows pressure contours on the surface of the sphere; Fig.10 (a) and (b) are the side and rear views respectively. The time development of the wake is shown in Fig.11. The computation time was 8 hours.

(iii) Circular Cylinder with a Slanted Base

The grid is made algebraically; the number of grid points is 30x32x30 and the Reynolds number is 10000. The base angle is 40°. Figure 12 shows equi-pressure surfaces. A pair of vortex tubes separated from the base is clearly seen. The vortex tubes flow down along the surface of the base. Pressure contours on the surface are shown in Fig.13. Figure 14 shows the rear view of velocity vectors on the grid plane twenty-mesh-point outside of the surface of the base. Particle paths are shown in Fig.15. Perpendicular vorticies are clearly seen in both figures. The computation time was 2 hours.

(iv) Rocket

An unsteady flow around a rocket is computed; the angle of attack is 75 degrees and the Reynolds number is 10000. The grid is generated following the same method as the case of a cone on a plate; the number of grid points is 40x33x30. Figure 16 shows the grid system. Figure 17 shows velocity vectors on a grid plane normal to the rocket. Figure 18 shows pressure contours on two grid planes normal to the rocket near its nose cone and rear end. Equi-pressure surfaces are shown in Fig.19. A pair of vortex tubes can be also seen in this case. Their roots are at the nose cone. They stay almost steadily near the nose cone but the asymmetry develops gradually as they flow down seen in the above figures. Figure 20 shows particle paths. The computation time was 10 hours.

Conclusion

From these computations, we can see that a pair of vortex tubes separated from a body plays the most important role in the wake. Near the body the vortex tubes are rather stable, however, they gradually become disturbed as they flow down.

To investigate the structure of a three dimensional flow, it is very important to visualize it well. For this purpose, a three-dimensional color graphic system is inevitable. To visualize a three dimensional flow, contour surfaces of the scalar quantities such as pressure and absolute value of the vorticity might be better than the vectors such as velocity. The vectors are too complicated to visualize on a two dimensional plane.

References

1) M. Van Dyke: "An Album of Fluid Motion", Parbolic Press, 1982.
2) D.P.Telionis; "Unsteady Viscous Flows", Springer-Verlag, 1981.
3) T.Kawamura and K.Kuwahara: AIAA paper 84-0340, 1984.
4) T.Kawamura and K.Kuwahara: AIAA paper 85-0376, 1985.
5) A.J.Chorin: Math. Comp. 22, p745, 1968.
6) H.Takami and K.Kuwahara: J.Phys.Soc.Japan 37, p1695, 1974.
7) H.Sato: "Turbulence", Kyoritsu Press, Tokyo, 1982. (in Japanese)

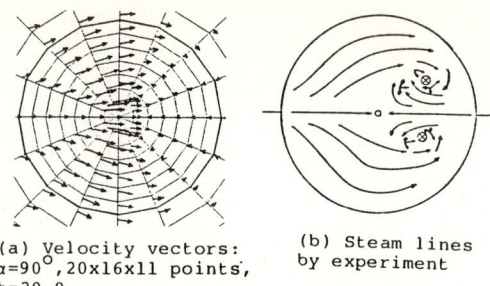

(a) Velocity vectors: $\alpha=90°$, 20x16x11 points, t=20.0

(b) Steam lines by experiment

Fig.1 Flow fields on a cone.

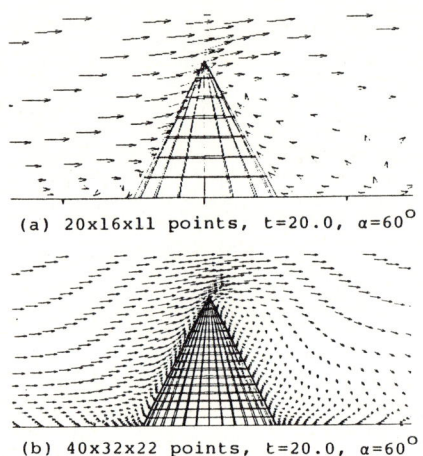

(a) 20x16x11 points, t=20.0, $\alpha=60°$

(b) 40x32x22 points, t=20.0, $\alpha=60°$

Fig.2 Comparison of the velocity distribution between the coarse and fine grids.

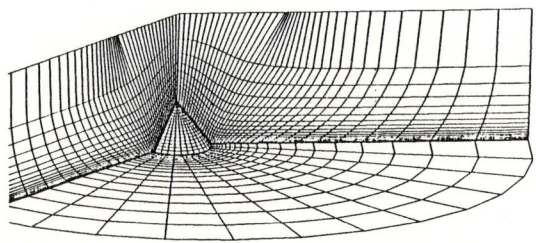

Fig.3 Grid system for the case of $\alpha=90°$. (40x32x20 points)

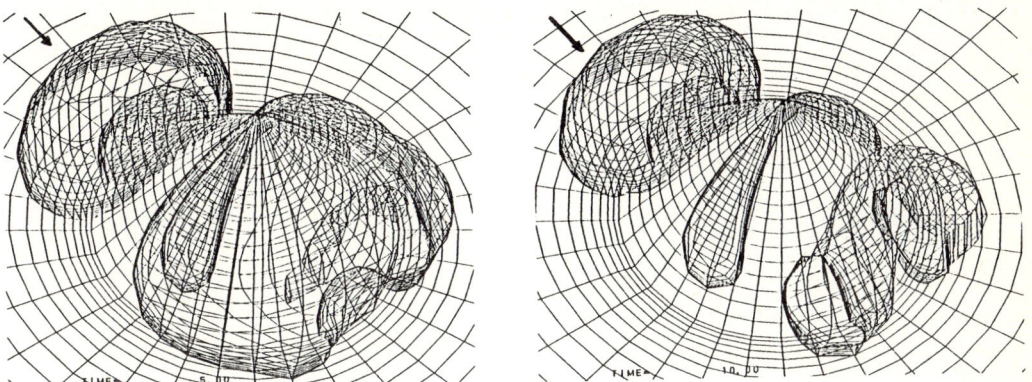
Fig.4 Time development of the equi-pressure surfaces.

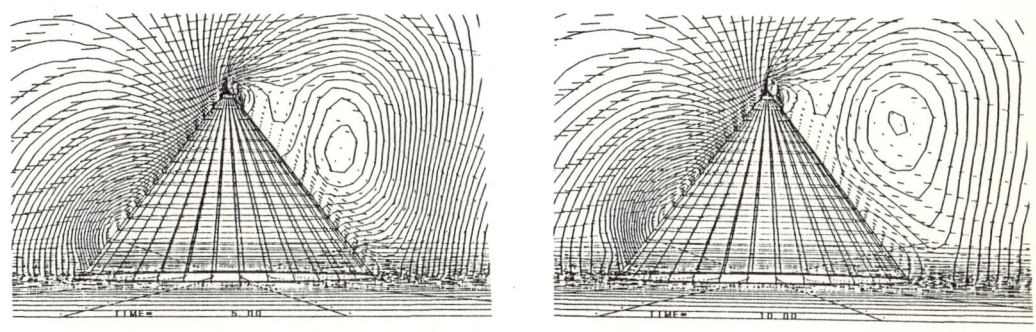
Fig.5 Velocity vectors and pressure contours on the central plane and velocity vectors on the body.

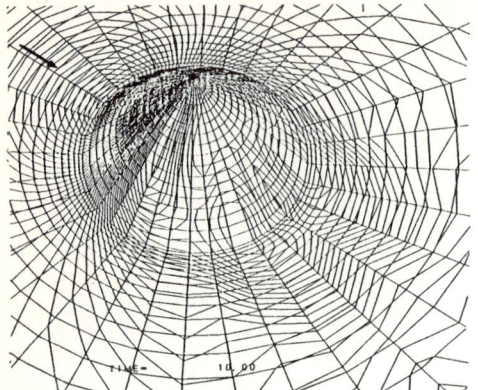

Fig.6 Pressure contours on the surface.

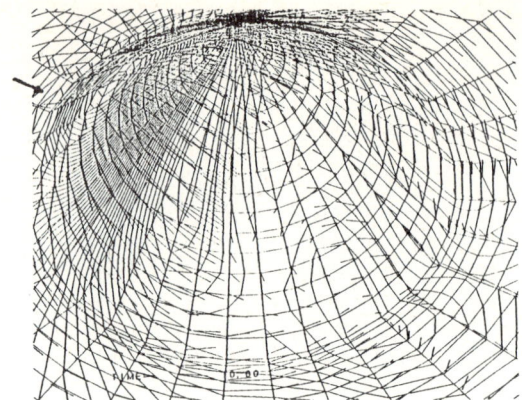

Fig.7 Pressure contours and velocity vectors on the surface.

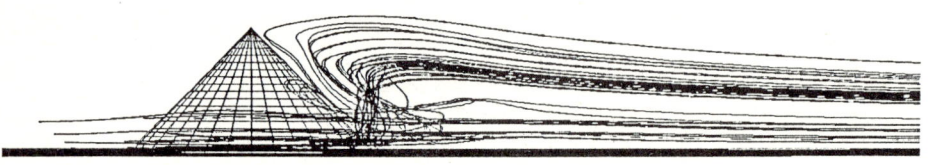

(a) Side view.

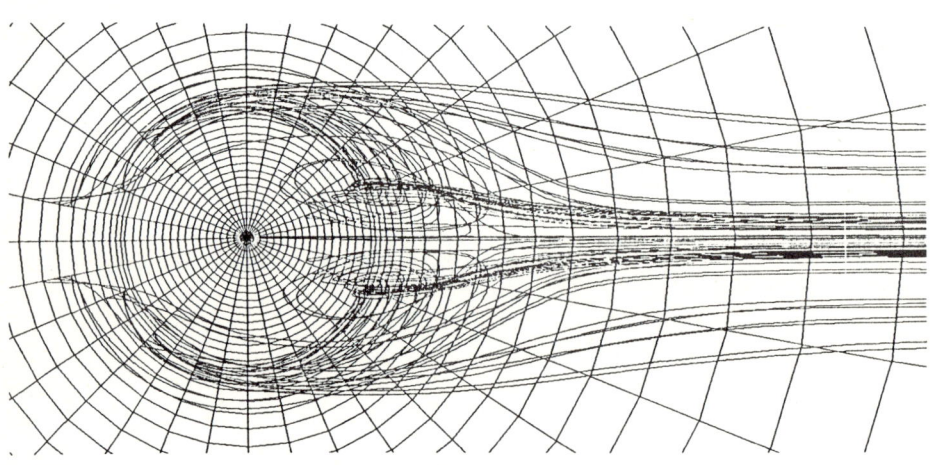

(b) Top view.

Fig.8 Particle paths drawn under the condition that the flow field be frozen at $t=10.0$.

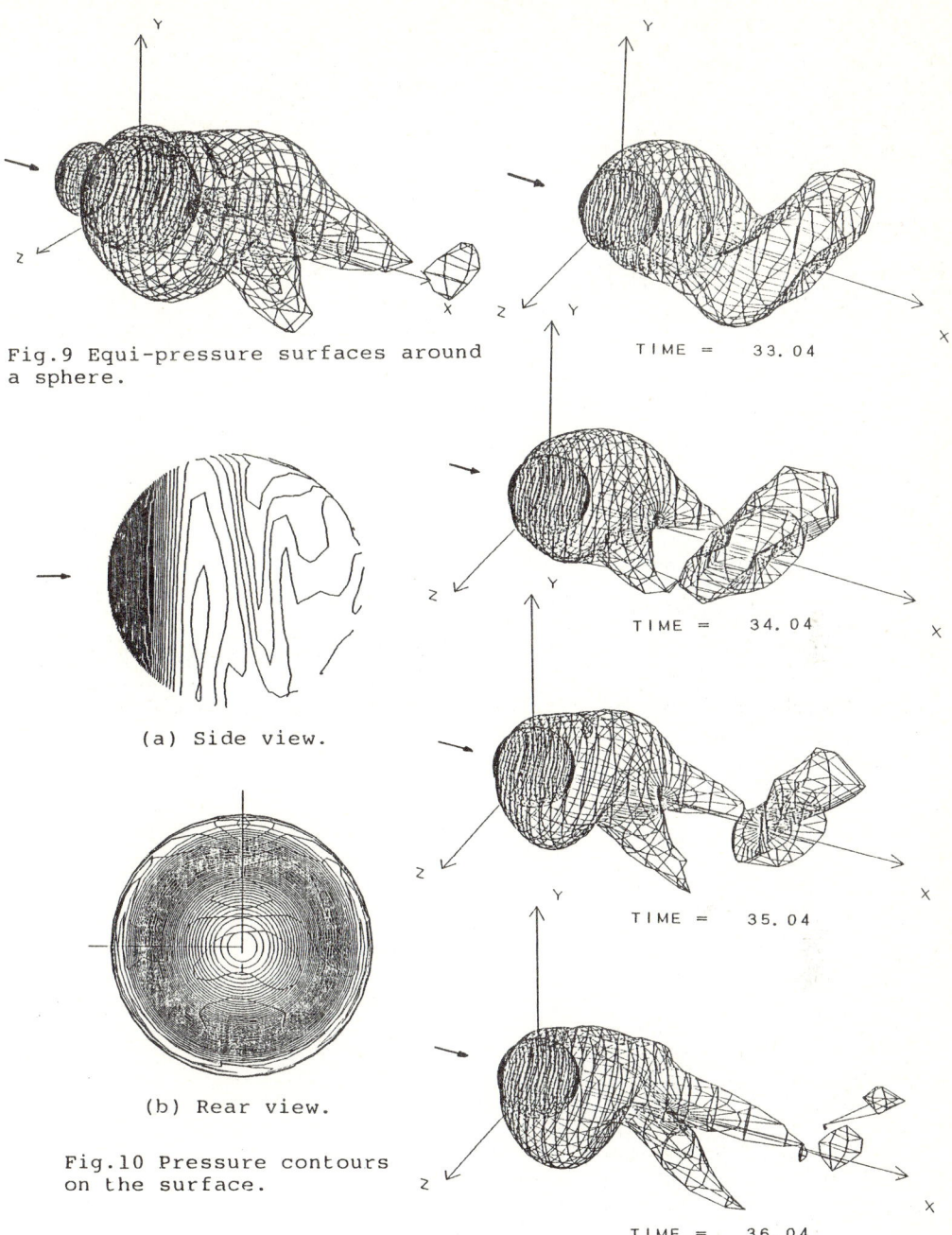

Fig.9 Equi-pressure surfaces around a sphere.

(a) Side view.

(b) Rear view.

Fig.10 Pressure contours on the surface.

TIME = 33.04

TIME = 34.04

TIME = 35.04

TIME = 36.04

Fig.11 Time development of the equi-pressure surface.

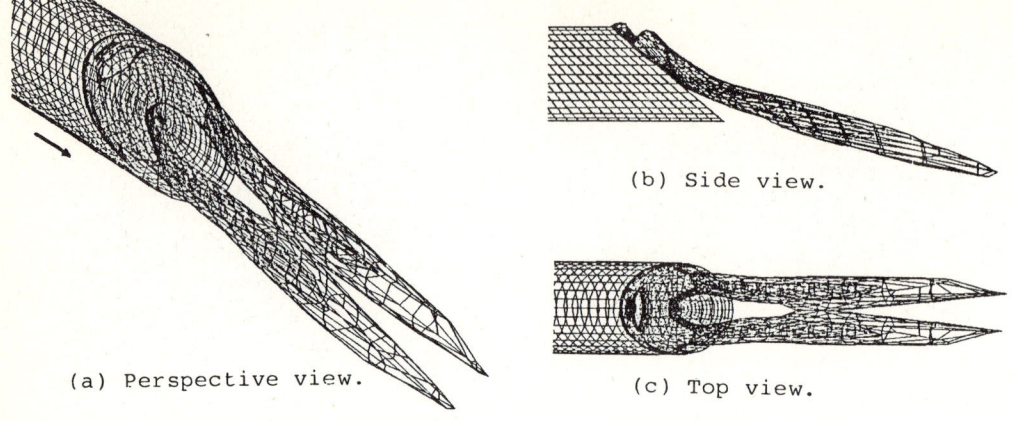

(a) Perspective view.

(b) Side view.

(c) Top view.

Fig.12 Equi-pressure surfaces in the wake. (Base angle: $\alpha=40°$, t=20.)

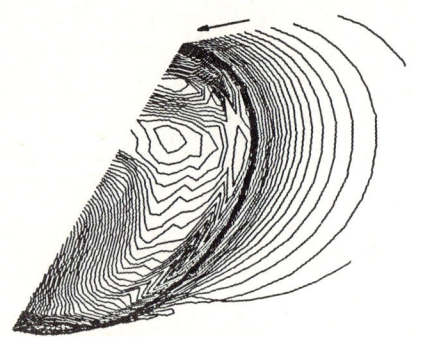

Fig.13 Pressure contours on the surface at t=20.

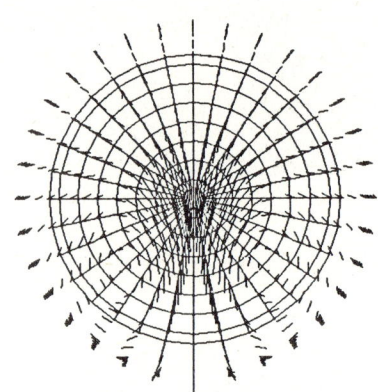

Fig.14 Velocity vectors on the grid plane twenty-mesh-point outside of the surface of the base at t=20.

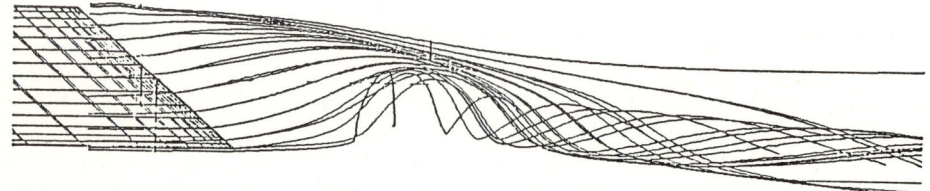

Fig.15 Particle paths. (Base angle: $\alpha=40°$, t=48.)

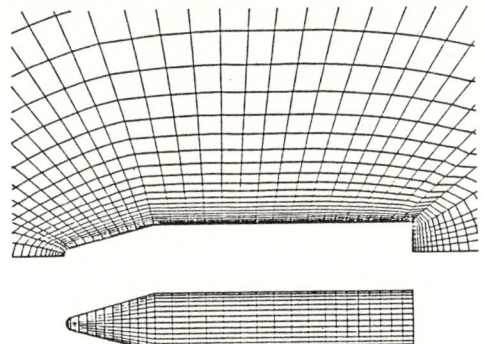

Fig.16 Grid distributions around a rocket and on its surface. (40x32x30 grid points)

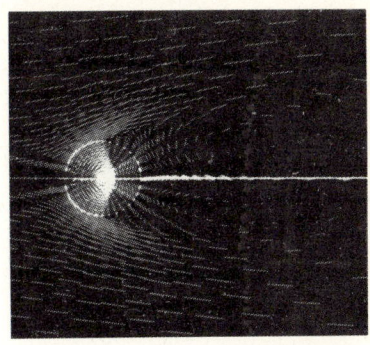

Fig.17 Velocity vectors on a grid plane normal to the body at 80.0 percents of its length (t=59.97).

(a) 50.0 percents of its length.

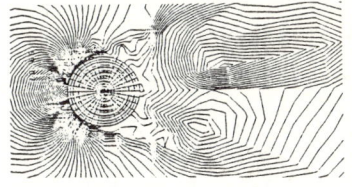

(b) 80.0 percents of its length.

Fig.18 Pressure contours on two grid planes normal to the body.

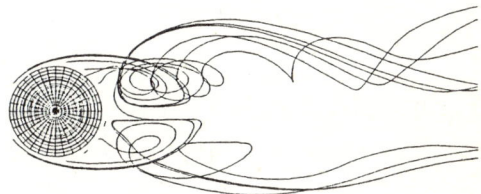

(a) Top view.

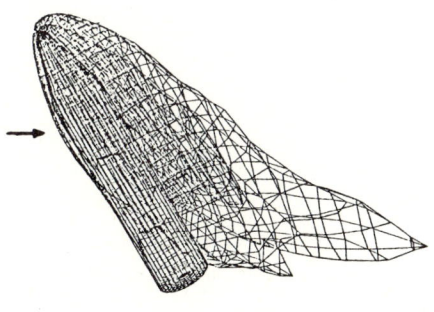

Fig.19 Equi-pressure surfaces around a rocket at t=59.97.

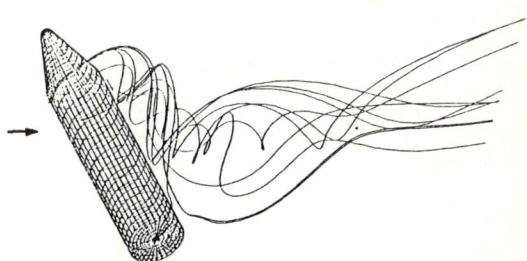

(b) Perspective view.

Fig.20 Particle paths at t=59.97.

A SEMI-ELLIPTIC ANALYSIS OF INTERNAL VISCOUS FLOWS[†]

U. Ghia, R. Ramamurti* and K.N. Ghia*
Department of Mechanical and Industrial Engineering
*Department of Aerospace Engineering and Engineering Mechanics
University of Cincinnati
Cincinnati, Ohio 45221/USA

INTRODUCTION

The increased demands placed presently on the performance of compressors and turbines of gas-turbine engines have, for some time, pointed the need for accurate analysis of viscous flows in turbomachinery. With the recent developments of advanced computational facilities, much effort has been made to respond to this need. Various mathematical formulations, grid systems and numerical techniques have been developed for the numerical solution of the viscous flow equations (Refs. 1-4). The full Navier-Stokes equations as well as their corresponding thin-layer approximate form have been employed in H- as well as C-grids, using explicit or implicit methods, including convergence enhancement techniques based on multi-grid methodology. Nevertheless, obtaining converged solutions for general geometries on acceptably refined grids remains a computationally demanding task.

The present paper discusses a reduced form of the governing equations which can capture much of the physics, while requiring less computer resources than the full Navier-Stokes equations. It belongs to the category of semi-elliptic analyses, one form of which was proposed and employed in Ref. 5. The formulation holds greatest promise for high-Re steady flows with a predominant flow direction. It should be mentioned, however, that the procedure can be extended easily to include consideration of unsteady flows. But the most unique feature of the method is its ability to compute low-Mach number flows. Although it is a density-based method, it is not plagued by computational difficulties for $M_\infty \to 0$, as are the other density-based methods available. Also, no use is made of any externally added artificial viscosity. The method is applicable to 3-D flows as well.

OUTLINE OF MATHEMATICAL MODEL

The governing differential equations used in the present study are derived from the Navier-Stokes equations, together with the continuity equation and the energy equation, for steady flow of a compressible fluid. With Cartesian decomposition of the vector quantities, these equations are expressed, in terms of a general coordinate system (ξ,η) in the following strong-conservation law (SCL) form:

[†] This research was supported, in part, by NASA-Lewis Grant NAG-3-194 and, in part, by AFOSR Grant No. 85-0231.

$$E_\xi + F_\eta = (E_v)_\xi + (F_v)_\eta \tag{1}$$

where E, F are the inviscid flux vectors and E_v, F_v represent the viscous contributions. These quantities are defined as

$$E = \frac{1}{J}\left[\rho U, (\rho uU + \xi_x p), (\rho vU + \xi_y p), (\rho e_t + p)U\right]^T ;$$

$$F = \frac{1}{J}\left[\rho V, (\rho uV + \eta_x p), (\rho vV + \eta_y p), (\rho e_t + p)V\right]^T ; \tag{2a}$$

$$E_v = \frac{1}{J}\left[\xi_x \bar{E}_v + \xi_y \bar{F}_v\right] \quad \text{and} \quad F_v = \frac{1}{J}\left[\eta_x \bar{E}_v + \eta_y \bar{F}_v\right]. \tag{2b}$$

Here, u, v are the Cartesian velocity components along the x, y coordinate directions, respectively, and $\bar{E}_v$, $\bar{F}_v$ are the Cartesian viscous quantities given as

$$\bar{E}_v = [0, \tau_{xx}, \tau_{xy}, (u\tau_{xx} + v\tau_{xy} - q_x)]^T$$

and

$$\bar{F}_v = [0, \tau_{yx}, \tau_{yy}, (u\tau_{yx} + v\tau_{yy} - q_y)]^T , \tag{3}$$

where the τ's and q's represent the Cartesian components of the shear-stress tensor and heat-flux vector, respectively. Finally, U, V are the contravariant velocity components along the ξ, η directions, respectively, and J represents the Jacobian of the transformation between the (x,y) and (ξ,η) coordinate systems. These quantities are defined as follows.

$$J = \xi_x \eta_y - \xi_y \eta_x ; \tag{4}$$

$$U = \xi_x u + \xi_y v \quad \text{and} \quad V = \eta_x u + \eta_y v . \tag{5}$$

Expressing the transformed governing differential equations in the SCL form [Eq. (1)] requires that the coordinate transformation metrics satisfy the following conditions.

$$(\xi_x/J)_\xi + (\eta_x/J)_\eta = 0 \quad \text{and} \quad (\xi_y/J)_\xi + (\eta_y/J)_\eta = 0 . \tag{6}$$

In an analytical formulation, these are identically satisfied, since they correspond to the identities

$$(y_\eta)_\xi - (y_\xi)_\eta = 0 \quad \text{and} \quad (x_\eta)_\xi - (x_\xi)_\eta = 0 . \tag{7}$$

In a discretized formulation, satisfaction of these relations is ensured by the use of appropriate differencing.

The semi-elliptic formulation used in the present work is obtained from Eq. (1) by invoking the approximation that, for flows with a predominant flow direction, streamwise diffusion is negligible relative to normal diffusion. Consequently, Eq. (1) is reduced to the following parabolized form.

$$E_\xi + F_\eta = (F_v)_\eta \quad . \tag{8}$$

At this juncture, it is important to make two observations. First of all, it is no longer possible to satisfy the conditions given in Eq. (6) associated with the viscous terms, except for a very special orientation of the (ξ,η) coordinates, namely, those for which the metrics x_ξ, y_ξ are independent of η, e.g., sheared Cartesian coordinates. This implies that, for a general (ξ,η) system, the viscous terms in Eq. (8) may not be retained in the SCL form but should be expressed in their corresponding chain-rule conservation law (CRCL) form. Hence, the parabolized Eq. (8) should be written as

$$E_\xi + F_\eta = [\eta_x (\bar{E}_v)_\eta + \eta_y (\bar{F}_v)_\eta]/J \quad . \tag{9}$$

The second point of note is that a large class of flows, for which streamwise diffusion may well be negligible, are significantly influenced by upstream interactions, and may not be adequately represented by mathematically parabolic equations. In the present formulation, upstream interaction is provided for via appropriate treatment of the streamwise pressure gradient term contained within $\partial E/\partial \xi$. Hence, the formulation may also be termed an <u>interacting parabolized Navier-Stokes (IPNS) model</u>. The viscous-inviscid interaction is included by composite consideration of the viscous and inviscid flow regions through the use of the PNS equations; upstream interactions are propagated and included through the pressure field, as discussed next.

Following Vigneron et al. (Ref. 6), the term E_ξ is represented as

$$E_\xi = E^*_{\xi_b} + a\, p_{\xi_f} \tag{10}$$

where

$$E^* = [\rho U, (\rho u U + \xi_x \omega p), (\rho v U + \xi_y \omega p), (\rho e_t + p)U]^T/J \quad , \tag{11}$$

$$a = [0, (1-\omega)\xi_{x_f}, (1-\omega)\xi_{y_f}, 0]^T/J \tag{12}$$

and

$$\omega \leq \gamma M^2/[1 + (\gamma-1)M^2] \triangleq f(M), \text{ with } \omega = 1 \text{ if } f(M) > 1, \tag{13}$$

and subscripts b and f denote that the subsequent numerical solution procedure should use backward and forward differencing, respectively, for these derivatives.

Since the term $(a\, \partial p/\partial \xi)$ in Eq. (10) is not in the SCL form, the term containing $\partial p/\partial \eta$ within $\partial F/\partial \eta$ should also not be in the SCL form. Hence, the final form of the governing equations is obtained as

$$E^*_{\xi_b} + F^*_\eta + b\, p_\eta - F_{v_\eta} = -a\, p_{\xi_f} \tag{14}$$

where

$$F^* = [\rho V, (\rho u V + \eta_x \omega p), (\rho v V + \eta_y \omega p), (\rho e_t + p)V]^T/J \tag{15}$$

and
$$b = [0, (1-\omega)\dot{n}_x, (1-\omega)n_y, 0]^T/J . \qquad (16)$$

Boundary Conditions

Three different types of boundary pairs are encountered in the present work. At the <u>inflow and outflow boundaries</u>, for the subsonic flows considered here, the total pressure, total temperature and streamline slope are prescribed at inflow and the static pressure is prescribed at outflow. At the <u>wall-wall boundaries</u>, the conditions of zero slip and zero suction/injection, together with a specified temperature condition, provide a total of six boundary conditions. However, Eq. (14) is a seventh-order system of differential equations for ρ, u, v, T, with respect to η. The one additional boundary condition needed is provided by an approximate form of the normal momentum equation obtained by neglecting the viscous terms in that equation. This last condition is applied in the cells adjacent to the wall, rather than at the wall itself, thus avoiding the need for any one-sided differences for the normal derivatives. The <u>wake-wake boundaries</u> are the periodic boundaries occurring in cascade flows. The periodicity condition requires that the corresponding values of all four flow variables, and the η-derivatives, u_η, v_η and T_η, of the velocities and temperature which are governed by second-order differential equations, be the same at corresponding periodic points along the wake boundaries. It is important to mention that, in terms of the conserved variables (ρ, ρu, ρv, ρe_t) comprising the solution vector $\bar{Q}$, the repeating condition on the η-derivatives must be satisfied for all four elements of $\bar{Q}_\eta$.

Using these boundary conditions, Eq. (14) is solved to determine the flow for a variety of configurations. Space limitations prevent the presentation of a discussion of the numerical solution technique. The equations are quasilinearized carefully and discretized consistently and solved by an alternating-direction method, requiring that a term (a p_t) be included in the right-hand side of Eq. (14). The boundary conditions are treated implicitly.

RESULTS

The analysis described was employed to determine the flow in several channel and cascade configurations. Some of the results obtained are presented here in terms of the two most sensitive quantities, namely, the static pressure and wall shear. Unless otherwise stated, the Mach number M_∞ is approximately 0.008.

Constricted-Channel Flow

The constricted channel considered was formed by straight parallel boundaries everywhere, except in the region of the constriction where the lower and upper boundary profiles $y_{b,\ell}$ and $y_{b,u}$ were given by

$$y_{b,\ell} = (\frac{t_{max}}{2h}) \exp[-(x-x_m)^2/d^2] \quad \text{and} \quad y_{b,u} = h - y_{b,\ell} , \qquad (17)$$

respectively, where x_m is the x-location of the maximum constriction; d controls the streamwise extent of the constriction; t_{max} is the total maximum constriction, and h is the channel height away from the constriction. Figure 1 shows the distribution of the surface pressure p_b (= $p_{w_{inlet}}$ -p_w) and wall-shear parameter, τ_w (= $\partial u_s/\partial n$), obtained for a channel with $t_{max}/h = 0.2$ and Re ≈ 1500. Of particular significance is the presence of a finite region of small reversed flow indicated by negative τ_w, downstream of the constriction and the completely non-singular behavior of the present IPNS solution for this configuration with upstream interaction.

Cascade of Finite Flat Plates

The performance of the IPNS model in the presence of sharp leading and trailing edges was evaluated by application of the model to a cascade of finite flat plates. Figure 2 shows the distribution of the pressure p_b and shear parameter τ_w for Re ranging from 1500 to 15,000. The corresponding behavior of p_w is inferred easily from Fig. 2a. As the leading edge (LE) is approached, the pressure rises to its maximum value and then drops sharply immediately past the LE, followed by a region of more gradual pressure drop, until the trailing edge (TE) where a sharp dip occurs in the pressure. Thereafter, the pressure rises to smoothly approach the prescribed value at the outflow boundary. Sharp peaks are also observed in τ_w distribution near LE and TE. Through all this highly nonlinear behavior, including that due to abrupt change in the boundary conditions across LE and TE, the solution of the IPNS model is quite regular as upstream interactions are appropriately included in it.

Cascade of Exponential Airfoils

The exponential airfoils were constructed using the profiles given by Eq. (17) with h replaced by the airfoil chord c. The corresponding results for p_b and τ_w are shown in Fig. 3 for various values of Re. Again, the correct behavior has been computed in the LE and TE regions. The region and intensity of the reversed flow are now smaller than for the exponential channel, because of the upstream influence due to the higher velocity of the fluid downstream of TE as compared to that of the fluid downstream of the constriction in the channel with zero slip at the walls.

Cascade of Parabolic-Arc Airfoils

Results in the form of distribution of p_b and τ_w are shown in Fig. 4 for parabolic-arc airfoils for various thickness ratios (Fig. 4a) and for various Reynolds numbers (Fig. 4b). The behavior of the flow in the wedge-shaped TE region of these airfoils is considerably different from that for the exponential airfoil which possesses a cusped TE. The effect of varying M_∞ up to nearly 0.5 has also been examined. It is found to be minimal on the shear parameter τ_w, but becomes evident in the pressure distribution at the highest value of M_∞ considered. The details of these results are not included here. However, Fig. 4c shows the static pressure contours for the case with $M_\infty = 0.49$, $Re = 15,000$. The high-pressure region localized near the LE is evident from the concentration of the contours in this region, as is the more widespread low-pressure regions downstream of the position of maximum thickness. From the values of the pressure along these contours, it is clear that the pressure varies rather minimally over the airfoil surface. Nevertheless, these variations have been very accurately computed in order to produce the contours which are well behaved and conform to the physics of this flow, especially in the LE and TE regions.

CONCLUDING REMARKS

A semi-elliptic formulation and solution procedure have been developed for the analysis of subsonic viscous flows, with upstream interaction included via the pressure field. Application to several flow configurations served to demonstrate that the technique is viable for flows with strong interactions occurring due to boundary-layer separation or the presence of sharp leading/trailing edges. The grids employed in the present calculations were reasonably fine. For example, for the parabolic-arc airfoil cascade, a grid of non-uniformly spaced (186x71) points was used so as to provide streamwise steps of 0.01 and 0.005 near the LE and TE, respectively. This resolution is within the guidelines of triple-deck theory providing the length scales of these strong-interaction regions, and was considered adequate also because results obtained with a modified (231x71) grid with $\Delta x_{TE} \approx 0.001$ remained essentially unchanged. As regards convergence rate, the maximum error was reduced by two to five orders of magnitude, depending upon the flow configuration and the grid considered, within 150 iterations. The choice of the time step Δt as well as its spatial variation had a significant influence on the convergence behavior of the solutions.

Experiences with application to cascades of airfoils with rounded LE region led to difficulties which were tracked down to the use of an H-grid for such geometry. For example, attempts to analyze a cascade of Joukowski airfoils were successful only when the rounded LE region was modified to a wedge-shaped region. This has led the present authors to develop a hybrid C-H grid (Fig. 5) which is more appropriate for such cascades. Here, a narrow C-region is wrapped around each of the airfoils; the second family of C-grid coordinates emanating from the LE region extends upstream to the inflow boundary. The coordinate system is completed by H-grid topology occupying the remainder of the cacade passage. The hybrid grid is generated using a composite, not patching, procedure. Flow solutions on this grid are presently being developed and should be reported in the near future. For the present, it is important to recall that the procedure developed uses no externally added artificial viscosity and is capable of producing satisfactory solutions for compressible (subsonic) viscous flows, with no modification needed for analyzing nearly incompressible flow as well.

REFERENCES

1. Chima, R.V., <u>AIAA Paper</u> 84-1663, June 1984.

2. Shamroth, S.J., McDonald, H. and Briley, W.R., <u>ASME Journal of Engineering for Power</u>, Vol. 106, pp. 383-390, April 1984.

3. Hah, C., <u>ASME Journal of Engg. for Power</u>, Vol. 106, pp. 421-429, April 1984.

4. Chima, R.V. and Johnson, G.M., <u>AIAA Journal</u>, Vol. 23, No. 1, January 1985.

5. Ghia, U., Ghia, K.N., Rubin, S.G. and Khosla, P.K., <u>International Journal of Computers and Fluids</u>, Vol. 9, pp. 123-142, 1981.

6. Vigneron, Y.C., Rakich, J.V. and Tannehill, J.C., <u>AIAA Paper</u> 78-1137, July 1978.

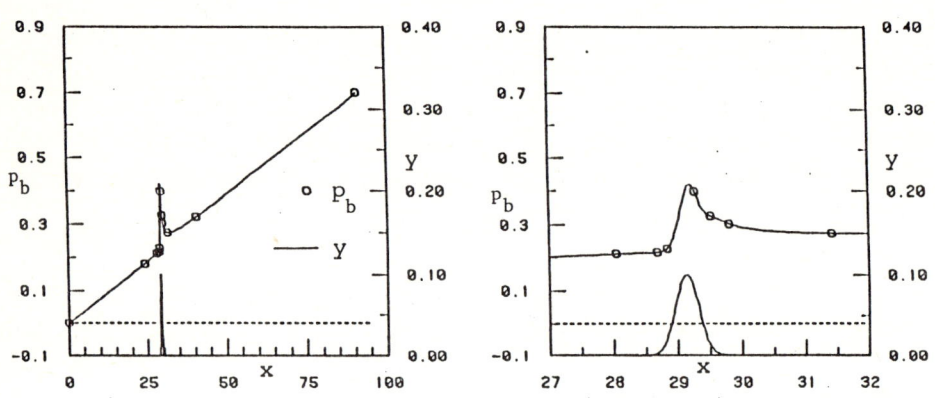

SURFACE PRESSURE DISTRIBUTION

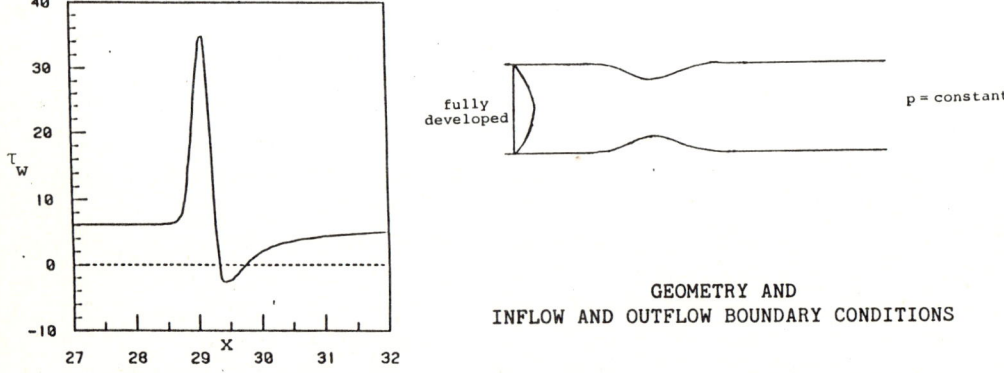

SURFACE SHEAR PARAMETER

GEOMETRY AND
INFLOW AND OUTFLOW BOUNDARY CONDITIONS

FIG. 1. RESULTS FOR SYMMETRIC CHANNEL WITH EXPONENTIAL CONSTRICTION; Re = 1500, t_{max}/h = 0.2, (201 x 61) GRID.

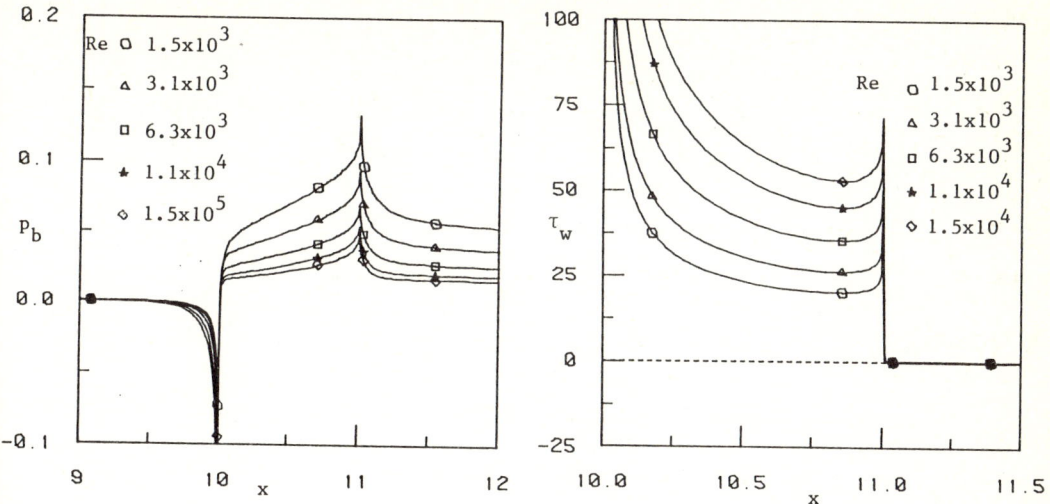

FIG. 2. RESULTS FOR FLAT-PLATE CASCADE FOR VARIOUS REYNOLDS NUMBERS, (186 x 71) GRID.

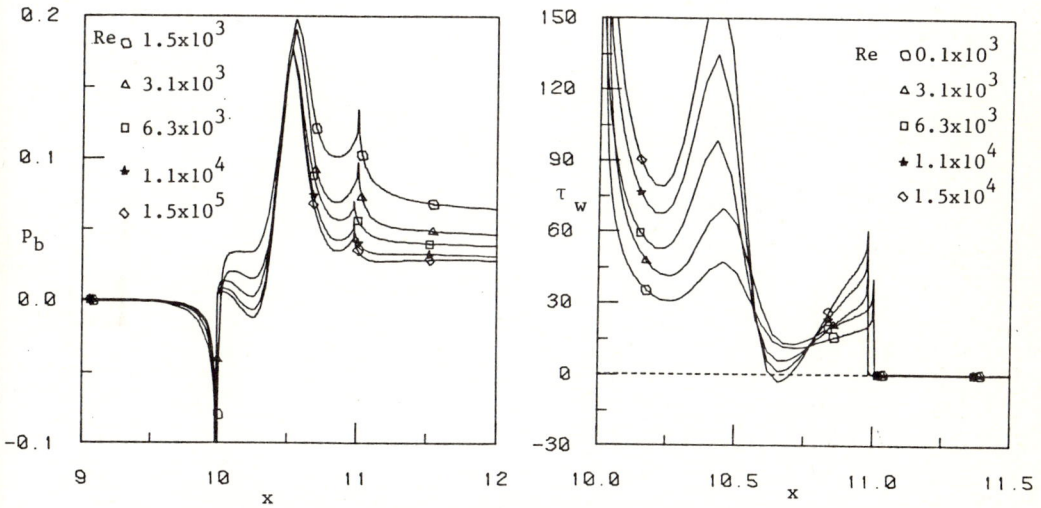

FIG. 3. RESULTS FOR SYMMETRIC CASCADE OF EXPONENTIAL AIRFOILS FOR VARIOUS REYNOLDS NUMBERS; $t_{max}/c = 0.05$, (186 x 71) GRID.

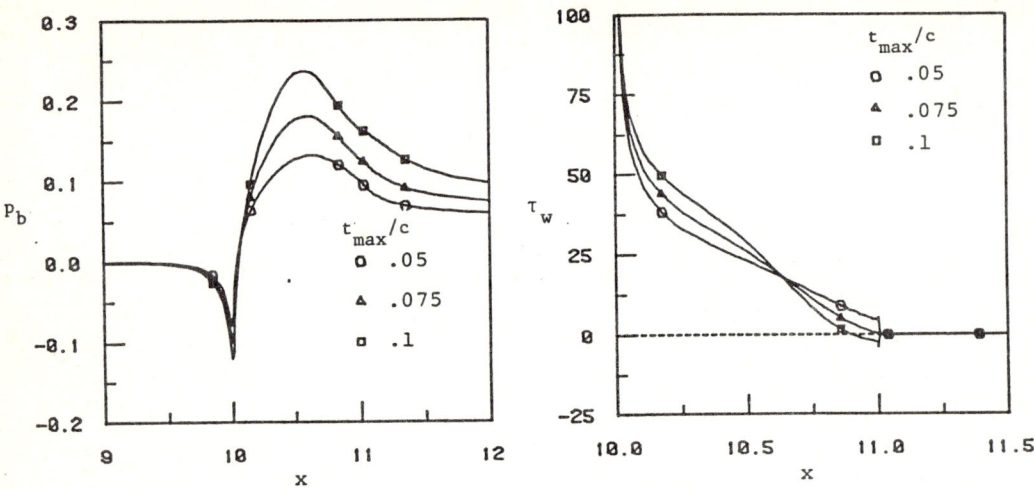

FIG. 4a. RESULTS FOR SYMMETRIC CASCADE OF PARABOLIC AIRFOILS FOR VARIOUS t_{max}/c; Re ≈ 1500, (186 x 71) GRID.

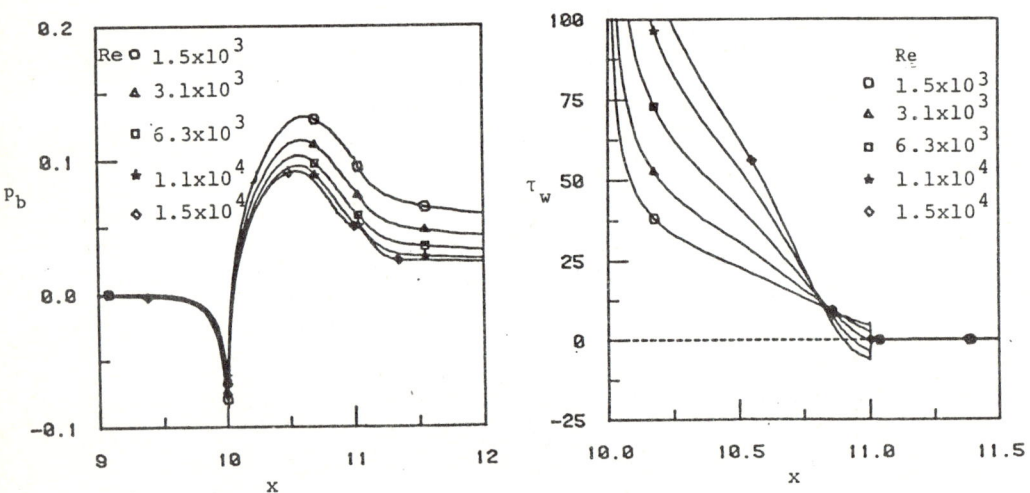

FIG. 4b. RESULTS FOR SYMMETRIC CASCADE OF PARABOLIC AIRFOILS FOR VARIOUS REYNOLDS NUMBERS; t_{max}/c = 0.05, (186 x 71) GRID.

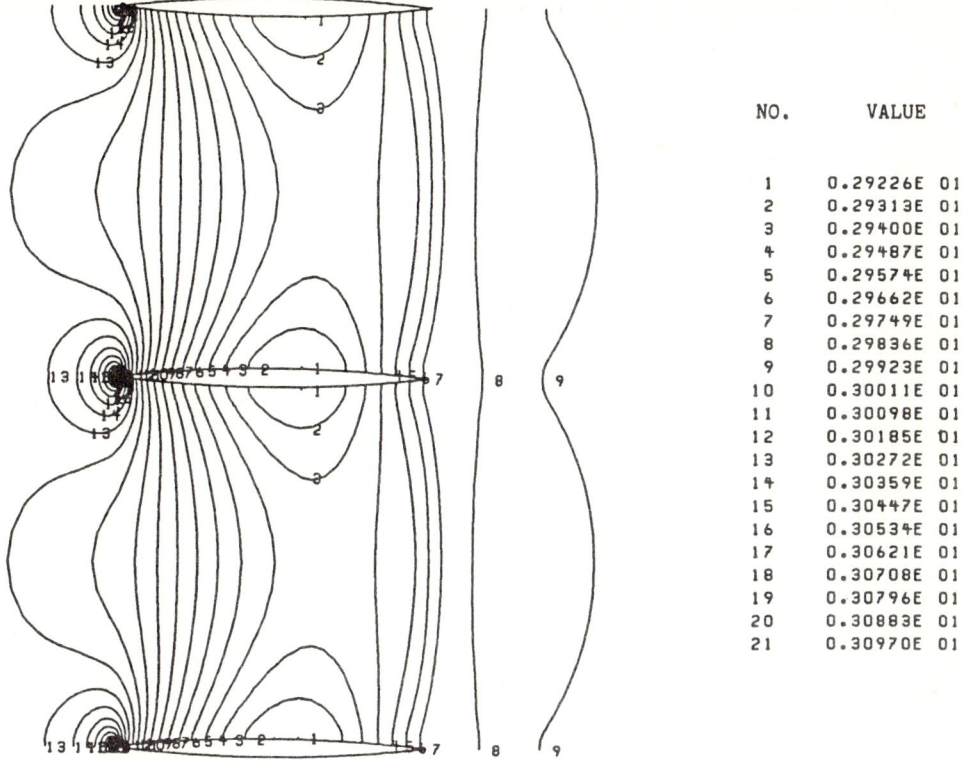

FIG. 4c. PRESSURE CONTOURS FOR SYMMETRIC CASCADE OF PARABOLIC AIRFOILS; $t_{max}/c = 0.05$, $M_\infty = 0.49$, $Re = 15,000$.

NO.	VALUE
1	0.29226E 01
2	0.29313E 01
3	0.29400E 01
4	0.29487E 01
5	0.29574E 01
6	0.29662E 01
7	0.29749E 01
8	0.29836E 01
9	0.29923E 01
10	0.30011E 01
11	0.30098E 01
12	0.30185E 01
13	0.30272E 01
14	0.30359E 01
15	0.30447E 01
16	0.30534E 01
17	0.30621E 01
18	0.30708E 01
19	0.30796E 01
20	0.30883E 01
21	0.30970E 01

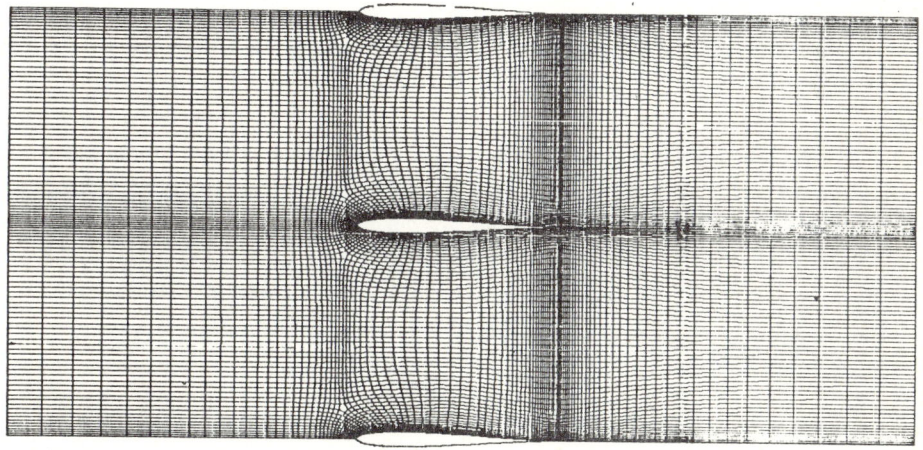

FIG. 5. HYBRID C-H GRID FOR A CASCADE OF SYMMETRIC JOUKOWSKI AIRFOILS.

SIMULATION OF SELF-INDUCED UNSTEADY MOTION IN THE NEAR WAKE OF A JOUKOWSKI AIRFOIL[†]

K.N. Ghia*, G.A. Osswald* and U. Ghia**
*Department of Aerospace Engineering and Engineering Mechanics
**Department of Mechanical Engineering
University of Cincinnati
Cincinnati, Ohio 45221/USA

INTRODUCTION

Recent impetus for research in unsteady separated flows stems from a wide range of applications from low- to high- Reynolds number, Re. The physics of high-Re flows, in general, is quite complex and often involves multiple nonuniqueness and chaos, beyond simple unsteady separation. For the low-Re case, e.g. in the manuevering of fighter aircraft at high angle-of-attack in near- and post-stall regime, the vortex interaction dominates the flow field. The passage of vortices over the suction surface and their subsequent shedding leads to self-excited persistently unsteady flows. This flow field is extremely complicated due to the global effect of unsteady separated flow, coupled with the presence of hydrodynamic instabilities which may trigger transition and eventually lead to chaos. Besides supermaneuverability, interest also lies in this low-Re case because of the need for design of efficient airfoil sections for Re in the range of 10^5-10^6, for improving the performance of mini-RPV's (remotely piloted vehicles) operating at low altitudes, jet engine compressor and turbine blades, helicopter rotor blades, etc.

For low-speed viscous flow without body forces, Re is the key similarity parameter. For flow over lifting bodies, the flow pattern is unique and steady for Re < Re_{cr}, where Re_{cr} is the value of Re at which transition first occurs. Near and beyond Re_{cr}, the flow is highly unsteady and it becomes imperative that this unsteady flow be better understood. Recent developments in the dynamical theory of low-dimensional nonlinear systems have provided a new and stimulating viewpoint concerning the onset of turbulence, as computer simulations of three or more coupled nonlinear first-order ordinary differential equations have led to chaotic solutions. Such an observation led Ruelle and Takens (1971) to hypothesize that transition to turbulence can be quantitatively explained by deterministic equations. Their work has produced exciting and profound results and the resulting theory has become widely known as the Ruelle-Takens theory of turbulence. They showed mathematically that, for a nonlinear initial-boundary value problem, with a large critical parameter such as Re, chaos resulted from repeated bifurcations of the solution.

[†] This research was supported, in part, by AFOSR Grant No. 85-0231 and, in part, by NASA Grant No. NAG-1-465.

The chaotic solutions were referred to as "Strange Attractors", to distinguish them from other ordinary attractors such as fixed points and limit cycles, i.e. steady-state and periodic solutions, respectively. The strange attractors are geometric entities in the phase or state space of the governing differential equations. In this context, fixed points are zero-dimensional entities, limit cycles are one-dimensional entities in the sense that they can be parameterized by a single degree of freedom, and strange attractors are more-than-one dimensional, perhaps even of fractional dimension. The important point is that the dimension of a strange attractor is often quite low. Indeed, in this new approach, it is possible that the underlying mechanism responsible for chaotic behavior can be characterized by only a few degrees of freedom. This new theory contradicts the earlier statistical theory which treats turbulence as a broad (i.e., many degrees of freedom) spectrum of periodic disturbances. But it is conjectured that it should include the secondary instability theory of transition. Perhaps, time-dependent instabilities are the likely mechanism by which an attractor remains strange. The arguments leading towards the concept of strange attractors and the Ruelle-Takens theory of turbulence will become evident in the section on results and their discussion.

K. Ghia, Osswald and U. Ghia (1985a) analyzed massively separated flow past a 12 percent thick Joukowski airfoil using a symmetric C-grid. The Reynolds number ranged from 10^3 to 10^4 and the angle of attack α was varied up to 10°. For the configuration of Re = 10^3, $\alpha_f=15°$, the unsteady massively separated flow asymptoted to a limit cycle. Subsequently, Osswald, K. Ghia and U. Ghia (1985b) significantly improved the above analysis by introducing circulation in the computation of conformal clustered C-grid. This resulted in the branch cut approaching the wake centerline a few chords downstream of the trailing edge (TE). A numerical method was developed to treat the branch cut of the C-grid implicitly while also appropriately treating the vorticity singularity at the TE. The versatility and efficiency of the numerical method were demonstrated by providing the massively separated flow structure for Re=10^3 and $\alpha_f=30°$ and also the transient results, at early times, for Re=10^3 and $\alpha_f=53°$. The present study is a sequel to these earlier studies and has the following objectives:

i.   To provide the detailed flow structure of massively separated flow for Re=10^3, $\alpha=53°$, in the post-stall regime of the flow past a Joukowski airfoil,

ii. to obtain time-dependent aerodynamic lift, drag and moment coefficients for Re=10^3 and α_f between 15° to 53° and, finally,

iii. to understand the observed quasiperiodicity and bring forth any similarity possible with strange attractors.

ON THE ANALYSIS AND NUMERICAL METHODS

The conservative form of the unsteady Navier-Stokes equations in terms of vorticity and stream function in generalized curvilinear coordinates (ξ^1, ξ^2) is used. The far-field boundary conditions of uniform flow are, strictly, valid only at infinity. To circumvent the large values of ψ occurring in the far-field and also facilitate the numerical implementation of the far-field boundary conditions, the stream function ψ is decomposed into two parts such that $\psi = \psi_{in} + \psi_v$, neither of which need to be small in comparison to the other. Here, ψ_{in} is a solution of the stream function equation with zero vorticity and satisfies the free-stream condition at infinity and zero normal velocity at the surface of the airfoil. This decomposition is used so as to enable the far-field boundary condition to be placed at infinity for the viscous-flow calculations.

The Reynolds number used in this study is defined as $Re = U_\infty c/\nu$ where c is the airfoil chord. The characteristic time is given as $t = t^*/(c/U_\infty)$, with U_∞ being the undisturbed free-stream velocity. The boundary conditions correspond to uniform flow at infinity, together with the no-slip conditions along the body surface. The initial conditions for the viscous flow are taken as the corresponding steady-state inviscid solution.

A clustered conformal grid is generated; the clustering is controlled by appropriate one-dimensional (1-D) stretching transformations. An attempt is made to resolve many of the multiple scales of the unsteady flow with massive separation, while maintaining the transformation metrics to be smooth and continuous in the entire flow field. Typical clustered conformal grids consisting of (230, 46) points for a 12 percent thick symmetric Joukowski airfoil with α_g = 15°, 30° and 53° are shown in Fig. 1. Here, α_g is the grid angle of attack, i.e. the asymptotic slope of the coordinate line emanating from the TE; this may, or may not, be the same as the flow angle of attack α_f.

A fully implicit time-marching method is developed such that all spatial derivatives are approximated using central differences and no use is made of any artificial dissipation. The numerical method solves the discretized equations using the alternating-direction implicit-block Gaussian elimination (ADI-BGE) method and has overall $O[\Delta t, (\Delta\xi^1)^2, (\Delta\xi^2)^2]$ accuracy. The boundary conditions on the vorticity are so implemented as to maintain second-order spatial accuracy. The results obtained for this study are discussed next.

RESULTS AND DISCUSSION

A 12 percent thick symmetric Joukowski airfoil is used in this study and has two especially attractive features. (i) The Joukowski airfoil can be accurately represented using conformal transformations; the details of these and the clustering transformations used were given by Osswald, K. Ghia and U. Ghia (1985a). (ii) The presence of a sharp TE leads to a much stronger interacting region and, hence, truly tests the analysis developed. This unsteady Navier-Stokes analysis and the corresponding numerical method are used to study three flow configurations in detail. All of these configurations have the same Re = 1,000 but the value of the free-stream incidence varies such that α_f = 15°, 30° and 53°, respectively. As stated earlier, a C-grid with (230x46) mesh points has been used; this number was arrived at based on the available full-core capacity of the supermini Perkin Elmer 3250 MPS computer system; this then also precluded a mesh refinement study. Hence, an attempt* was made to convert the program to run on the CYBER 205 VPS/32 computer at NASA Langley Research Center; this effort is still in progress. The CPU time τ require to advance the solution by one time step per spatial grid point is referred to as a "computational effort" index; the value achieved for τ was 2.14×10^{-3} seconds for a Perkin Elmer 3250 MPS supermini computer system.

Flow in Post-Stall Regime: Re = 1000, α_f = 53°

There are two critical parameters in the flow past an airfoil, namely, Re and α_f. In the present study, Re is held constant and only α_f is increased from 15° to 53°, so that α_f becomes the critical parameter in this discussion. For the high angle-of-attack case with α_f = 53°, the Joukowski airfoil appears, to the oncoming stream, as an apparent bluff body. The massively separated vortex-dominated flow in the post-stall regime for this configuration of the Joukowski airfoil, is exceedingly complex and, from the results available so far, it is feasible to conjecture two hypotheses; see Fig. 5. One possibility is that the solution has still not asymptoted to an exact limit cycle but may do so subsequently. The second possibility, based on the results for α_f = 30 to be discussed later, is that the solution may asymptote to a quasiperiodic state, with anywhere from 3 to 8 incommensurate frequencies. The second hypothesis is more likely to prevail and some arguments in its favor will be presented later. However, the discussion for this configuration is presently considered speculative in nature, since the results in Fig. 5 do not permit identifying a limit-cycle and describing its evolution. Hence, the time instants at which the results are presented, are selected arbitrarily to show the spatial structure between the LE-TE-LE sheddings.

The instantaneous stream function contours presented in Figs. 2a, c, e, g show massively separated flow with large eddies present over the suction surface as well as in the wake. The stagnation streamline on the pressure surface fluctuates and is closer to LE when the LE eddy is stronger in strength (see Fig. 2a) as compared to Figs. 2c, e where the clockwise rotating eddy has already been shed and is in the process of strong interaction with the counterclockwise eddy from the TE. The corresponding vorticity contours are shown in Figs 2b, d, f, h and are of greater

---

* This effort was made in August 1985, while the present investigators were in residence at ICASE. Subsequently, the computer program has been made fully operational and, it is anticipated that the much-needed grid refinement in the normal direction will be carried out shortly.

significance, since they are independent of the observer's reference frame and, hence, permit more meaningful assessment of the convection and diffusion of the vortices. Figure 2b shows the intense TE vortex and also the weaker LE vortex. As compared to the cases with α_f = 15° and 30°, the interaction between these two vortices is initially of a weaker nature.

Figure 2d corresponds to intense interaction between the LE vortex and a part of the TE vortex, while the remaining part of the TE vortex is elongated and its shedding is imminent. Still there is a substantial strength elongated vortex that has remained as seen in Fig. 2f and it is about to shed at t = 52.7; also, the shear layer from the LE has thickened. Finally, in Fig. 2h, both the LE and TE vortices are beginning to intensify and the earlier interacting vortices are on the verge of separating from the LE shear layer. The subsequent flow structure at t = 54.5, not shown here, is very similar to that at t = 50.4 and corresponds to shedding of the vortex at the LE. This evolution process could have been visualized more clearly, had color contour plots been available to distinguish the LE and TE vortices.

Limit Cycle Analysis

i. **Coefficients of Lift, Drag and Moment for Re = 1000, α_f = 15°, 30° and 53°**

Originally, the aerodynamic coefficients were computed only at intervals of 0.1 characteristic time. This was quite satisfactory for qualitative assessment of the flow evolution but too coarse for its detailed analysis. Subsequently, the computer program has been modified to provide the coefficients of lift C_L, drag C_D and moment C_M (nose-up positive about the quarter chord point) at every Δt increment. The configuration with α_f = 15°, which requires minimum time to reach the time-asymptotic limit cycle solution has been completely recomputed, using a slightly improved grid near the TE. The flow configuration with α_f = 30° has been recomputed between t = 45 and t = 58, whereas, due to limitation of availability of CPU time on host computer system, the configuration with α_f = 53° is currently available with C_L, C_D and C_M computations at the interval of 0.1t only. Figures 3a, b, c show C_L, C_D and C_M corresponding to α_f=15°. As seen in this figure, C_L rises initially but drops very sharply during the transient phase and asymptotes to a near-limit-cycle solution corresponding to the dominant frequency for the shedding of vortices from the TE. The L_2 norm of the entire vorticity and stream function fields were carefully examined to ensure that the near-limit-cycle has been achieved. This limit-cycle solution is an "ordinary attractor", the attractor being the 1-D object to which the phase-space trajectories are attracted at all times. The complete motion is known once the geometry of the attractor is determined. Hence, it is also possible to compute the mean flow by averaging the flow over one complete cycle; similarly, it is possible to determine the Reynolds stresses from first principles, although these computations have not been performed in the present study.

For the flow configuration with α_f=30°, the physics changes dramatically, as seen in Figs. 4a, b, c. The curves for the force coefficients show that one limit cycle consists of two TE vortices sheddings. There are now two shedding frequencies, or modes, associated with this more complex attractor. As shown in Fig. 4a, the first frequency is associated with the shedding which takes place at point 1, whereas the second frequency is associated with the shedding which takes place at point 3. The LE shear layer associated with the first frequency is thinner and more intense, as compared to that associated with the second frequency. The energy now oscillates between the two unstable modes through a nonlinear coupling. The appearance of subharmonics signifies small modulations in the shedding frequency. This flow field, with its two natural incommensurate frequencies, is referred to as a quasiperiodic flow, also known as "Hopf bifurcation" into an invariant torus. From Fig. 4a, it is clear that the initial state at point 10 of a new cycle is slightly different from that at point 8. If the phase-space trajectories were drawn, this solution may very well show the tendency to fill a rather significant surface area of the torus. Finally, it should be noted that the C_D peaks in Fig. 4d correspond to points 2 and 9 in Fig. 4a.

For the case with $\alpha_f=53°$, the results obtained up to t=74 may be far from approaching an asymptotic state. Figure 5a shows some resemblance of quasiperiodic flow with three incommensurate frequencies, this fact being further supported by the curves in Figs. 5b, c. From their numerical experiments, Grebogi, Ott and Yorke (1983) have also shown the existence of quasiperiodicity with three incommensurate frequencies. The state of the system at a given time instant in one cycle is not quite repeated at the corresponding time instant in the subsequent cycle. The phase-space portrait, not shown here, is very complex, where the surface has folded repeatedly onto itself, so that it appears to be a strange attractor. This is an indication, although preliminary, that the flow may be exhibiting a route to chaos. There are a few rigorous approaches to characterize a strange attractor. These are the determination of (i) the Lyapunov exponent, (ii) the fractal dimension of the attractor, which is related to the number of degrees of freedom; and finally, (iii) the Kolmogorov entropy. These indices still need to be studied thoroughly in order to rigorously analyze the route to chaos in a meaningful way.

ii. **Entire State of the System**

Analysis of lift, drag and moment histories by themselves is not sufficient to examine limit-cycle behavior since it is quite possible that two different dynamic states of the system may produce the same values of C_L, C_D and C_M. To avoid such a possibility, the L_2 norms of the difference between the evolving stream function and vorticity fields and their corresponding values at some designated initial time were computed at each time step. Only when this measure of the internal dynamic state of the system reached a value below a specified tolerance, was it considered that an initial state of the system had actually re-occurred. To date, this analysis has been carried out only for the configuration with Re=1,000 and $\alpha_f=15°$. Here, a near-limit-cycle (within the specified tolerance) does occur, with a period of 1.416

characteristic-time units and a nondimensional shedding frequency of 0.706. The corresponding Strouhal number, $S = fc\sin\alpha/U_\infty = 0.18$, (see K. Ghia, Osswald and U. Ghia (1985b)), agrees well with the universal wake-based number of Roshko (1954). From Figs. 6a and c, as well as 6b and d, it is clear that the large as well as small-scale motion repeats itself and that a limit cycle has been nearly established. For the case of Re=1000 and $\alpha_f = 30°$, the L_2-norm of the solution has yet to be examined. Instead, the limit cycle was arrived at from visual observation of the variation of aerodynamic coefficients presented in Fig. 4. As seen in Fig. 4a, the two Strouhal numbers are S=0.15 and S=0.20, corresponding to two shedding frequencies. Considering the two sheddings per cycle, the overall Strouhal number S is obtained as 0.17 which, again, is in the correct range. The stream-function and vorticity contours in Figs. 7a-d for t=45.1 closely resemble those at 50.98, but the two states are not identical, implying a slightly different initial state each time. Finally, for Re=1000 and $\alpha_f = 53°$, the results obtained so far are not sufficient to warrant a limit-cycle analysis. It is likely that the flow field may asymptote to quasiperiodicity with three incommensurate frequencies, as can be inferred from Fig. 5b. However, this is a very weak justification and, hence, no attempt is made to compute the Strouhal number yet. In order to understand the degree to which this motion repeats itself, points 1 and 14, corresponding to LE shedding after three sheddings, have been plotted in Figs. 8a-d at t=46.2 and 58.6. The stream-function and vorticity contours are similar, but there are sufficient differences. This leads to the conjecture that the motion may be quasiperiodic with three frequencies, and may be on the route to chaos.

CONCLUSION

The unsteady Navier-Stokes analysis is shown to be capable of analyzing the massively separated, persistently unsteady flow in the post-stall regime of a Joukowski airfoil for angle of attack as high as 53°. The analysis has provided the detailed flow structure, showing the complex vortex interaction for this configuration. The aerodynamic coefficients, C_L, C_D and C_M for lift, drag and moment, respectively, have been calculated; these aid further in characterizing this unsteady flow. The use of α_f as the critical parameter appears to be appropriate, but further computations are needed to convincingly demonstrate the state of the flow for $\alpha_f = 53°$. The phase-space portrait not shown for this case does, at least qualitatively show that the asymptotic solution is a strange attractor. This study has so far only computed the spatial structure of the vortex interaction. It is now important to potentially use the large-scale vortex interactions, an additional energy source, to improve the aerodynamic performance. To achieve this, a quantitative analysis must be carried out from the results obtained so far to analyze the dependence of vortex evolutions, their growth and strength, and the various interactions amongst vortices and with the airfoil. This latter study would aid in carefully characterizing the flow field as a function of the airfoil geometry. It is only after this phase that the undesirable aerodynamic features can be appropriately controlled and the energy of the unsteady vortex-dominated flow harnessed to improve the aerodynamic performance as desired under critical operating conditions.

REFERENCES

Ghia, K.N., Osswald, G.A. and Ghia, U. (1985a), "Analysis of Two-Dimensional Incompressible Flow Past Airfoils Using Unsteady Navier-Stokes Equations," Proceedings of Third Symposium on Numerical and Physical Aspects of Aerodynamic Flows, Long Beach, California.

Ghia, K.N., Osswald, G.A. and Ghia, U. (1985b), "Analysis of Two-Dimensional Incompressible Flow Past Airfoils Using Unsteady Navier-Stokes Equations," to appear in Numerical and Physical Aspects of Aerodynamic Flows, Editor: T. Cebeci, Springer Verlag, New York.

Grebogi, C., Ott, E. and Yorke, J.A. (1983), "Are Three-Frequency Quasiperiodic Orbits to be Expected in Typical Nonlinear Dynamical Systems?" Physcial Review Letters, Vol. 51, No. 5, pp. 339-342.

Osswald, G.A., Ghia, K.N. and Ghia, U. (1985a), "A Clustered Conformal Grid Generation Technique for Symmetric Joukowski Airfoils at Arbitrary Angle of Attack," AFL Report 85-1-69, University of Cincinnati, Cincinnati, Ohio.

Osswald, G.A., Ghia, K.N. and Ghia, U. (1985b), "An Implicit Time-Marching Method for Studying Unsteady Flow with Massive Separation," AIAA CP 854, pp. 25-37.

Roshko, A. (1954), "On Drag and Shedding Frequency of Two-Dimensional Bluff Bodies," NACA TN-3169.

Ruelle, D. and Takens, F. (1971), "On the Nature of Turbulence," Commun. Math. Phys., Vol. 20, pp. 167-192.

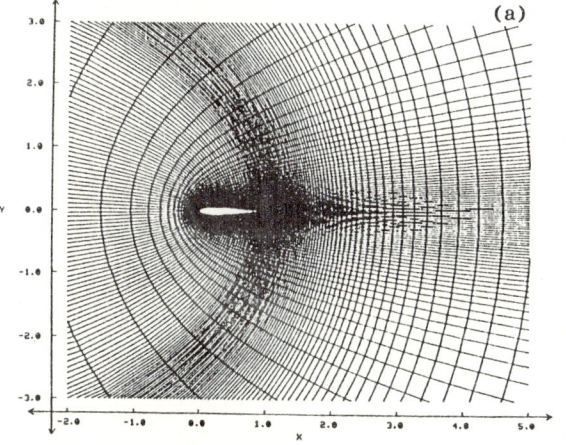
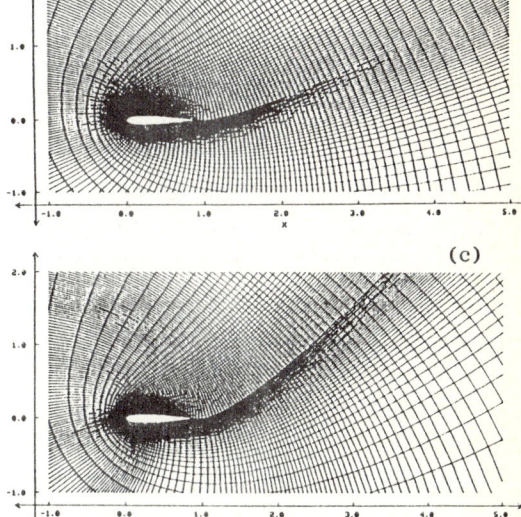

Fig. 1. Typical Grid Distributions for Symmetric Joukowski Airfoil; (229,45) Mesh, τ_{max}=0.12.
(a) α_g = 15°; (b) α_g = 30°; (c) α_g = 53°.

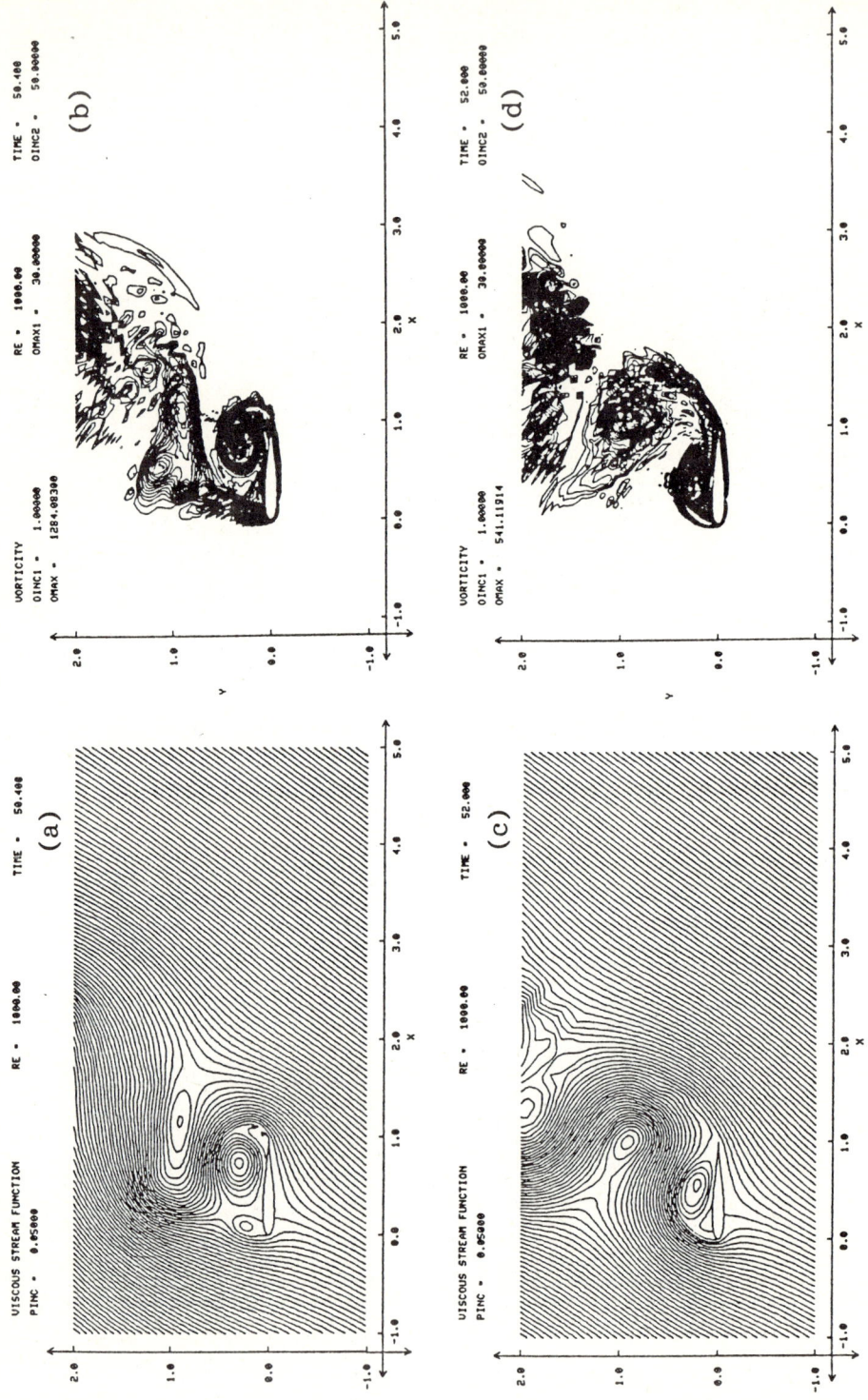

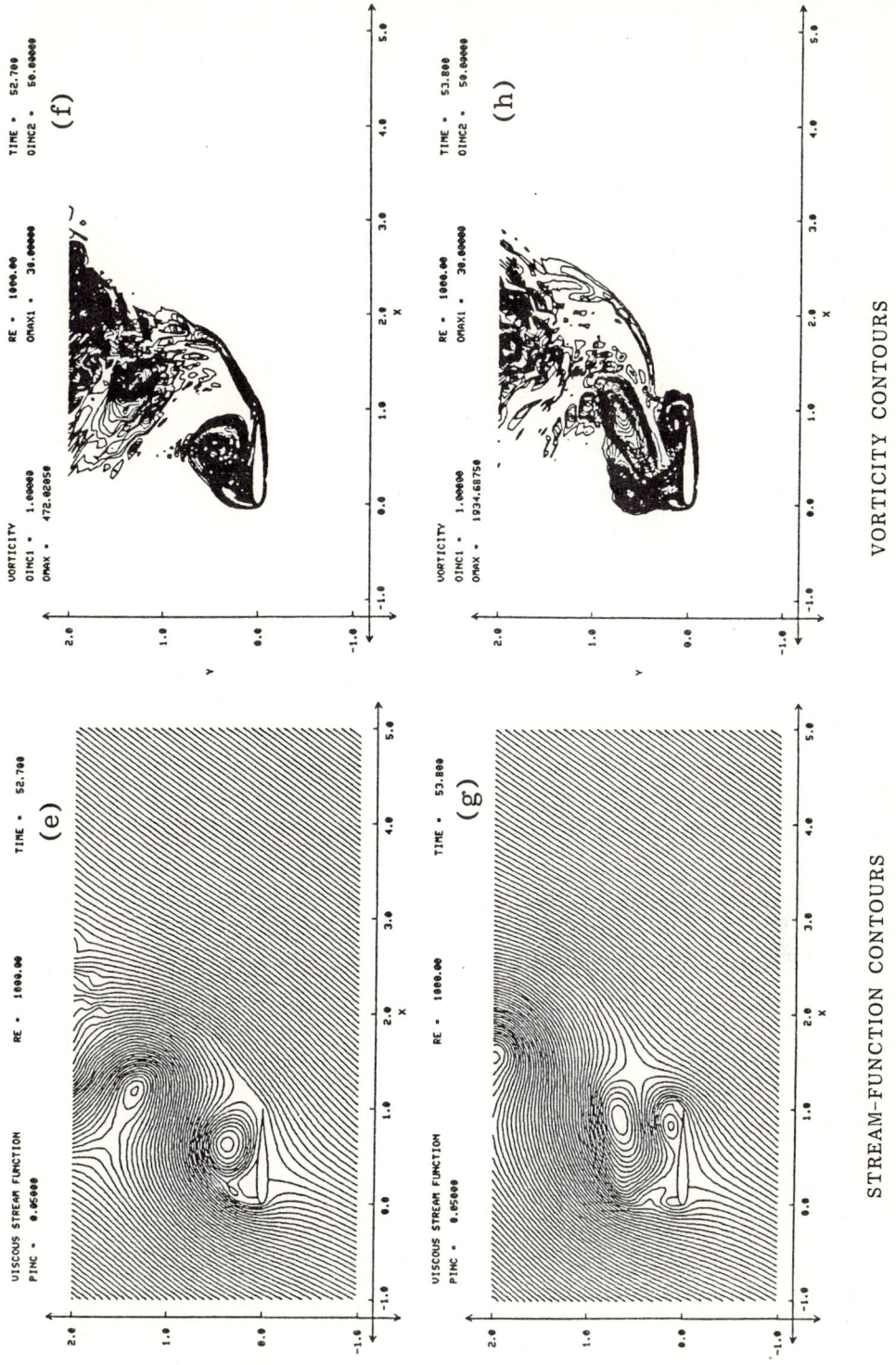

STREAM-FUNCTION CONTOURS   VORTICITY CONTOURS

Fig. 2. LE-TE-LE Vortex-Shedding Cycle for Joukowski Airfoil at Re = 1,000, $\alpha_f = 53°$.

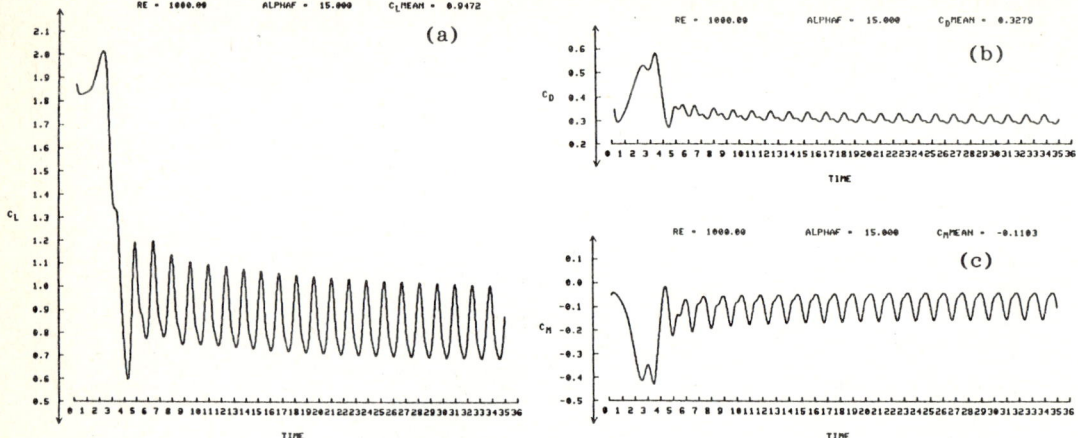

Fig. 3. Instantaneous Aerodynamic Coefficients at Re = 1,000, $\alpha_f = 15°$.
(a) Lift C_L, (b) Drag C_D, (c) Moment C_M.

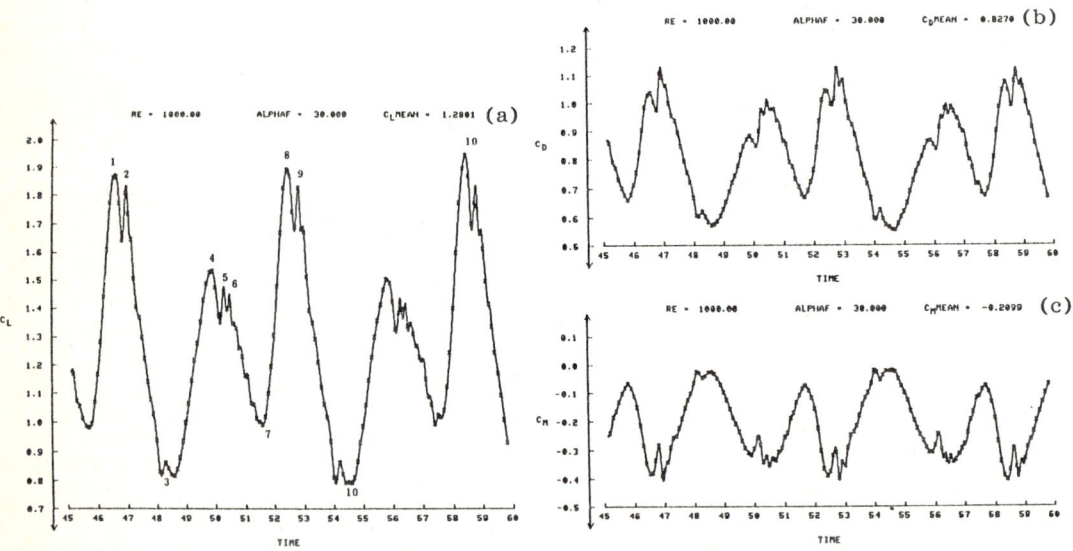

Fig. 4. Instantaneous Aerodynamic Coefficients at Re = 1,000, $\alpha_f = 30°$.
(a) Lift C_L, (b) Drag C_D, (c) Moment C_M.

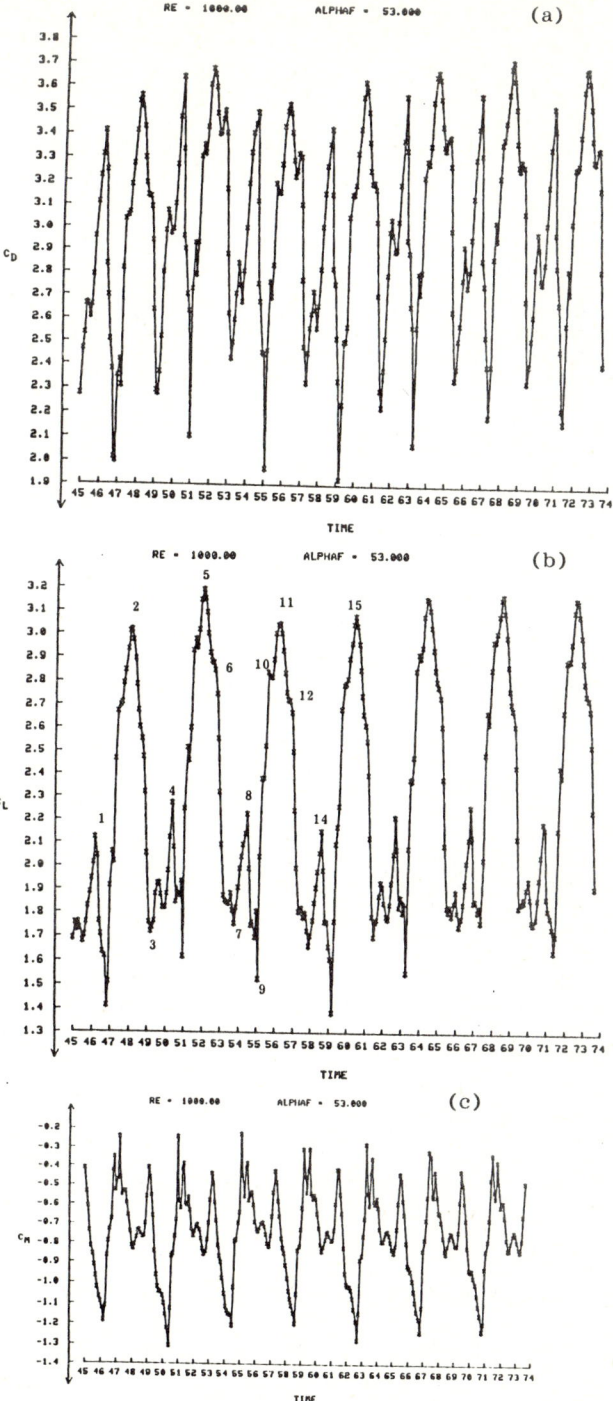

Fig. 5. Instantaneous Aerodynamic Coefficients at Re = 1,000, α_f = 53°.
(a) Lift C_L, (b) Drag C_D, (c) Moment C_M.

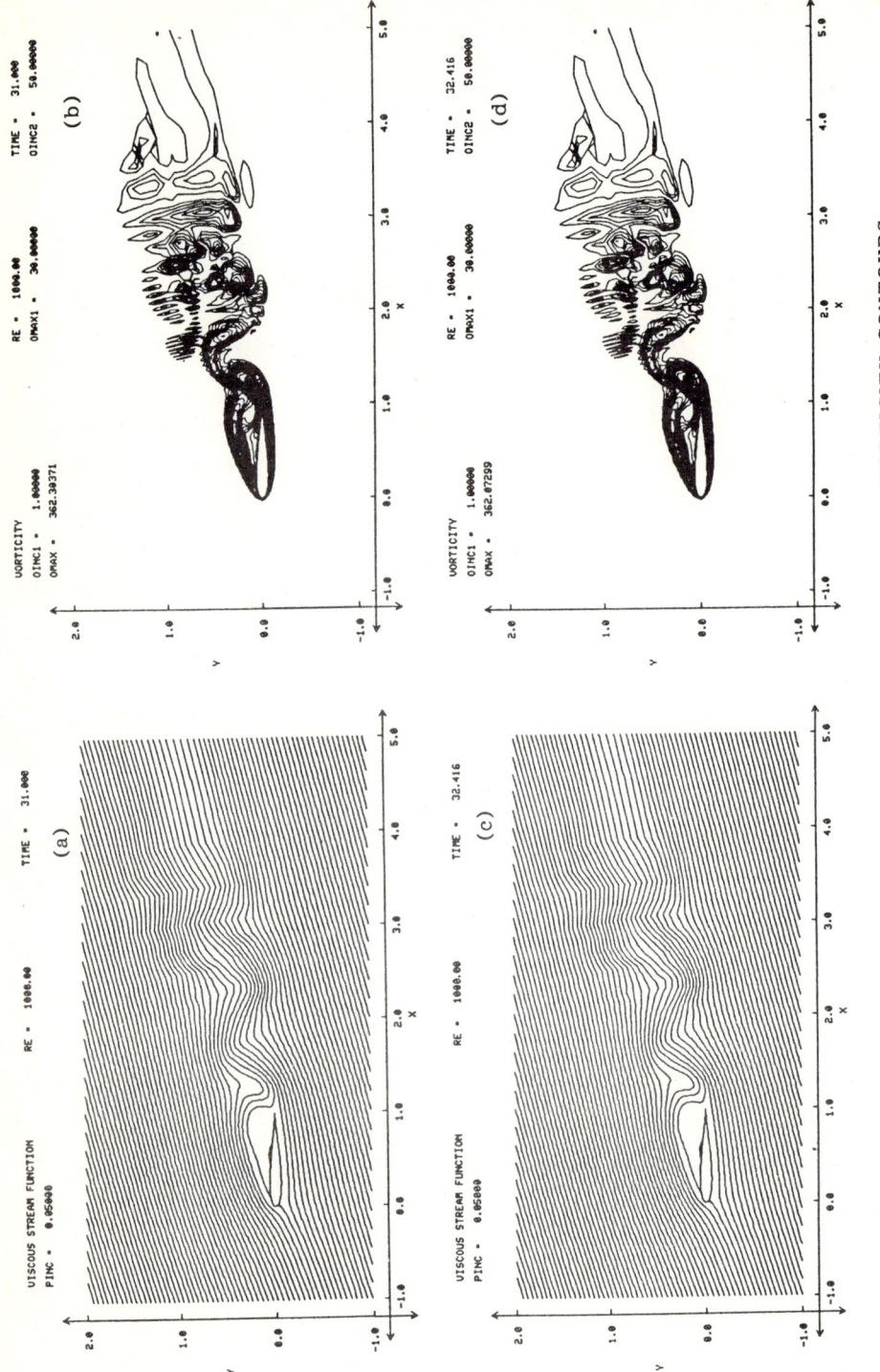

Fig. 6. Limit-Cycle Analysis for Joukowski Airfoil at Re = 1,000, $\alpha_f = 15°$, S = 0.18.

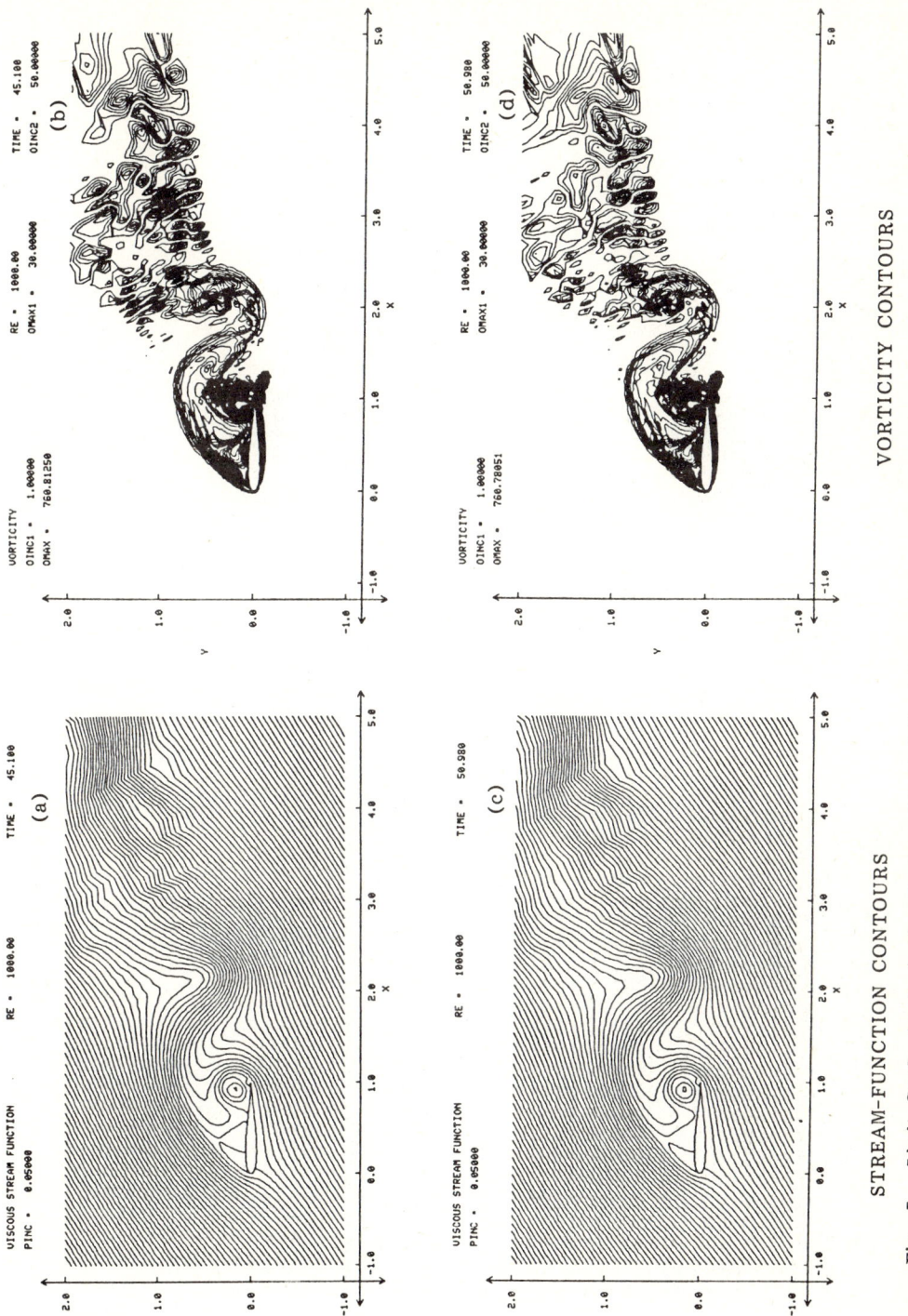

Fig. 7. Limit-Cycle Analysis for Joukowski Airfoil at Re = 1,000, $\alpha_f = 30°$, S = 0.17.

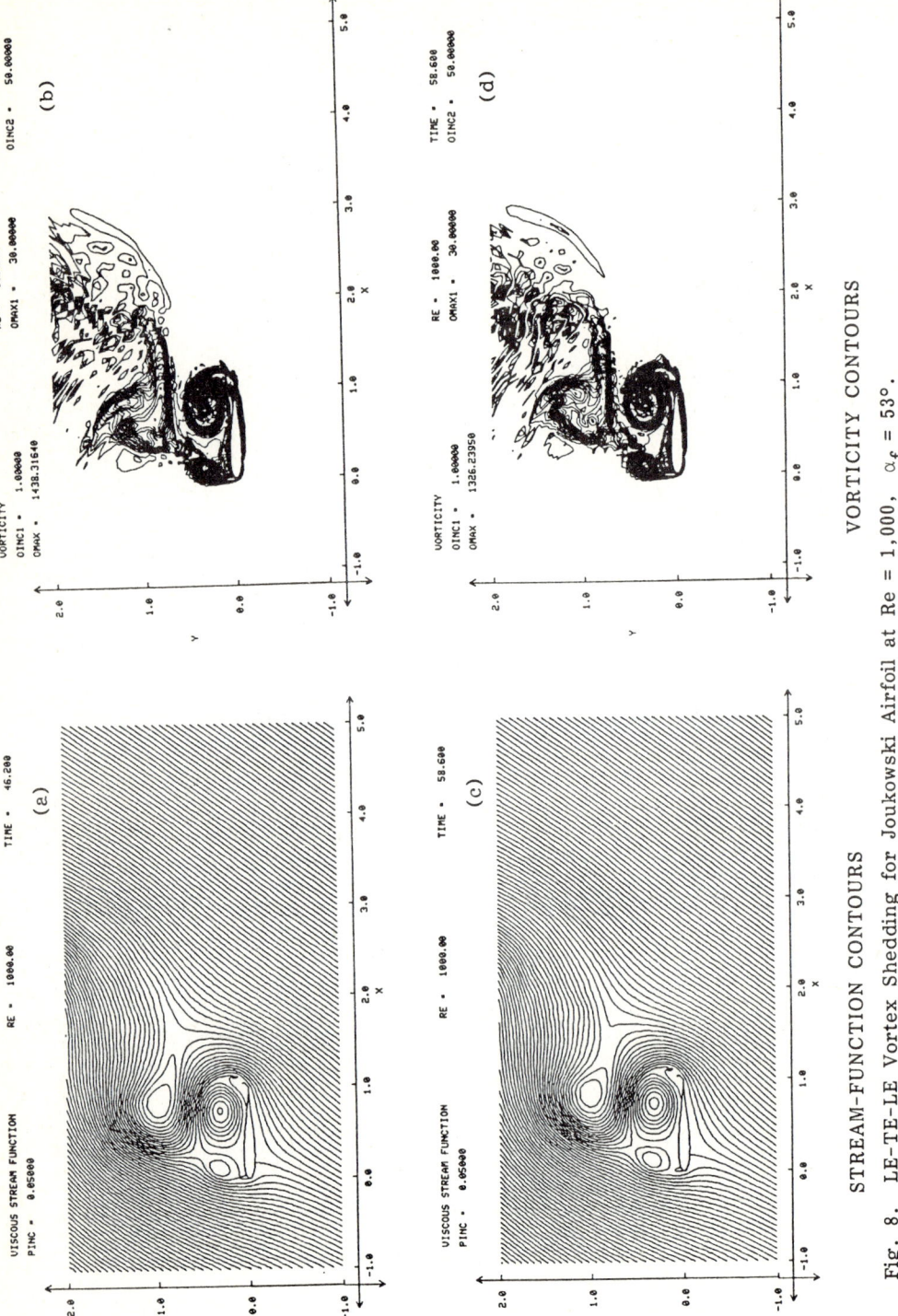

STREAM-FUNCTION CONTOURS   VORTICITY CONTOURS

Fig. 8. LE-TE-LE Vortex Shedding for Joukowski Airfoil at Re = 1,000, $\alpha_f = 53°$.

VISCOUS COMPRESSIBLE FLOW SIMULATIONS USING SUPERCOMPUTERS

Kozo Fujii

Second Aerodynamics Division
National Aerospace Laboratory
Chofu-city,Tokyo,Japan

1. Introduction

The appearance of supercomputers accelerated the development of the sophisticated Computational Fluid Dynamics for the practical use. Even the "Reynolds-averaged" Navier-Stokes computations are in the matured stage with the help of supercomputers. For instance, two-dimensional Navier-Stokes code called 'ARC2D' developed by T.H.Pulliam and J.L.Steger at NASA Ames Research Center requires only 5 minutes to obtain the converged solution with 27000 grid points on CRAY XM-P[1]. The two-dimensional code called 'LANS2D' developed by Obayashi and the present author currently requires less than 1 minute with 6400 grid points and is becoming faster using Japanese supercomputer, Fujitsu VP-400[2]. Now, it seems that two-dimensional Navier-stokes codes such as these can be used as one of the design tools. Actually, Mitsubishi Heavy Industry is using the code 'NSFOIL' developed by the National Aerospace Laboratory,Japan for the design of a transonic airfoil, the detail of which was presented at the AIAA 3rd Applied Aerodynamics Conference with the experimental data[3].

Flow field simulations using three-dimensional Navier-Stokes equations are presently still in the stage of research. However, the number of the reports about the development of the three-dimensional Navier-Stokes codes appearing in the AIAA conferences are rapidly increasing and the progress of the supercomputers and numerical techniques will enable the use of such codes as a design tool pretty soon.

In parallel to the applications of the developed codes to more and more practical problems, the improvements of these codes are also underway in the sense that both cpu time for the computation should be reduced and the solution should be more accurate. The LU-ADI factored scheme used here was originally developed by Obayashi and Kuwahara[4] for the purpose of reducing the left-hand side operations of the Beam and Warming algorithm. The cpu time has been reduced about as half as that of the Beam and Warming algorithm. In this LU-ADI scheme, the flux Jacobian matrices which appear in the left-hand side operators in the Beam and Warming algorithm are decomposed to the product of the lower and upper bidiagonal matrices by the LU factorization based on the idea of the flux vector splitting[5]. Since local diagonalization is used for each operator, the inversion of the original block tridiagonal matrices reduces to those of the scalar bidiagonal matrices and the matrices multiplications. The right-hand side is left to be the same, and, thus, the steady state solutions must be the same when the convergence is good enough. The scheme was next applied to the problems in the generalized coordinate system[6], and the three-dimensional extension has been done by S.Obayashi and the present auther [7].

The purpose of the present paper is to show the capability of the original LU-ADI code and the recent improvements of the code structure. In general, the LU factorization based on the flux vector splitting reduces stability of the code, compared to the original block tridiagonal solver. To maintain the stability, the diagonally dominant LU factorization which was originally proposed as scalar DDADI factorization by Lombard, et al.[8] is adopted in the improved version. The three-point upwind differencing is also used to improve the stability for large CFL numbers[2]. These modifications are done both for the two-dimensional code and the three-dimensional code in the same manner since the LU-ADI scheme is based on the ADI type factorization.

In the following section, the original and improved versions of the LU-ADI scheme is preseted. The applications are done not only for the two-dimensional transonic viscous flows but also for the three-dimensional flows. Japanese supercomputer named Fujitsu VP 200 and VP 400 are used for the practical flow field simulations in three-dimensions. The results indicate the capability of the codes named "LANS2D" and "LANS3D" based on the LU-ADI scheme.

2. Basic Equations and the LU-ADI schemes

2.1 Basic Equations and the Original LU-ADI scheme

The scheme is presented for the two-dimensional equations because the formulation for the three-dimensional equations are almost the same. Basic equations are written in the strong conservation-law form in the generalized coordinate system. A thin-layer viscous model is employed and two layer algebraic eddy viscosity model developed by Baldwin and Lomax[9] is used for evaluating the turbulent effect.

$$\hat{U}_\tau + \hat{E}_\xi + \hat{F}_\eta = \hat{S}_\eta / Re . \qquad (1)$$

where $U = J^{-1}(\rho, \rho u, \rho v, e)^T$ (See Ref.1 for instance, in detail.). In Eqs.(1), k= 0 corresponds to the inviscid flow and k = 1 corresponds to the thin-layer viscous flow. Only the viscous applications are shown in this paper although the validation of the inviscid computations have been confirmed. The pressure, density, and velocity components are related with the energy for an ideal gas by the following equations.

$$p = (\gamma - 1)(e - \rho(u^2 + v^2)/2). \qquad (2)$$

The metrics are evaluated using second-order, central-difference formulas for interior-points and three-point, one-sided formulas at the boundaries.

The original LU-ADI scheme applied to the basic equations is described as,

$$(I + h\nabla_\xi \hat{A}^+ + \varepsilon_i J^{-1}\nabla_\xi J)(I + h\Delta_\xi \hat{A}^- - \varepsilon_i J^{-1}\Delta_\xi J)$$
$$(I + h\nabla_\eta \hat{B}_\nu^+ + \varepsilon_i J^{-1}\nabla_\eta J)(I + h\Delta_\eta \hat{B}_\nu^- - \varepsilon_i J^{-1}\Delta_\eta J) \Delta \hat{U}^n \qquad (3)$$
$$= - h [\delta_\xi \hat{E}^n + \delta_\eta (\hat{F}^n - k \hat{S}^n/Re)] - \varepsilon_e J^{-1}[(\nabla_\xi \Delta_\xi)^2 + (\nabla_\eta \Delta_\eta)^2] J \hat{U}^n .$$

where h= Δt, δ is the central finite-difference operator, and Δ and ∇ are forward and backward difference operators, respectively. The basic algorithm is first-order accurate in time and second-order accurate in space.

Equations (3) can be obtained through the following process. The Jacobian matrices $\hat{A}$ and $\hat{B}$ that appear in the implicit operators in the Beam-Warming's ADI scheme can be splitted into two matrices having all positive and negative eigenvalues. For $\hat{A}$ matrix, for instance,

$$\hat{A} = \hat{A}^+ + \hat{A}^-, \qquad (4)$$

where

$$\hat{A}^\pm = T_\xi \hat{D}_A^\pm T_\xi^{-1},$$
$$\hat{D}_A = \text{diag}(U, U, U + c\, r_\xi, U - c\, r_\xi),$$
$$r_\xi^2 = \xi_x^2 + \xi_y^2.$$

Thus, each ADI operator can be decomposed to the product of two one-sided operators. For ξ-direction,

$$(I + h\, \delta_\xi \hat{A}) = (I + h\, \nabla_\xi \hat{A}^+)(I + h\, \Delta_\xi \hat{A}^-). \qquad (5)$$

In order to maintain the stability of the thin-layer viscous terms, the splitted Jacobian matrices $\hat{B}^\pm$ are modified as follows,

$$\hat{B}_v^\pm = T_\eta (\hat{D}_B^\pm \pm \nu I) T_\eta^{-1}, \qquad (6)$$

where

$$\nu = 2\mu r_\eta^2 / \text{Re}\, \rho \Delta \eta.$$

Equations (3) are thus derived using Eqs.(5) and (6).

The solution procedure for an LU-ADI operator is described in the diagonal form;

$$(I + h(\hat{D}_A^+ + \varepsilon_i I)) \Delta \hat{\underline{u}}_j^n = \underline{RHS}_j^n + T_\xi^{-1} h\, T_\xi (\hat{D}_A^+ + \varepsilon_i I) \Delta \underline{U}_{j-1}^n. \qquad (7)$$

where $\Delta \hat{\underline{U}}^n = T_\xi^{-1} \Delta \hat{U}^n$ and $\underline{RHS}^n = T_\xi^{-1} RHS^n$.

The similar procedure is used for the other operator. The block bidiagonal inversions are reduced to the scalar bidiagonal ones and the matrix multiplications by means of the local similarity transformation. The resultant code is effectively explicit. It has no storage problem, and is easy to program and vectorize.

2.2 Improved version of the LU-ADI scheme

The original LU factorization is based on the simple operator splitting. The main disadvantage of this splitting is that the resulting scheme becomes less stable than the original block tridiagonal solver. In order to improve stability of the code, the following two modifications are basically implemented.

One is the use of the three-point upwind differencing in the implicit part[2]. The fourth-order smoothing terms are included implicitly in the left-hand side with the coefficient chosen carefully by the use of the three-point upwind differencing as shown below. No third order derivatives are produced with these coefficients. The stability of the resultant code was improved about twice or three times compared to that of the original version of the code. It should be noted that the use of the three points makes no much difference for the computational time for the LU-ADI scheme since only one more scalar addition is required in addition to the operations in the original code.

The other is the use of the diagonally dominant LU factorization. This basic idea was proposed as DDADI factorization by Lombard et al.[8]. The scalar bidiagonal factorization is the most efficient one in the several types of factorization proposed there. The bidiagonal factorization in their paper is due to the two-point upwind differencing, and is straightforward extended to the LU factorization for the three-point upwind differencing in this paper.

The implicit matrix system, for instance in the ξ-direction, can be written for the $\hat{A}$ matrices using the notation of block penta-band matrix:

$$(\widetilde{A}^+, - 8\widetilde{A}^+, I + 7(\widetilde{A}^+ - \widetilde{A}^-), 8\widetilde{A}^-, - \widetilde{A}^-) \Delta \hat{U}^m = RHS^m. \qquad (8)$$

where $\widetilde{A} = h \hat{A}/6$ and the first-order three-point upwind differencing is used so as to be consistent with the fourth-order differencing in the right hand side. The block-matrix system can be simplified to the scalar-matrix one when the implicit nonconservative form is used as well as Pulliam-Chaussee's diagonal form,

$$(\widetilde{D}_A^+, - 8\widetilde{D}_A^+, I + 7(\widetilde{D}_A^+ - \widetilde{D}_A^-), 8\widetilde{D}_A^-, - \widetilde{D}_A^-) \Delta \underline{\widetilde{U}}^m = \underline{RHS}^m, \qquad (9)$$

where $\Delta \underline{\hat{U}}^m = T_\eta^{-1} \Delta \hat{U}^m$ and $\underline{RHS}^m = T_\xi^{-1} RHS^m$. The diagonally dominant factorization results in the following form:

$$(\widetilde{D}_A^+, - 8\widetilde{D}_A^+, \widetilde{N}) \widetilde{N}^{-1} (\widetilde{N}, 8\widetilde{D}_A^-, - \widetilde{D}_A^-) \Delta \underline{\widetilde{U}}^m = \underline{RHS}^m. \qquad (10)$$

where $\widetilde{N} = I + 7(\widetilde{D}_A^+ - \widetilde{D}_A^-)$. The operation for the $\hat{B}$ matrix in the other direction can be derived in the same way.

It should be noticed that the original DDADI factorization in the two dimensions produces the block-matrix inversion in addition to the ADI operators. This block matrix is neglected, and thus, the simple ADI factorization is used here in order to maintain the advantage of scalar inversion process.

3. Two-Dimensional Applications

The original code was used to check the validity of the LU-ADI scheme. The comparison of the LU-ADI factored method and the Beam-Warming one was carried out. Figure 1 shows the computed Cp distributions over the surface of the NACA 0012 airfoil. The flow conditions consist of a free stream Mach number of 0.75, an angle of attack of 2°, and a Reynolds number of 6.7×10^6. The result obtained using the Beam-Warming algorithm is shown in Fig.2. Both results are in good agreement each other, which indicates the validity of the LU-ADI code. The triangular plots are experimental data by Takashima[10] at National Aerospace Laboratory in Japan. No angle of attack and the Mach number correction was made and thus, the difference between the computations and the experiment may come from the wind tunnel wall effect.

The result for the improved version of the code is shown in Fig.3. In this two-dimensional code, the nonlinear mixed 2nd and 4th order smoothings suggested by Pulliam and Steger[1] was used and the use of it deleted a spike at the shock wave.

The efficiency can be found by comparing the actual cpu time to obtain a nearly steady-state solution. In the above test case of 161x41 grid points, the original code took about one hour on Fujitsu M-380 computer. The improved code took about 15 minutes. The improved version of the code was also run on the Fujitsu VP400 supercomputer and the converged solution was obtained within one minute^2.

4. Three-Dimensional Applications

The original version of the code was applied to two kinds of the flow field. The first one is the slightly supersonic viscous flow over an hemisphere-cylinder, and the other is the viscous transonic flow over the simple wing having NACA0012 wing section with the swept angle of 20 degrees. The results were presented at the AIAA 7th Computational Fluid Dynamic Conference at Cincinnati[7]. Total number of grid points are about 200,000 for the first case and 13,4000 in the second case. The detail of the computational conditions are shown in Ref.7. In this paper, some of the new graphic results are shown.

The result for the first case is shown in Figs. 4 and 5. Since the angle of attack is relatively large and the free-stream is in the transonic regime, there occurs a shock wave in the leeward side as well as the bow shock wave in front of the body, and there also occurs a large separation vortex in the leeward side of the body. In Fig.4, the oil flow patterns over the surface of the hemi-sphere cylinder is given. Very complicated flow pattern can be recognized especially in the nose region from this figure. The axial separation line is seen in this region and the primary separation line and the secondary separation lines can also be observed in the cylindrical region. Figure 5 shows the so called "particle path traces" that show the vortical flow in the leeward-side of the body. Clear vortical motion is observed by these kind of plottings. The original figures are the colored ones that help much more to understand the fluid physics.

Two figures of the second case are shown in Figs. 6 and 7 for reference. Figure 6 shows the pressure contours over the upper surface of the wing and in the 75 percent spanwise location. The existence of the strong shock wave is clearly seen. Figure 7 shows the particle path traces near the upper surface of the wing. The strong spanwise flow occurs just after the shock wave, and the three-dimensional flow separation appears.

These computations were carried out using Japanese new supercomputers named Fujitsu VP 200 and VP 400. There are two versions of the code. First version of the code is the code where no special efforts were made for utilizing the benefit of the longer vector length even though these machine's capability becomes much better when using very long vector length. Cpu time per one iteration per one grid point required about 12 μsec for this code on VP 400, and the cpu time per iteration is about 25 times smaller on the VP 200 and 30 times smaller on the VP400 than the cpu time of the original code on the Fujitsu scalar machine the M 380 that has the capability of 8 MFLOPS for this kind of practical programs. It should be noted that VP machines are based on this scalar machine. Thus, it can be said that the code is well vectorized. For the second version of the code, the efforts were made for utilizing the longer vector length. In other words, one dimensionalization was done for the other two directions when sweeping in one direction. In this code, the cpu time per iteration per grid is about 6.6 μsec, and the ratio to the M 380 computation is about 35 times on VP 200 and nearly 55 times on the VP 400. Pretty good speed was obtained on this one-dimensionalized version. It should be remembered that the ratios shown above are the ratio of the original code on the M 380 and the modified code on the VP 200 and 400. Honestly speaking, these ratio might be a little different if the ratio were measured about the same code on the scalar and the vector modes of the VP supercompuers. The direct comparison of the scalar mode and the vector mode is done for the improved version and will be presented below.

An improved code has been developed and the computations were done for the practical wing configuration. The wing is named W-14 which was designed as a wing of the new transportation aircraft. Figure 8 shows the wing shape which has the aspect ratio of 9.42, the tapered ratio of 0.246, the swept angle at 25 % chord of 23.71 degrees, the dihedral angle 7 degrees. The relative thickness of the root chord is 14.6 % and 11% at the kink point (0.377 relative spanwise location). The C-H topology for the grid system is adopted, and the grid generation is done two-dimensionally for each spanwise location using an algebraic procedure developed by S.obayashi and present author. The detail will appear in Ref.2. Three chordwise grid distributions are shown in Fig.9 for the root symmetric plane, abut 50 % spanwise station an the wing-extension region. The topological cut in the wing-extension is treated as a permeable surface. Figure 10 shows the overall grid distributions. The number of the grid point used here is 123 in the ξ-direction (101 points over the surface), 41 points in the η-direction (33 poins over the surface), 41 points from the body to the outer boundary.

The computed pressure contour is shown in Fig.11 for nearly the design point (M_∞= 0.82, angle of attack α = 0.35°). The Reynolds number was chosen to be 2.0×10^6 corresponding to the experiment carried out at the National Aerospace Laboratory. Pressure contours over the upper surface and two typical spanwise stations are also plotted in Fig.11. At this design point, only weak shock wave appears followed by the small expansion. No strong shock wave is seen except near the tip. The Cp comparison with the experimental data is shown in Fig.12 for several spanwise stations. The agreement is quite good.

Another case corresponds to the case close to the buffet limit where M_∞ =0.82, and the angle of attack α =2.46 degrees. The computed pressure contours over the upper surface and two typical spanwise stations are also plotted in Fig.13. At this buffet boundary, there appears a relatively strong shock wave and a small separation bubble. There appears a tip shock in addition to the main shock wave. Isobar patterns are observed after the shock wave and thus, the three-dimensionality is pretty weak after the shock wave except near the root. The comparison of the Cp distributions with the experimental data at several spanwise stations with the experimental data is shown in Fig.14. The agreement is pretty good when the difficulty of the case is rememberd.

The third case is the case of Mach number 0.82 and the angle of attack 4.66 degrees which is over the buffet boundary. The result is shown in Fig.15. The very strong curved shock wave is observed, and again the tip shock wave can be seen. Unfortunately, the experimental data is not available for this case, and the comparison with the experiment is not made. The flow even after the shock wave is three-dimensional as is seen from the figure. It should be noted that the flow should be unsteady in this case, whereas the computed result is the steady state solution and shows no unsteadiness. The reason might be the use of the turbulence model which overestimates the eddy viscosity in the computation.

The final case is the case of Mach number 0.82 and the angle of attack 7.50 degrees as is shown in Fig.16. At this high angle of attack, the flow is fully three-dimensional. The location of the shock wave over the upper surface is curved in the spanwise direction.

Surface oilfow patterns for each case is presented in Fig.17. It can be seen that the no strong shock wave exists in the design point, whereas there exists for the other three cases. Near the design point, there exists a strong spanwise flow only near the trailing edge, and trailing-edge separation occurs. For the other three cases, shock-induced separation takes place and three dimensionality is very important. Tip shock wave is also noticed for these three cases. Figure 18 show the computed particle path traces for the last three cases. The vortival flow is clearly seen and the three-dimensionality is well recognized.

The prediction of the integrated values are very important for the design of the wing. The CL-α curve is plotted in Fig.19. The agreement with the experiment is excellent. The potential code for instance would predict the straight line, which fails to predict the flow field for the relatively high angle of attack range. The CL-CD curve is plotted in Fig.20 which also shows the good agreement with the experiment.

So far, no much efforts have been made for the vectorization of the improved code. The code was run on the VP 200 and the VP400 and the cpu time per grid per iteration is currently 8.6 μsec on the VP 200, and 6.7 μsec on the VP400. The reason of this acceleration is mainly due to the use of the diagonal form and the Fujitsu compiler improvements. The comparison of the scalar mode and the vector mode was checked on the VP 400, and the result indicates the vector mode is about 40 times faster than the scalar mode. The special effort like the original one for utilizing the longer vector length is under going and the cpu time per grid per iteration would be decreased to be about 4 or 5 μsec.

The application of the code to the wing-fuselage combination is currently going and the preliminary result will appear in Ref.[11]. The application to more practical wing-fuselage configuration, the wing of which is used in this study will appear soon[12].

Throughout these studies, it turns out to be promising that the three-dimensional Navier-Stokes codes are used as a design tool. The time will soon come when the simulation of the flow field over the whole aircraft in transonic regime becomes possible using the "Reynolds-averaged" three-dimensional Navier-Stokes equations.

Conclusions

The recent development of the two-dimensional and three-dimensional Navier-Stokes codes using LU-ADI scheme has been described. The computed results indicated that these codes are very efficient and reliable. The codes have been well-vectorized easily and the efficiency is enhanced when using Fujitsu supercomputers.

Acknowledgement

This work was done as a cooperative work with Mr. Shigeru Obayashi, the graduate student of University of Tokyo. His contribution to this study may be more than the present author's. The author would like to express his appreciation to Mr. S. Shirayama, University of Tokyo for his help about the development of the graphic programs. Especially for the three-dimensional computations, the display of the results is very important and his help is very appreciated. The author also thanks Prof. K. Kuwahara at the ISAS for a fruitful discussions concerning the several aspects of the present study.

References

1) Pulliam,T.H. and Steger,J.L., "Recent Improvements in Efficiency, Accuracy, and Convergence for Implicit Approximate Factorization Algorithms," AIAA Paper 85-0360, Reno, Nevada, January, 1985.

2) Obayashi,S., Matsushima,K., Fujii,K., and Kuwahara,K., "Improvements in Efficiency aand Reliability for Navier-Stokes Computations using the LU-ADI Factorization Algorithm," to appear as AIAA Paper 86-0338, Reno, Nevada, January, 1986.

3) Miyakawa,J., Hirose,N., and Kawai,N., "Comparison of Aerodynamic Characteristics of Transonic Airfoil by Navier-Stokes Computation and by Wind Tunnel Test at High Reynolds Number," AIAA Paper 85-5025, Coloradosprings, Colorado, Sept., 1985.

4) Obayashi,S. and Kuwahara,K., "LU Factorization of an Implicit Scheme for the Compressible Navier-Stokes Equations" AIAA Paper 84-1670, Snowmass, Colorado, June, 1984.

5) Steger,J.L. and Warming,R.F., "Flux Vector Splitting of the Inviscid Gasdynamic Equations with Application to Finite-Difference Methods," J. Comp. Phys., Vol. 40, pp. 263-293, 1981.

6) Obayashi,S., Kuwahara,K. and Yoshizawa,Y., "A New LU Factored Method for the Compressible Navier-Stokes Equations," Proc. 9th ICNMFD, Saclay, France, June, 1984.

7) Obayashi,S. and Fujii,K., "Computation of Three-Dimensional Viscous Transonic Flows with the LU Factored Scheme," AIAA Paper 85-1510, Cincinnati, Ohio, July,1985.

8) Lombard,C.,K., Bardina,J., Venkatapathy,E., and Oliger,J., "Multi-Dimensional Formulation of CSCM - An Upwind Flux Difference Eigenvector Split Method for the Compressible Navier-Stokes Equations," AIAA Paper 83-1895, Danvers, Massachusetts, July, 1983.

9) Baldwin,B.S. and Lomax,H., "Thin Layer Approximation and Algebraic Model for Separated Turbulent Flows," AIAA Paper 78-257, Jan., 1978.

10) Takashima,K., to appear in Techniocal Memorandum of National Aerospace Laboratory, Japan.

11) Fujii,K and Obayashi,S., "Practical Applications of Improved LU-ADI Scheme for the Three-Dimensional Navier-Stokes Computation of Transonic Viscous Flows," to appear as AIAA Paper 86-0513, Reno, Nevada January,1986.

12) Fujii,K and Obayash,S., "Navier-Stokes Simulation of Transonic Flows over Wing-Fuselage Combinations," submitted to the presentation at the AIAA 4th Applied Aerodynamics Conference to be held at San Diego, California,June,1986.

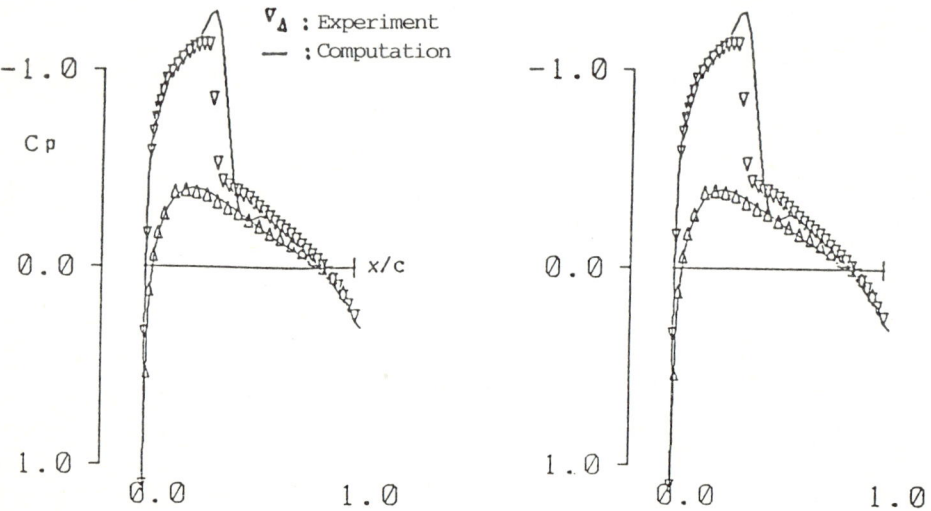

Fig.1 Cp distribution over an NACA 0012 airfoil; Original LU-ADI scheme, $M_\infty = 0.75$, $\alpha = 2.0°$, $Re_c = 6.7 \times 10^6$.

Fig.2 Cp distribution over an NACA 0012 airfoil; Beam and Warming scheme, $M_\infty = 0.75$, $\alpha = 2.0°$, $Re_c = 6.7 \times 10^6$.

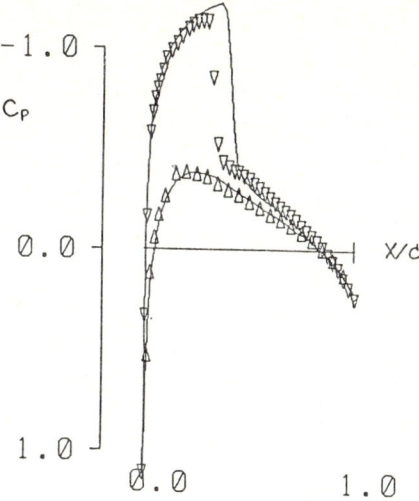

Fig.3 Cp distribution over an NACA 0012 airfoil
Improved LU-ADI scheme, $M_\infty = 0.75$, $\alpha = 2.0°$, $Re_c = 6.7 \times 10^6$.

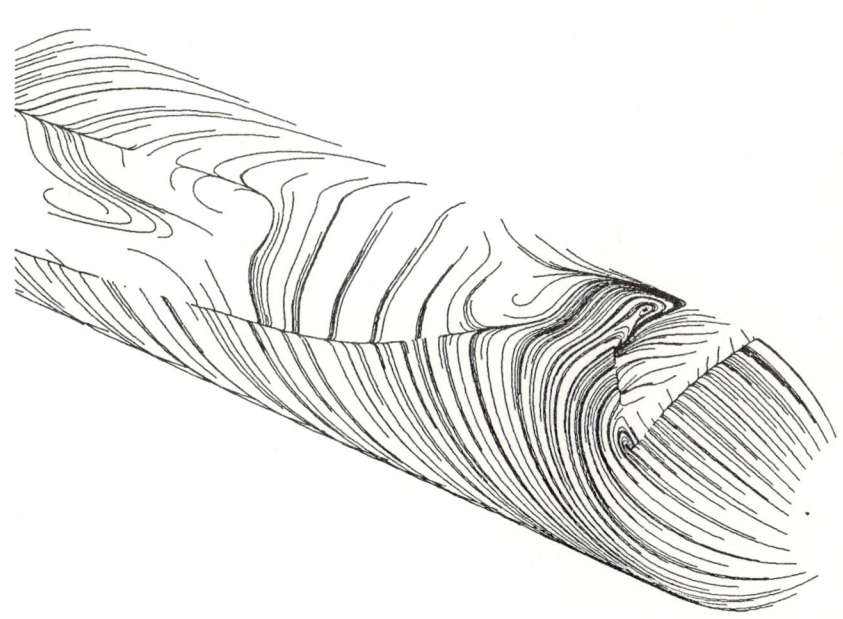

Fig.4 Computed oilflow patterns near the body surface:
Hemi-sphere cylinder ($M_\infty = 1.2$, $\alpha = 19.0°$, $Re_r = 222,500$).

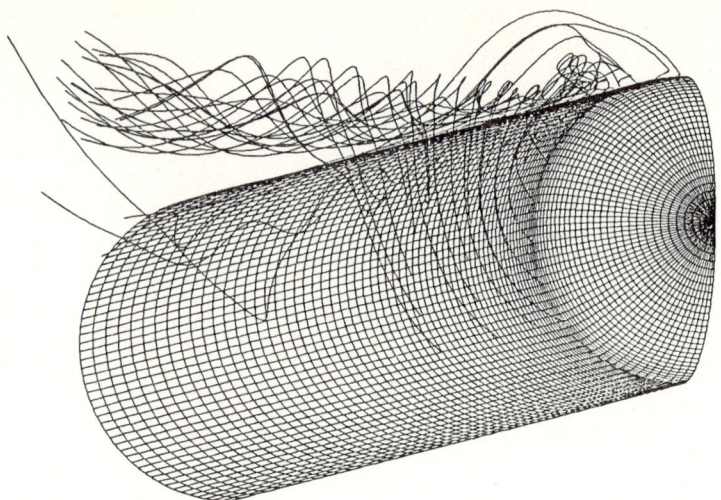

Fig.5 Particle path traces: Hemi-sphere cylinder
($M_\infty = 1.2$, $\alpha = 19.0°$, $Re_r = 222,500$).

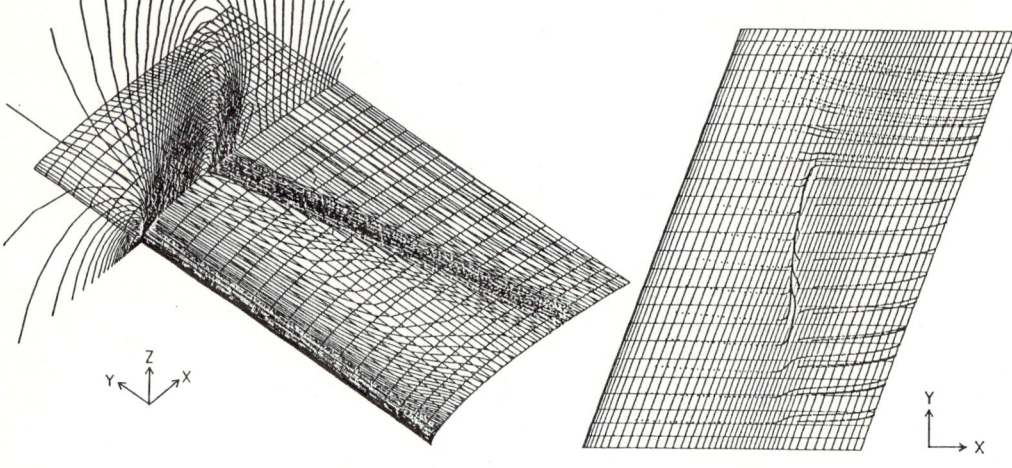

Fig.6 Pressure contour plots both on the upper surface and on the spanwise station of $y/s = 0.742$: Wing with NACA0012 cross section ($M_\infty = 0.836$, $\alpha = 2°$, $Re_c = 8 \times 10^6$).

Fig.7 Computed oilflow patterns near the upper surface: Wing with NACA0012 cross section ($M_\infty = 0.836$, $\alpha = 2.0°$, $Re_c = 8 \times 10^6$).

Fig.8 W-14 transonic wing geometry.

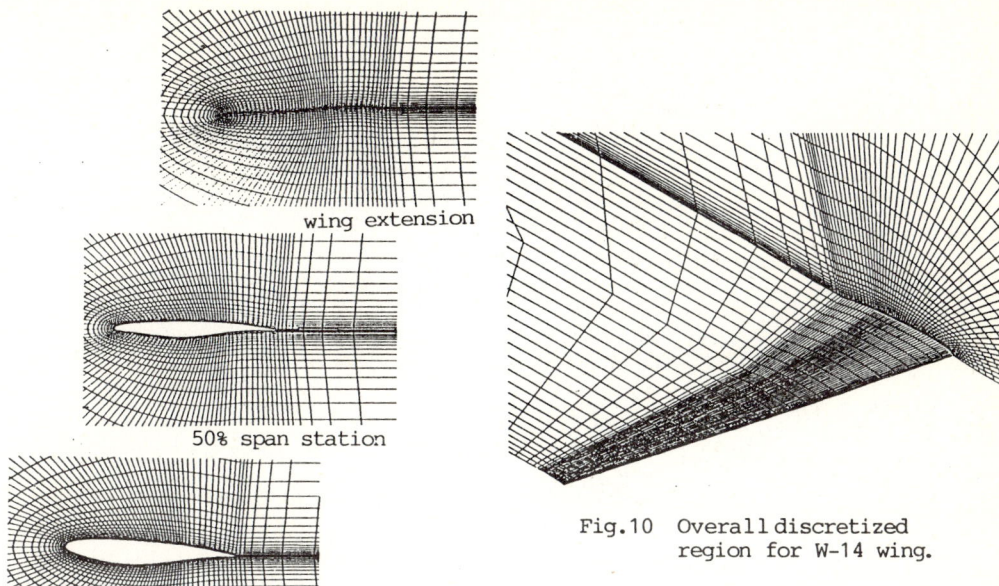

wing extension

50% span station

root section

Fig.9 Grid distributions at three spanwise stations.

Fig.10 Overall discretized region for W-14 wing.

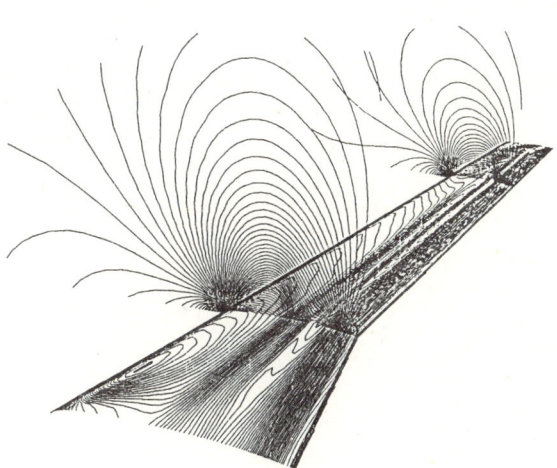

Fig.11 Pressure contour plots both on the upper surface and two spanwise stations: W-14 Wing (Nearly design point; M_∞= 0.820, α = 0.35°, $Re_{\bar{c}}$= 2x10^6).

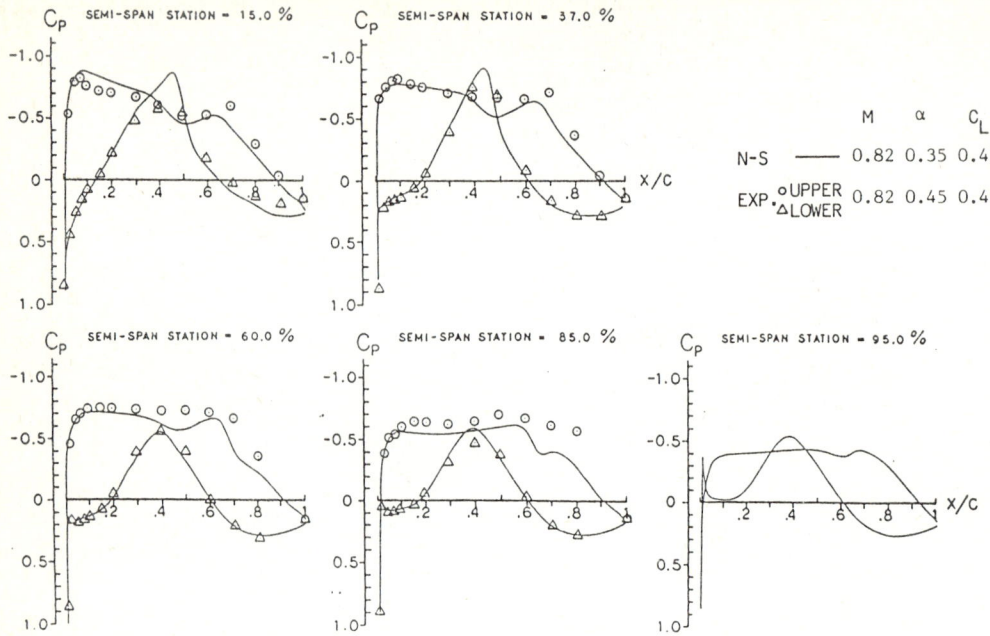

Fig.12 Comparison of the Cp distributions with the experimental data at several spanwise locations
(Nearly design point; $M_\infty = 0.820, \alpha = 0.35$, $Re_{\bar{c}} = 2 \times 10^6$).

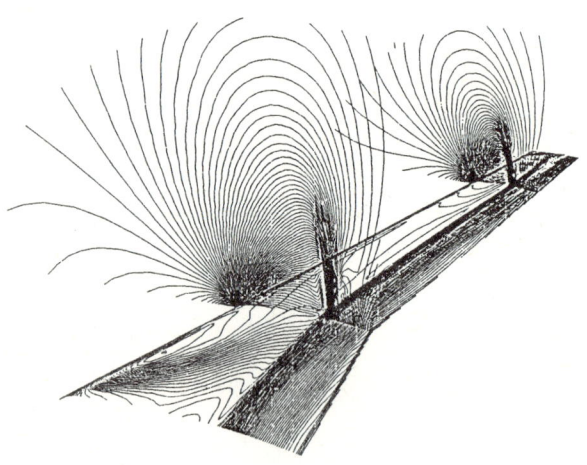

Fig.13 Pressure contour plots both on the upper surface and two spanwise stations: W-14 Wing
(Nearly buffet boundary; $M_\infty = 0.820, \alpha = 2.46$, $Re_{\bar{c}} = 2 \times 10^6$).

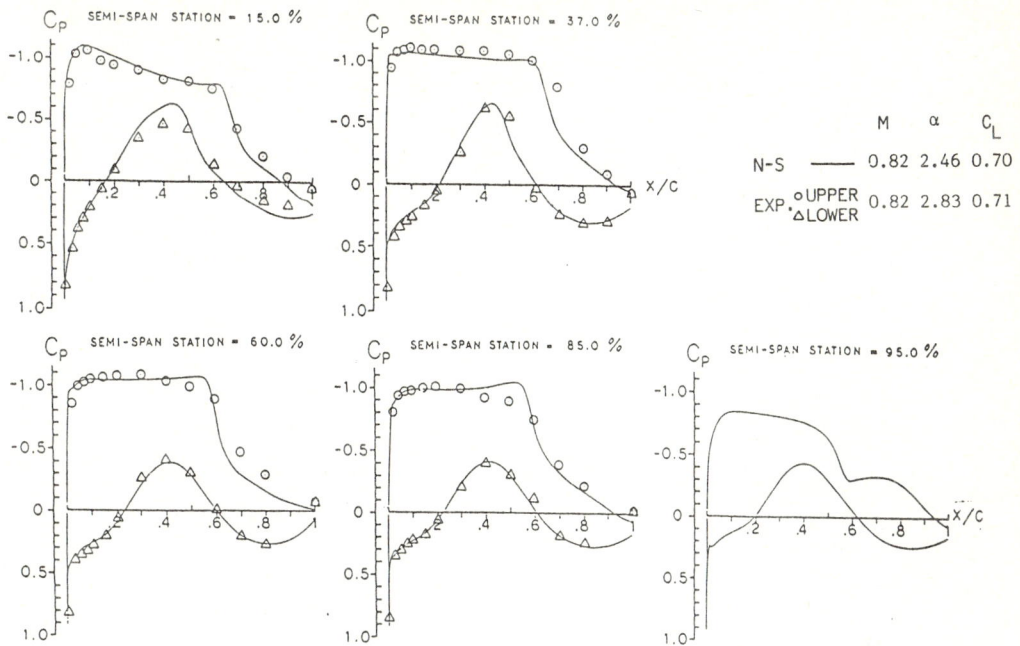

Fig.14 Comparison of the Cp distributions with the experimental data at several spanwise locations
(Nearly buffet boundary; $M_\infty = 0.820, \alpha = 2.46°, Re_{\bar{c}} = 2\times 10^6$).

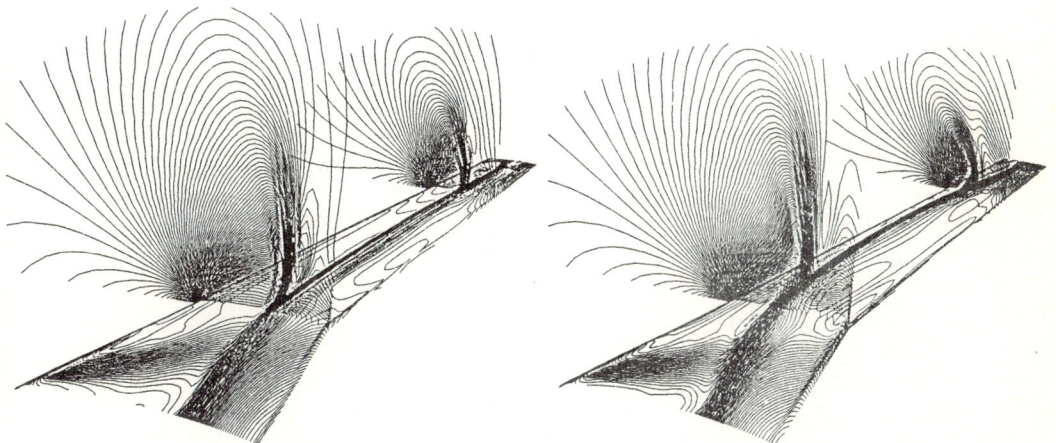

Fig.15 Pressure contour plots both on the upper surface and two spanwise stations: W-14 Wing. (Over buffet boundary; $M_\infty = 0.820, \alpha = 4.66°, Re_{\bar{c}} = 2\times 10^6$).

Fig.16 Pressure contour plots both on the upper surface and two spanwise stations: W-14 Wing. (Over buffet boundary; $M_\infty = 0.820, \alpha = 7.50°, Re_{\bar{c}} = 2\times 10^6$).

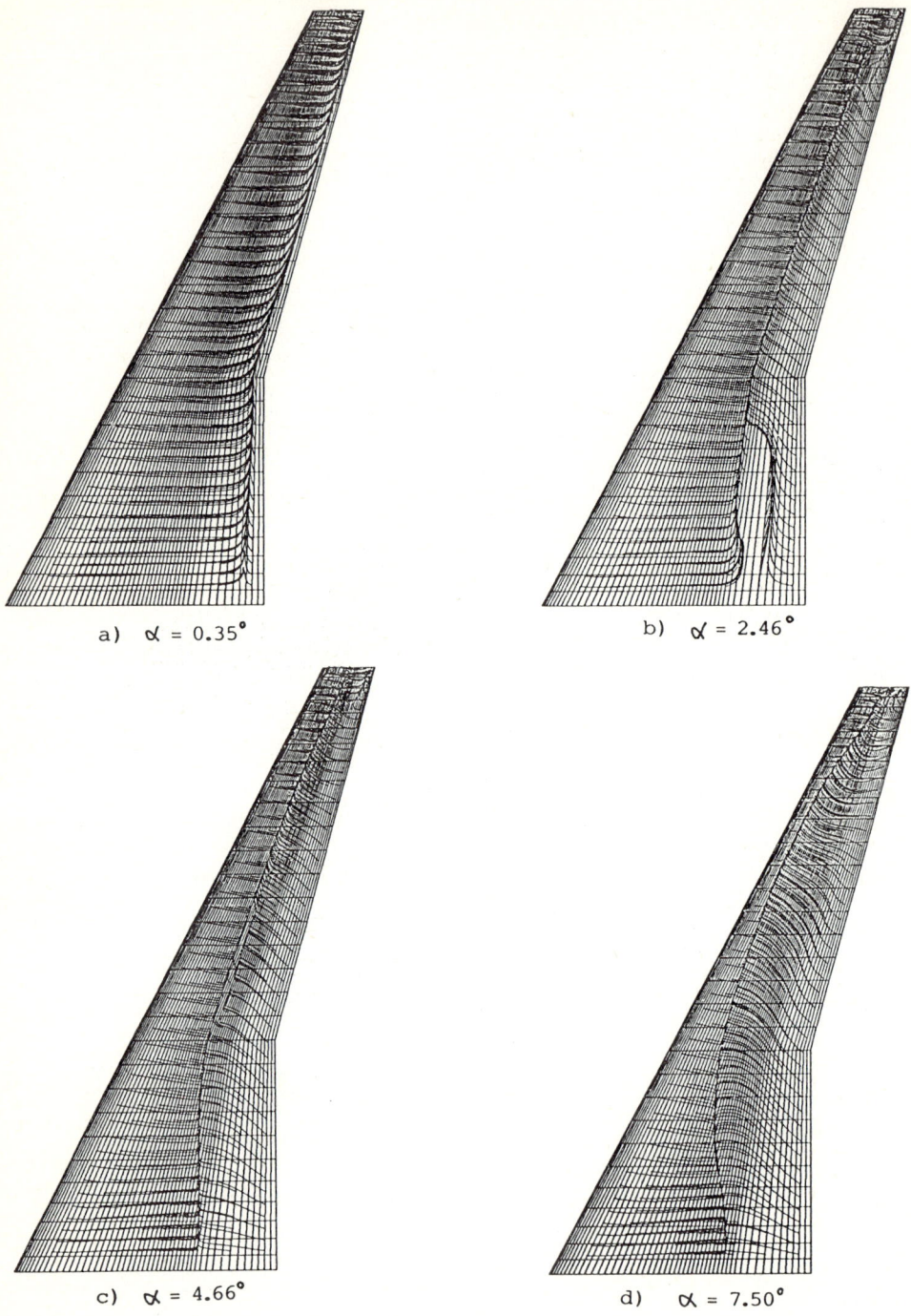

Fig.17 Computed surface oilflow patterns over the upper surface of the W-14 wing, ($M_\infty = 0.820$, $Re_{\tau c} = 2 \times 10^6$).

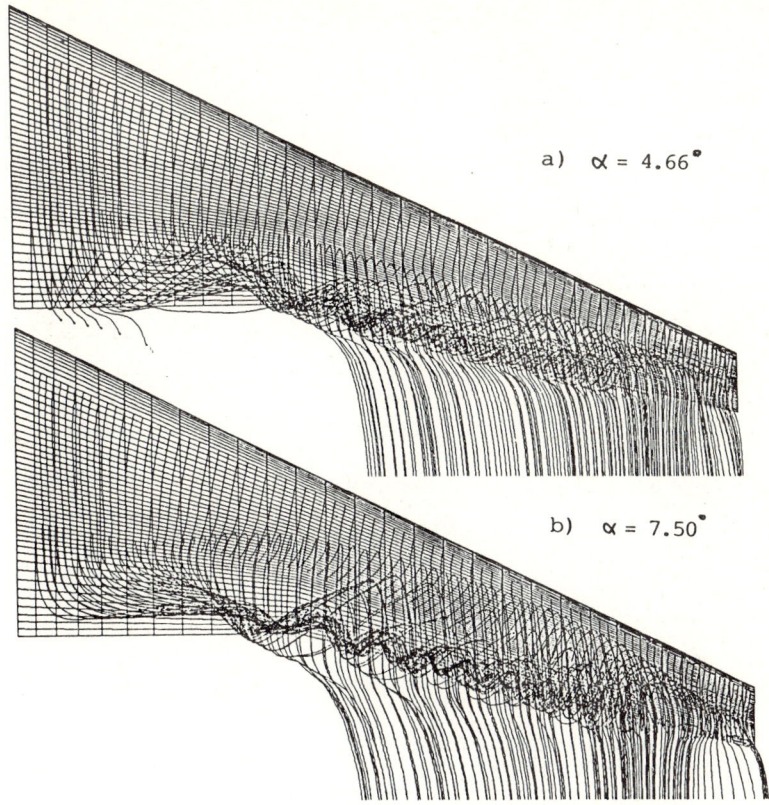

Fig.18 Computed particle path traces over the upper surface of the wing (M_∞ = 0.820, Re_{rc} = 2×10^6).

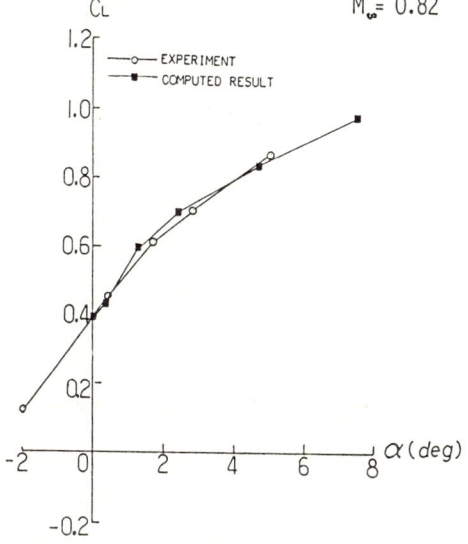

Fig.19 CL vs. α curve for the W-14 wing.

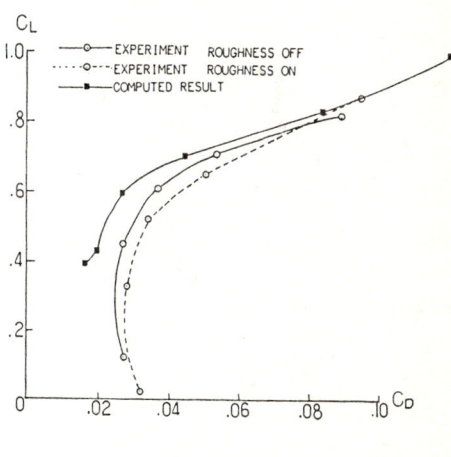

Fig.20 CD-CL curve for the W-14 wing.

THE SCALAR PERFORMANCE OF THREE SUPERCOMPUTERS
CRAY'S X-MP/2, FUJITSU'S VP-200 AND NEC'S SX-2

Raul H. Mendez

Since the first delivery, late in 1983, of the Cray X-MP/2, Fujitsu VP-200 and Hitachi S-810/20 supercomputers, the race in the scientific computing area has considerably accelerated its pace. In 1984, both the Fujitsu VP-400 and the Cray X-MP/4 were first introduced and in the Fall of 1985 the Cray2 and the NEC SX-2 supercomputers were first brought into the market. The total number of systems delivered up to now include more than 120 Cray systems, about 30 CDC systems, about 30 VP systems, 4 Hitachi systems. So far, 3 NEC SX systems have been shipped in Japan and one SX-2 system will be delivered to the Houston Area Research Center this year, it will be the first delivery of a Japanese system to an Academic Institution in the US. In this article we shall give an introduction to the SX-2 system, compare some of its features with those of the Fujitsu VP-200 and CRAY X-MP/2 supercomputers (although not discussing in detail the latter systems) and survey the scalar performance of these three systems on five fluid dynamics codes used as benchmarks. A vector performance study of these three systems will be postponed to a later article.

It should be emphasized that ours are by no means detailed throughput tests and that our goal was not to obtain a detailed profile of the scalar performance of these systems but rather to sketch its most important features. Results on other benchmarks might yield different conclusions.

The results of our tests suggest that the SX-2 is a powerful processor of scalars the fastest single processor in scalar performance in all of our tests, these were all single processor tests and they were run on one single processor of the X-MP/2 that we tested (we shall refer to this single processor as the X-MP/1). The performance of the SX-2 was most notable in regards to the processing of scalars. In fact, the NEC's system's scalar performance ranges in our tests from 1.9 to 2.9 times the scalar speed of the other systems tested. The scalar processing power of the SX-2 system is evidenced also by its outperforming in scalar mode each of the other two systems's performance in vector mode in two of our tests.

EFFECTIVE SPEED OF A VECTOR PROCESSOR

It has been widely recognized that the effective performance of a vector processor in real applications codes differ widely, often by an order of magnitude, from the advertised theoretical speed of the system. Gene Amdahl traced the source of this apparent paradox to the scalar bottleneck. The effective speed of a vector processor depends on both its scalar and vector speed. The time required to run the scalar portion of any workload is inversely proportional to that system's scalar speed and the same can be said of the time needed to process the vector portion of the workload. Since the total time required to run the workload is quite close to the net of these two times, it follows that no matter how fast the vector box of a supercomputer, the scalar portion will contribute significantly to the total time required to run a workload unless its scalar portion its negligible (in real applications the scalar portion will contribute the most). Therefore, unless the scalar speed is well balanced with the vector speed of a system, it can act as a bottleneck to the system's performance.

To illustrate the importance of scalar processing speed to the effective speed of a vector processor we shall use the above ideas to compare three hypothetical supercomputer systems, labelled A, B, C. In the following example the three systems are assumed to process a workload which is assumed to be 85% vector and 15% scalar. The scalars and vector speeds are assumed to be as listed in table 1, while the effective overall speeds are determined from Amdahl's law.

TABLE 1

Characteristics Speeds in MFLOPS of three hypothetical supercomputers for a workload which is 85% vector and 15% scalar

System	Scalar Speed	Vector speed	Effective Speed
A	2.5	300	15.9
B	5.0	150	28.0
C	10.0	300	56.1

It can be seen that the scalar speed of system B is twice that of system A, while exactly the opposite relation holds between their vector speeds. As the table shows, despite the comparatively high vector ratio of this workload the effective speeds of systems A and B more closely reflect their scalar, rather than their vector speeds (the same can be said when comparing the effective speed of system C to that of systems A and B). This simple example points out that the effective speed of a supercomputer on a given application code is critically impacted by its scalar speed(in this case system A is an instance of a system with poor balance of scalar and vector speeds).

ARCHITECTURE AND HARDWARE OF THE SX-2 SYSTEM

This system design has targeted the scalar processing bottleneck and to implement that goal the SX-2 designers have been guided by the ideas of distributed and RISC architectures (the number of vector instructions is 88 while that of scalar instructions is 83).

The system consists of two processors that can operate concurrently, the control and arithmetic processors. The control processor runs the operating system, the compiler and executes other supervising tasks. The control processor's design is based on that of NEC's ACOS mainframe computer, a general purpose computer with an advertised performance in the 30 MIPS range, for the single processor configuration.

The arithmetic processor consists of two subunits each running at a clock speed of 6 nsec. The scalar unit includes a set of four fully segmented pipelines including floating point add and multiply. Scalar memory accesses are speeded up by a 64 K-byte cache, as in the VP-200 system. Operands and instructions are routed to cache from memory and from there instructions are transferred to an 2k byte instruction buffer from which they are sent to the instruction processor. Scalar operands are directed from the general purpose cache to the scalar registers (128 of these are available, there eight scalar S registers in the X-MP/1) and from there routed to the scalar pipelines. Thus, the SX-2 as the X-MP/2 processes scalars, in pipeline fashion. This pipeline feature as well as the large number of scalar registers has a direct impact on scalar performance.

Since this paper is concerned with scalar processing with shall make no reference to the vector architecture of the systems tested.

MEMORY

The SX-2's memory has a maximum capacity of 256 megabytes, the same maximum capacity as in the VP-200 while the maximum is 128 Megabytes on the X-MP/2. The X-MP/2 memory is interleaved in 16 banks while the SX-2 is interleaved in effectively 256 banks, the same level of interleaving as in the VP-200. In addition to the main memory, the control processor includes 64 Megabytes of local memory. Both local and main memory are addressable by the control processor.

The bandwidth of the main memory as stated earlier is 8 words per clock or 1.33 gigawords as opposed to 315 million words on the X-MP/1 (three words per cycle) and 565 million words per second on the VP-200. The main memory is supported as in the X-MP/2 by an SSD device (no SSD is available on the VP-200). The maximum capacity of the SSD is 2 gigabytes. The transfer rate between the main memory and the SSD is 1.3 gigabytes per second in the SX-2 and 2 gigabytes per second on the X-MP/2. The availability of the SSD should have considerable impact on I/O handling but none of our tests tested this capability.

BASIC TECHNOLOGY USED IN THE SX-2 SYSTEM

The achievement of the 6 nsec clock in the SX-2 is possible through the implementation of very fast densely packaged logic. Liquid convection technology allows high gate density packaging.

The main memory devices are 64 Kbit static RAMs with 40 nsec access times, while 256 dynamic RAMs with 120 nsec access times are used in the SSD. Vector registers and cache are implemented in 1 Kbit 3.5 nsec access time bipolar LSI. Logic is implemented in 1000 gate arrays chips with gate delays of 250 picoseconds.

Memory is packaged in 3-d modules, each with a capacity of two megabytes. Logic is cased in special purpose thermal cooling modules which house up to 36 LSI, for a maximum 36000 gates per package. Air cooling is used to cool the main memory device and a water cooling convection system is used to convect the over 200 Watts dissipated by each LSI package (there are in total 92 of these packages).

PERFORMANCE

Five fluid dynamics applications codes gathered from different sources were used as testing instruments. The same five programs were used in an earlier comparison study of the Fujitsu VP-200 and Cray X-MP/2 systems. These codes do not represent any given workload and are characteristic only of the types of fluid dynamics modeling used in these programs. Two of them, MHD-2D and SHEAR3 have been used extensively in turbulence simulations in two and three dimensions and developed on Cray systems. BARO is a two dimensional shallow water mode of the atmosphere, which has been developed on the CDC CYBER 205. EULER is a one-dimensional spectral code used to model the shock-tube problem, developed on a TI's ASC system and VORTEX is a particle simulation code developed on an IBM 3033 main-frame.

In our testing the following ground rules were used. Codes BARO and VORTEX were run unmodified in all three systems, slight tuning was allowed in EULER (up to twenty lines) and about the same amount of time was given to the three makers to tune the other two codes, MHD-2d and SHEAR3.

SCALAR PERFORMANCE

One of the strongest features of the SX-2 system lies in its strong scalar processing power. Table 2 shows that the floating point operations run faster on the SX-2 than on the other two systems. However, the speedup obtained in our tests is far from that suggested by scalar speeds alone. Thus, the fast scalar performance is attributable not only to the fast clock only but to other features such as the large number of scalar registers, pipelined functional units and the ability of the compiler to schedule scalar operations with a high degree of concurrency. The scalar unit's cache memory, also available on the VP-200, is a very important performance factor. It was observed that when the workload requires frequent memory access of operands which cannot be mantained in cache the slow scalar clock of the VP-200 will result in long load and store times which degrade the performance of the VP system. The impact of the faster SX-2 clock is felt most on tranfers of data to and from memory when a cache miss takes place. The SX-2 superior performance in scalar mode can be attributable to a higher degree of parallellism in its pipelined scalar floating point units an to the larger number of scalar registers to minimize transfers rather than to faster processing of floating point operations.

TABLE 2

TIMINGS OF FLOATING POINT OPERATIONS

	SX-2	VP-200	X-MP
	1clock=6nsec	1clock=14nsec	1clock=9.5nsec
Operation	nsec (clocks)	nsec (clocks)	nsec (clocks)
Floating Point Add	36 (6)	42 (3)	57 (6)
Floating Point Multiply	54 (9)	56 (4)	66.5 (7)

RESULTS

Table 3 summarizes the scalar performance results. These scalar timings were obtained with the VP's V10L10 compiler, the CRAY'S CFT 1.13 compiler and Version 20 of the SX-2's compiler. All runs were in dedicated mode, at the NEC Fuchu plant (11/85), the Numatsu Fujitsu plant (11/83) and the NASA Ames research Center (1/84). Although these are not the most recent versions of the three compilers it is expected that scalar timings will not differ significantly from performance obtained via the most recent versions of these systems' compilers (vector timings will, however, show significant changes).

The memory configuration of the systems used was as follows, in the Cray X-MP/2 system there were 16 Megabytes, in the Fujitsu's VP-200 there were 64 Megabytes and in the NEC's SX-2 there were 128 Megabytes.

In summary, on our benchmarks, on the average the SX-2 was more than twice as fast than either the VP or X-MP/1 system (in scalar mode).

In two of the codes, SHEAR3 and EULER, the SX-2 was 2.9 times faster than the X-MP/1. Most of the work in these two codes is done on FFT routines, processing arrays that can be kept in cache on the SX-2 throughout the computation. The VP-200 perhaps because of its larger cache processes these two codes faster than the X-MP but it is slower than the SX-2 by a factor of 2.03 in EULER and 2.50 in SHEAR3.

In MHD-2d most of the work is done on a FFT routine processing two-dimensional 256x256 arrays which cannot be kept in cache. In this program the SX-2 was 2.13 than the X-MP/1 and 2.36 faster than the VP-200.

In BARO most of the work is done on arrays too large to be kept in cache continuoulsly. In this program, the number of operations and the number of loads pers store is rather large (about ten). This type of computation can more efficiently use the scalar registers and pipelines available on the SX-2 and to a lesser extent in the X-MP/1. The number of loads also slow down its performance on the VP-200, perhaps because of this, this program suffered a performance degradation when run on a VP-100 with half the number of banks used in the VP-200 that these tests were run on. The SX-2's speed up over the X-MP/1 is 1.9 on BARO and the SX-2 is 2.78 times faster than the VP-200 on BARO.

In VORTEX the speedup of the SX-2 over the VP-200 (the timing for the X-MP/1 is not available) was 1.91, the lowest speed up over all. This performance is consistent with the above results. Program VORTEX spends over 90% of its work on a subroutine which processes three arrays of size 500 which can be easyly kept in cache in both systems. VORTEX is probably the program with the lowest number of memory loads.

TABLE 3

SCALAR TIMINGS IN SECONDS

V/S stands for X-MP to SX-2 timing ratio, and V/S stands for VP-200 to SX-2 timing ratio

Code	SX-2	VP-200	X-MP/1	X/S	V/S
BARO	398.8	1107.8	765.9	1.92	2.78
EULER	3.1	6.3	9.0	2.90	2.03
MHD2-D	18.4	43.4	39.2	2.13	2.36
SHEAR3	65.7	164.4	190.3	2.90	2.50
VORTEX	76.7	146.39	NA	NA	1.91

CONCLUSIONS

The SX-2 system is an outstanding system in regard to the processing of scalars, it was more than two times as fast as the othe systems in scalar mode on all of our tests. In later work we shall discuss the vector performance of the three systems using the same set of benchmarks.

NEC Supercomputer SX System

Tadashi WATANABE
Computer Engineering Division
NEC Corporation
1-10, Nisshin-cho, Fuchu
Tokyo 183 JAPAN

1. Introduction

   NEC Supercomputer SX System was developed to meet the demands for high-speed and large-scale computations in the fields such as aerodynamics, meteorology, molecular science and structural analysis.
   The SX system consists of three models, SX-1E, SX-1 and SX-2, and is one of the most powerful supercomputers ever built. SX-2, in particular, has the vector peak performance of 1.3 billion floating-point operations per second (1.3 Gflops). SX-1 and SX-1E can operate at a speed of up to 570 and 285 million floating-point operations per second (Mflops) respectively.
   Table 1 lists the major characteristics of the SX system. The principal features of the SX system are:
   - A 6 nanosecond machine cycle both in vector and scalar operations.
   - 16 vector arithmetic pipelines which can operate in parallel.
   - 256 Mbytes of main memory unit with a transfer speed of 11 Gbytes per second.
   - A semiconductor extended memory with a capacity of 2 Gbytes.
   - The integrated front-end processor, control processor, to perform the supervisory functions and improve the effective performance.
   - 1,000-gate LSI with 250 picosecond gate delay and a liquid-cooled LSI package with 36 LSIs.
   - FORTRAN77/SX with an automatic vectorization and various interactive tuning tools.

2. SX System Configuration

   The overview of the SX-2 is shown in Fig. 1 and its configuration is illustrated in Fig. 2.
   In Fig. 2, the Scientific Processing Unit (SPU), which corresponds to the conventional Central Processing Unit, consists of two indepen-

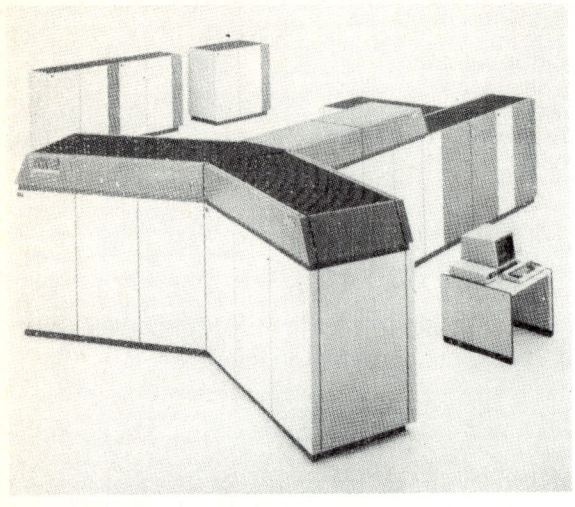

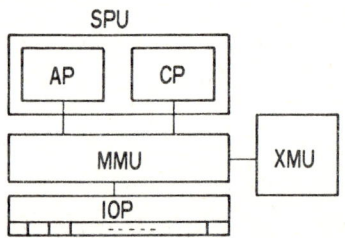

SPU : SCIENTIFIC PROCESSING UNIT
AP : ARITHMETIC PROCESSOR
CP : CONTROL PROCESSOR
MMU : MAIN MEMORY UNIT
IOP : INPUT OUTPUT PROCESSOR
XMU : EXTENDED MEMORY UNIT

Figure 1 Supercomputer SX-2   Figure 2 SX System Configuration

Table 1 SX System Characteristics

		SX-2	SX-1	SX-1E
Maximum Performance (64-bit floating-point operation)		1,300 Mflops	570 Mflops	285 Mflops
Machine Cycle		6 nsec.	7 nsec.	7 nsec.
Registers	Vector Register	80 Kbytes	40 Kbytes	20 Kbytes
	Vector Mask Registers	256 bits × 8	128 bits × 8	64 bits × 8
	Scalar Registers	128		
Vector Pipelines		16	8	4
Masked Vector Operation		Available		
List Vector Operation		Available		
Cache Memory		64 Kbytes		
Main Memory Unit	Arithmetic Processor Memory	128/256 Mbytes	64/128/256 Mbytes	32/64/128 Mbytes
	Control Processor Memory	16 ~ 64 Mbytes		
Logic LSI		1,000 gates/250 psec.		
Bipolar RAM LSI		1 Kbits/3.5 nsec		
Multi-chip Package		36 LSIs/36,000 gates		
Main Memory LSI		64 K bit static MOS LSI/40 nsec.		

dent processors, called Arithmetic Processor and Control Processor. The Control Processor performs the supervisory functions such as job scheduling, resource management and I/O management.

In addition, Fortran compiler and linkage editor also run on this Control Processor. On the contrary, the Arithmetic Processor executes both the scalar and vector operations of user's job programs. We can, therefore, obtain high throughput with such distributed function architecture.

The Main Memory Unit is a fast and large capacity storage and its maximum size is 256 million bytes, consisting of 512 independent banks.

The Extended Memory Unit functions as a fast access disk device using the semiconductor LSI memory, and it can transfer data at a peak speed of 1.3 billion bytes per second.

3. Vector Architecture

Fig. 3 shows the internal structure of the SX system. In this figure, the Arithmetic Processor is divided into the Scalar Unit (SU)

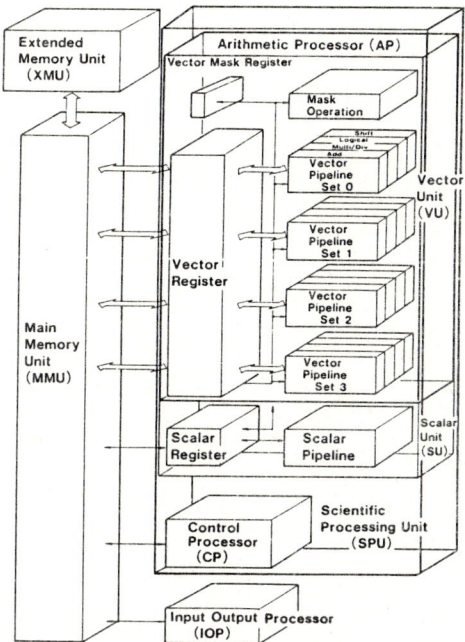

Figure 3 SX-2 Structure

and the Vector Unit (VU). The Scalar Unit executes the instruction fetch and decoding as well as the scalar instructions. The Vector Unit executes the vector instructions and includes the Vector Registers which hold the ordered vector data.

As Fig. 3 shows, there are four identical sets of vector pipelines, and each pipeline set consists of four arithmetic pipelined units which contain vector add, vector multiply, vector logical and vector shift unit. Then the Arithmetic Processor has 16 vector arithmetic pipelines. Using these pipelined units, the SX system achieves the vector peak speed of 1.3 billion floating point operations per second.

Each pipeline set handles every fourth vector elements. To speak more specifically, the first pipeline set is in charge of vector elements of 1st, 5th, 9th and so on. In the same way, the second pipeline set is in charge of vector elements of 2nd, 6th, 10th, etc. All these assignment of vector elements into the pipeline sets are automatically handled by hardware. Users, therefore, do not need to care about the detailed pipeline configurations to fully utilize the hardware capability.

All the vector arithmetic operations are performed in 64-bit length. In case of handling 32-bit floating-point data, 32-bit data is expanded to 64-bit when 32-bit data in memory is loaded into vector registers.

In addition, the SX system provides list vector functions for vectorizing loops with the vector subscripts, and masked vector operations and vector compress/expand functions for handling loops with IF statements.

4. Scalar Architecture

Even if the extensive and high speed vector operations are provided, there still remains unvectorizable part in the programs. As vector speed increases, the percentage of the time occupied by scalar operations increases. It is, therefore, quite important to speed up scalar execution for enhancing the effective performance in the actual processing environment.

SX system provides 128 scalar registers and employs arithmetic pipelines in scalar operations, too. In addition, branch instruction can be executed at high-speed by providing a fast and large instruction buffer. Moreover, the Scalar Unit and Vector Unit can be operated in parallel. With these features, the effective scalar performance is greatly enhanced.

5. LSI and Packaging

   LSI and packaging are the fundamental technologies to attain a 6 nanosecond cycle time. The SX system employs 1,000-gate LSI with 250 picosecond gate delay as the logic elements and 1 Kbit bipolar memory with 3.5 nanosecond access time for cache memory and vector registers. These logic LSIs and memory chips are mounted on the multi-layer ceramic substrate with the size of 10 centi-meter square, forming the LSI multi-chip package shown in Fig. 4. The LSI multi-chip package can contain up to 36 LSI chips. Thus it can have a maximum of 36,000 gates.

   As the gate density on the package increases, the power density also increases. To cool the package and enable the high density packaging, a liquid cooling system was employed. The cold-plate, which is the duct of water, is mounted on the LSI multi-chip package, forming the cooling module as shown in Fig. 5.

   In the Main Memory Unit, the 64 Kbit static MOS memory chip with 40 nanosecond access time is used to achieve a fast and large storage.

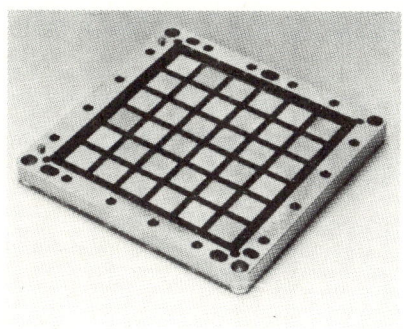

Figure 4 LSI Multi-chip Package   Figure 5 Liquid Cooling Module

6. FORTRAN77/SX and Tuning Tools

   The FORTRAN 77/SX is the standard FORTRAN 77 compiler which has a capability of automatic vectorization. The automatic vectorizor checks the inner DO loops of the source programs and translates those DO loops into the sequence of vector instructions.

The vectorizable DO loops include those containing IF statements, intrinsic functions and vector indices as well as the normal arithmetic assignment statements.

Users, therefore, can utilize the existing FORTRAN programs without modification and can program easily using standard FORTRAN without knowing the details of the machine structure.

The key factor to achieve high performance is to maximize the vectorizable part of the program and execute it at high speed with vector instructions. The SX system provides various support tools to obtain much higher vectorizing ratios and increased speedup.

VECTORIZER/SX is a vectorizing support tool designed to assist the user to increase the vectorizing ratio. It is an interactive tool which includes vectorization diagnosis and source program editing.

ANALYZER/SX analyzes and reports the static and dynamic characteristics of source programs such as the execution frequencies of statements and DO loops, the execution time and the vectorizing ratio.

7. Conclusion

This paper presented an overview of NEC's supercomputer SX system with a vector peak performance of 1.3 Gflops.

The SX system exhibits high performance over a wide range of applications with high-speed scalar and vector operations and distributed function architecture as well as sophisticated Fortran with automatic vectorization.

References

[1] "NEC Supercomputer SX-1/SX-2 General Description", NEC, Pub. No. GAZ01E-1, 1983.

[2] T. Furukatsu, T. Watanabe and R. Kondo: "Supercomputer SX system with a vector peak performance of 1.3 Gflops and 6 nanosecond cycle time", Nikkei Electronics, 1984.11.19, No. 356, pp237-272.

[3] T. Watanabe: "Architecture of Supercomputers-NEC Supercomputer SX System", NEC Research & Development, No. 73, pp1-6, April 1984.

FX: A CMOS-IMPLEMENTED DIGITAL SPECTRO-
CORRELATOR SYSTEM FOR RADIO ASTRONOMY

Kenichi Miura and Toshiro Nakazuru
Mainframe Division, Computer Systems, Fujitsu Limited,
1015 Kamikodanaka, Nakahara-ku, Kawasaki, 211, Japan

Yoshihiro Chikada
Nobeyama Radio Observatory,
Minamimaki, Mimamisaku, Nagano Pref., 384-13, Japan

1. INTRODUCTION

A special purpose digital spectro-correlator system, FX, has been developed to perform the real time digital signal processing for the five-element synthesis telescope at the Nobeyama Radio Observatory of Tokyo Astronomical Observatory[Chikada et al.,1983]. This paper outlines the algorithms, architecture and implementation of the FX system. The test and maintenance of the system is also described. This paper is a revised version of an invited paper to the 4th Australian Microelectronics Conference, "Migrating Systems to Silicon", held in Sidney, 13-15 May, 1985, sponsored by the Institution of Radio and Electronics Engineeres Australia.

2. OUTLINE OF SYSTEM

The design objective of the FX system is to perform the real time computations which are necessary for spectroscopy and interferometry of mm-wave signals from the stellar objects, with the the frequency resolution of 1024 points and with the maximum bandwidth of 320 MHz. In order to fulfil these requirements, the FX system employs a highly parallel and pipelined architecture. The total computational power is equivalent to approximately 120 Giga operations-per-second (GOPS).

The FX system consists of a Fourier transform section (F section), a correlation section (X section) and a control section (Figure 1). F and X sections are to be collectively called arithmetic section throughout this paper. The function of each section and FX-related equipment are briefly described as follows:

(a) Fourier transform section (F section)
　　It is composed of five FFT processors, each of which performs the real time 1024-point fast Fourier transform on the incoming complex digital data from one of the five movable antennas with 10 meter diameter, and produces 1024 complex frequency components. An extra FFT processor may be attached to the system, as an option, which receives data from a separate fixed antenna with 45 meter diameter.

(b) Correlation section (X section)
　　It is composed of fifteen correlators, each of which computes the auto- or cross-correlation for one of the fifteen combinations of outputs from five FFT processors. The (i,j)-th correlator, for example, performs the complex conjugate multiplications for 1024 complex frequency components and accumulates the results as follows;

$$\overline{X_{i,j}(k) = F_i(k) \times F_j(k)^*} \quad (k = 0,1,2,\ldots,1023),$$

where $F_i(k)$ and $F_j(k)$ are the k-th frequency components of the i-th and j-th FFT processors, respectively, * indicates the complex conjugate and ---- means accumulation of results over specified duration of time.

(c) Control section
　　It controls the operation of arithmetic section and the interfacing to a host computer system.

(d) FX-related equipment (Figure 1)
　-- Front-end receiver and filter: they convert the received mm-wave signals into the intermediate frequency signals, then down to the baseband complex signals by the in-phase/quadrature-phase mixing.
　-- A/D converter: it consists of five converter pairs (real and imaginary parts each) which convert the complex analog signals into 3 to 6 bit precision complex digital signals at the maximum sampling

rate of 320MHz.

3. ALGORITHMS, ARCHITECTURE AND IMPLEMENTATION

In order to perform 1024-point complex FFT's continuously at 3.2 microsecond pitch, it is necessary to map the FFT algorithm directly into hardware in a highly parallel and pipelined fashion. The best choice for the device technology for such purpose is the CMOS LSI, due to its very high circuit density and low power consumption. In the FX system, 32-way parallel structure has been adopted so that the system can operate at 10 MHz clock. The entire system forms a very long pipeline: data flow only in one direction.

3.1 Algorithms and architecture

The outline of the employed algorithms and the architecture of the FX system is as follows.

(a) FFT

A Fourier transform of 1024 point complex data is performed by two cascaded 32-point complex FFT circuits, with 32-way parallel input ports each (Figure 2). Prior to FFT computations in each circuit, 1024 point contiguous data are mapped into a 32*32 matrix which is then transposed so that the every 32nd element in the original sequence is now arranged in contiguous location. 32 sets of such data are time-multiplexed and fed to FFT circuit at every clock cycle. The internal structure of each 32-point FFT circuit is a straightforward and pipelined implementation of the signal flow graph of the 4-2-4 radix FFT.

(b) Correlation and accumulation

Correlation computation is also done in a 32-way parallel and pipelined fashion (Figure 3). Accumulation of the products is performed in three steps. The first two steps use the intermediate accumulators equipped with a 32 stage FIFO(first-in first-out) registers. Here, 32 frequency components are multiplexed. In the final step, on the other hand, all the 1024 frequency components can be multiplexed and accumulated into RAM (random access memory) sequentially, since the carry counting occurs at a much lower rate at this step.

3.2 Implementation using CMOS gate-arrays

The above algorithms have been implemented by mainly using Fujitsu's C-2000 and C-3900 series CMOS gate-array LSI's, which equivalently contain 2000 or 3900 2-input NAND gates, respectively. The typical on-chip delay time is from 5 to 15 nanoseconds per gate. Four types of LSI chips have been newly designed for the FX system. Most of the arithmetic circuits in the system have been implemented with the above four types of LSI's; 3700 LSI's have been used in the entire system (Table 1). TTL-MSI's have also been extensively used. The following paragraphs describe the four types of chips briefly. They all have the parallel and pipelined structure. Also note that the precisions in arithmetic operations are from 6 to 8 bits in all cases.

(a) Corner turner LSI (CT)

This LSI has two shift register planes whose shift directions are orthogonal to each other: one for inputs and the other for outputs. It performs the aforementioned transposition of data by transfering the data from the input plane to the output plane in a snap-shot fashion. Each shift register plane consists of 16 words by 16 bits.

(b) Butterfly LSI (BTF)

This LSI is a two point discrete Fourier transform circuit; it adds and subtracts two 7 bit precision complex numbers in parallel.

(c) Multiplier LSI (MPY)

This LSI multiplies two 6 bit precision complex numbers; the results are rounded to an 8 bit complex number.

(d) Accumulator LSI (ACC)

This LSI is a 9 bit complex word accumulator circuit with a 32 stage FIFO register, each stage being 9-bit complex number. It accumulates the 32 time-multiplexed data.

4. SYSTEM TESTING AND MAINTENANCE METHODOLOGY

As described above, the FX system is a large digital system containing 3700 CMOS LSI's, which are equivalent to about 12 million gates. Testing and maintenance are of prime importance for any system of such size.

Maintenance of the control section is done through the built-in maintenance panel, whereas testing of the arithmetic section, which requires a large amount of test data, is mainly performed through a host computer. For testing the entire arithmetic section, parallel structure of the FX system is fully utilized. That is, the identical test patterns are fed to more than one units (note that there are five FFT processors and fifteen correlators) and the results are compared with each other.

The detailed testing of arithmetic section is accomplished by incorporating in the pipeline structure the scan stages, which are composed of TTL universal shift registers. As an example, Figure 4 shows a schematic diagram of a 8-point FFT circuit; it illustrates the locations of scan stages in the pipeline structure. Shift registers are organized so that test patterns can be scanned in and results can be scanned out. Therefore, the LSI's between scan stages can be tested independently of the rest of the system.

5. CONCLUSION

The underlying algorithms, architecture of the FX system, and its implementation are outlined in this paper. The methodology for system testing and maintenance is also described. The FX system has been successfully installed at Nobeyama, and it is now operational for the observation of radio sources, while measurement of the S/N ratio is being continued.

6. ACKNOWLEDGEMENT

We wish to express our thanks to the researchers at the Nobeyama Radio Observatory, especially to Dr. M. Ishiguro for his helpful discussions, and to the engineers of Fujitsu Limited, especially Mr. T.Miyazawa for managing the production of FX.

7. REFERENCE

Chikada, Y. et al.,1983. A DIGITAL FFT SPECTRO-CORRELATOR FOR RADIO ASTRONOMY, URSI/IAU Symposium on Measurement and Processing for Indirect Imaging, Sydney, Australia, Aug.30-Sept.2.

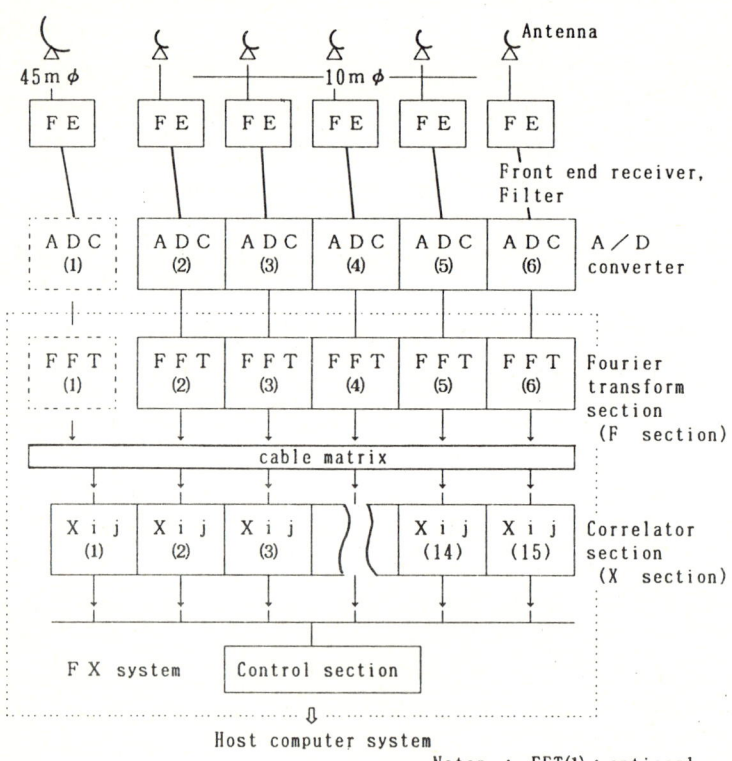

Figure 1   Block schematics of FX

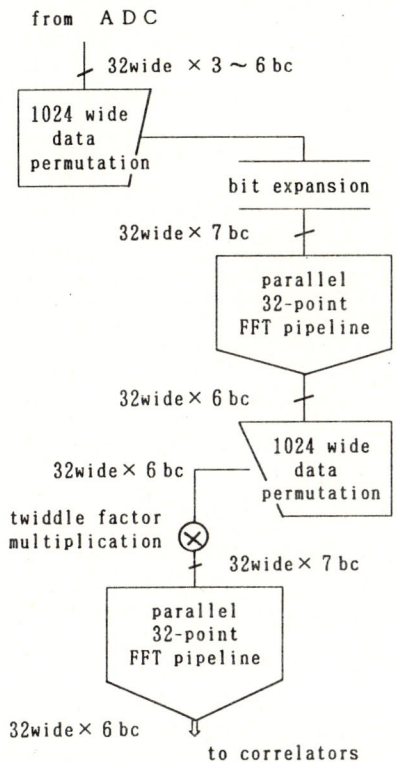

Figure 2 1024-point complex FFT pipeline

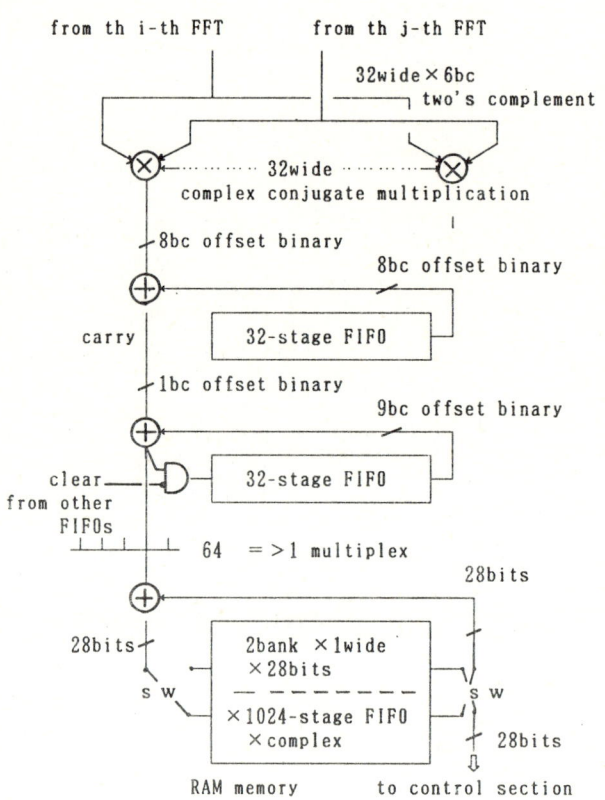

Figure 3 Correlator $X_{i,j}$

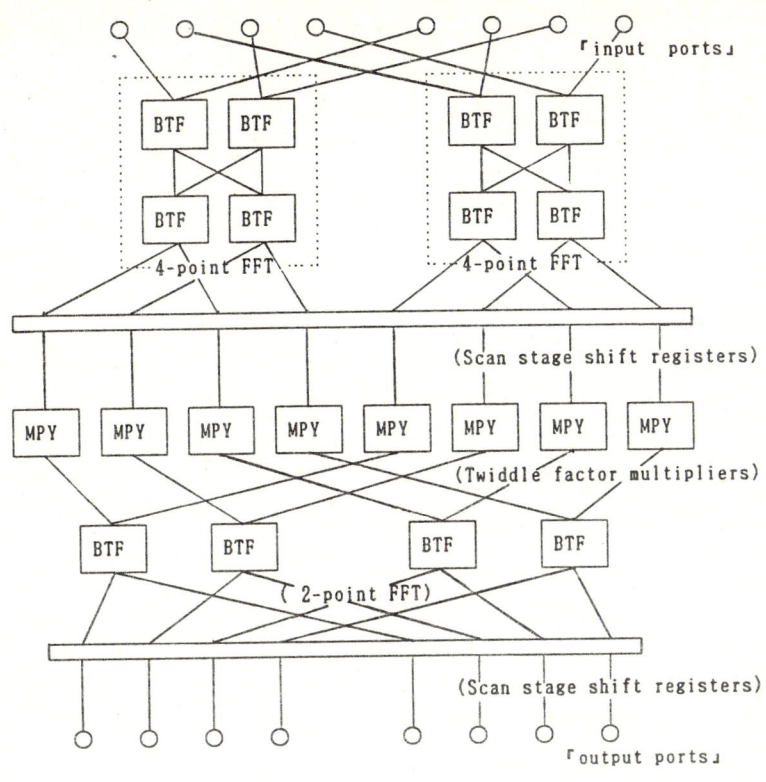

Figure 4 Schematic Diagram of 8-point FFT printed circuit board

Table 1 Gate counts and chip counts of FX

LSI Name		CT	BTF	MPY	ACC	Total
Gate count/chip (*)		3367	1897	3593	3671	---
Chip count	one FFT	116	176	160	0	452
	one Correlator	0	0	32	64	96
	System (**)	580	880	1280	9600	3700
Gate count ($\div 10^6$)	one FFT	.39	.33	.57	.0	1.29
	one Correlator	.0	.0	.11	.23	.34
	System (**)	1.95	1.65	4.5	3.5	11.55

Notes: (*) Gates are counted in terms of 2-input NAND gates.
       (**) System consists of 5 FFT's and 15 correlators.

THE CRAY-2: THE NEW STANDARD IN SUPERCOMPUTING

S. C. Perrenod
Cray Research, Inc.
5776 Stoneridge Mall Road
Pleasanton, California 94566

Abstract

An overview of the Cray-2 system, including its capability and performance, is provided. The Cray-2 consists of 4 background processors and a foreground processor for I/O. An extremely large multibank memory is a key feature, as is the cooling technology. The operating system is based on Unix System V*. The Cray-2 may be considered as the new standard in supercomputing because of its unprecedentedly large main memory and its Unix operating system.

Cray History

Seymour Cray's Cray-1 was introduced in 1976 and quickly set the standard in supercomputing (1). A key feature is the vector register set of 8 registers holding 64 words each. Functional units are pipelined in order to produce one result per the 12.5 nanosecond clock period in vector mode. Both functional unit overlap and chaining (the ability to use resultant quantities immediately as operands in another functional unit) are included. The Cray-1 has a single CPU with 1 port to a banked memory capable of supplying up to 1 word per clock period (80 million words per second). Peak performance is 160 Megaflops (2 floating operations per clock period) and performance on the 14 Livermore loops about 30 Mflops.

In 1982 Steve Chen introduced the Cray X-MP, a 2 CPU enhanced version of the Cray-1. The clock period was improved 30% to 9.5 ns and the memory bandwidth increased. Each CPU has 4 ports to memory allowing 2 loads, 1 store and I/O to all be overlapped (per CPU). Chaining was made more flexible and automatic. In addition, a large secondary memory with 10 Gigabit/sec peak transfer rate was introduced. The SSD (Solid-state Storage Device) was originally available with up to 32 Megawords. In 1984 this was increased to 128 MW, allowing very large problems to be solved. The SSD is logically accessed like a disk drive. The X-MP-2 has a peak performance of 420 Mflops and runs the Livermore loops at about 70 Mflops in a single processor.

* Unix is a trademark of AT&T Bell Laboratories.

In 1984 the 4 processor X-MP/48 with 8 MW of memory was introduced. This machine includes hardware gather-scatter to speed sparse matrix calculations. This X-MP has a peak rate of 840 Mflops and peak memory bandwidth of 1684 million words/second. Both the Cray-1 and X-MP use freon cooling technology. Both machines stand in a $270°$ C-shaped chassis about 7 feet high. The X-MP is a full product line with 1,2 and 4 CPU models and a range of memory options, now available up to 16 MW.

Hardware

The Cray-2 comes in one configuration: 4 Background processors and 256 Megawords (268 million words) of Common Memory (all of which is directly addressable by the operating system or a single user) (2). It is this extremely large memory (2 1/2 orders of magnitude larger than the Cray-1) which primarily justifies the phrase "New Standard in Supercomputing" for the Cray-2. The Background processors and memory, as well as the Foreground processor, disk controllers, network interface controllers, and power supplies are all contained in a C-shaped chassis 45" (1.14 m) high. The chassis circumscribes a $300°$ arc and is 53" (1.35 m) across. The dimensions of the Cray-1, by comparison, are 77" (1.96m) by 104" (2.64m). The mainframe weighs 2.75 tons (2500 kg), just over half the weight of the Cray-1.

CRAY-2 COMPUTER SYSTEM

Module Technology

The module technology in the Cray-2 is quite interesting. Modules are 3 dimensional, containing 8 board layers spaced only 1/8" (.3cm) between layers. Total module dimensions are 8"x4"x1" (20.3cm x 10.2cm x 2.5cm), and each module contains about 750 chips. There are 36 vertical pin interconnects (modules are mounted horizontally in the chassis) for each of the 8 layers. Thus the information traffic in the third dimension is quite significant.

A single memory module contains 2 MW, twice the maximum memory in the original Cray-1! The logic circuits used are 16-gate ECL arrays, as in the X-MP.

The key to the fast clock speed in the Cray-2 is the dense packing within the modules, and this is made possible only by the unique cooling technology for the Cray-2.

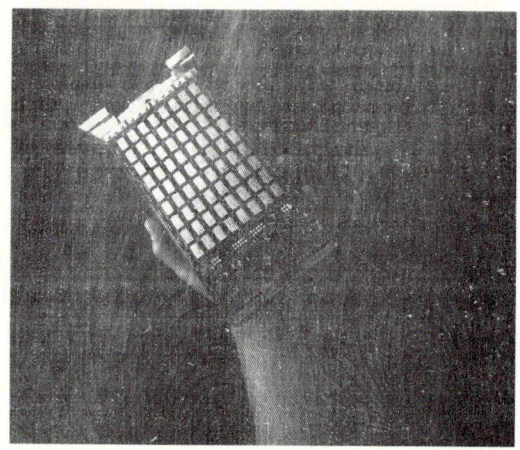

CRAY-2 Module

Cooling Technology

All of the electronic modules as well as the power supplies are cooled by immersion in an inert fluorocarbon (fluorinert) liquid at room temperature. The liquid enters the chassis at 70°F (21°C) and leaves at 80°F (27°C). Flow across the modules is primarily horizontal at 1"/sec (2.54 cm/sec). The flow is directed by vanes and is turbulent. Bubbles of air rise up through the liquid, along with the turbulent flow. This provides a very aesthetic effect. In fact, the first machine, installed at the Magnetic Fusion Energy Computer Center in Livermore, California, is nicknamed "Bubbles".

The cooling system is valveless to maintain high reliability. There are 200 gallons (727 liters) of the fluorinert in the chassis. The heat carried off by the fluorinert is exchanged to a conventional refrigeration unit. The power load of the mainframe is 195 kW. There are 10 reservoir standpipes to contain the excess fluorinert plus the chassis fluorinert if required. If it is necessary to replace a module in the system the chassis can be pumped down in about 90 seconds and the plexiglass panels removed. The electronic modules are always visible through the translucent panels, adding to the aesthetic quality of the machine.

The liquid immersion cooling technology is expected to result in very good hardware reliability. Chip temperatures remain at less than $100^\circ F$ ($38^\circ C$).

System Architecture

A diagrammatic overview of the system architecture is shown in Figure 1. The Foreground processor handles system supervision tasks and directs traffic along the 4 channel loops. Each channel loop has a bandwidth of 15.6 Gigabits/sec. Each loop (or bus) ties together the Common Memory, one Background processor (CPU) and 10 controller units (disk or network) to the Foreground processor.

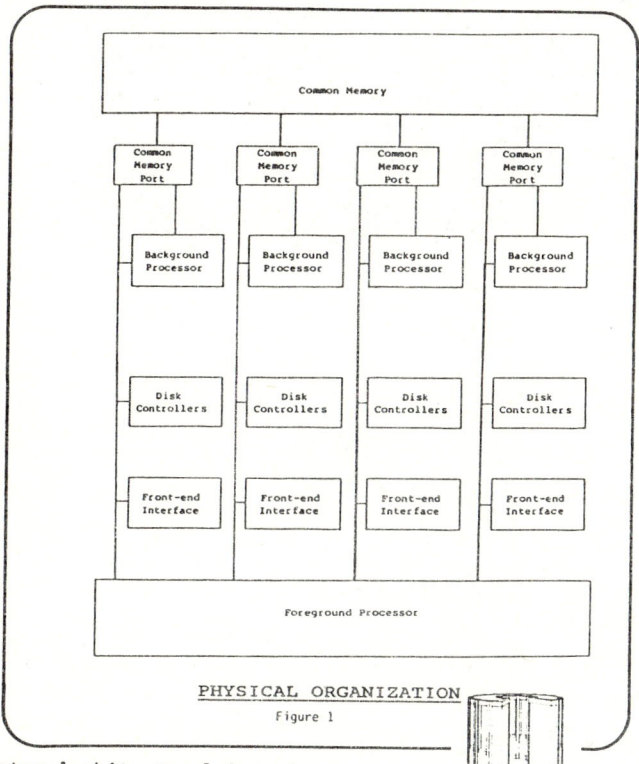

PHYSICAL ORGANIZATION
Figure 1

Cray-2 System Architectural Overview

The memory is segmented into 4 quadrants of 32 banks each, and there is one port to each quadrant. The 4 CPUs access successive quadrants each clock period in a round-robin scheme. The maximum bandwidth between Common memory and the CPUs is 1 word per processor per clock period, or 975 million words/sec.

The Foreground processor has a total I/O bandwidth of 15.6 Gigabits/sec. Up to 36 DD-49 disk drives (totaling 43.2 Gigabytes storage) can be attached to the system and data can be streamed to all simultaneously. This results in an aggregate transfer rate of over 3 Gigabits/sec.

Background Processors

Each of the 4 CPUs is qualitatively very similar to a Cray-1, but simpler in design and also faster (see Figure 2). The clock period is just 4.1 ns. Each

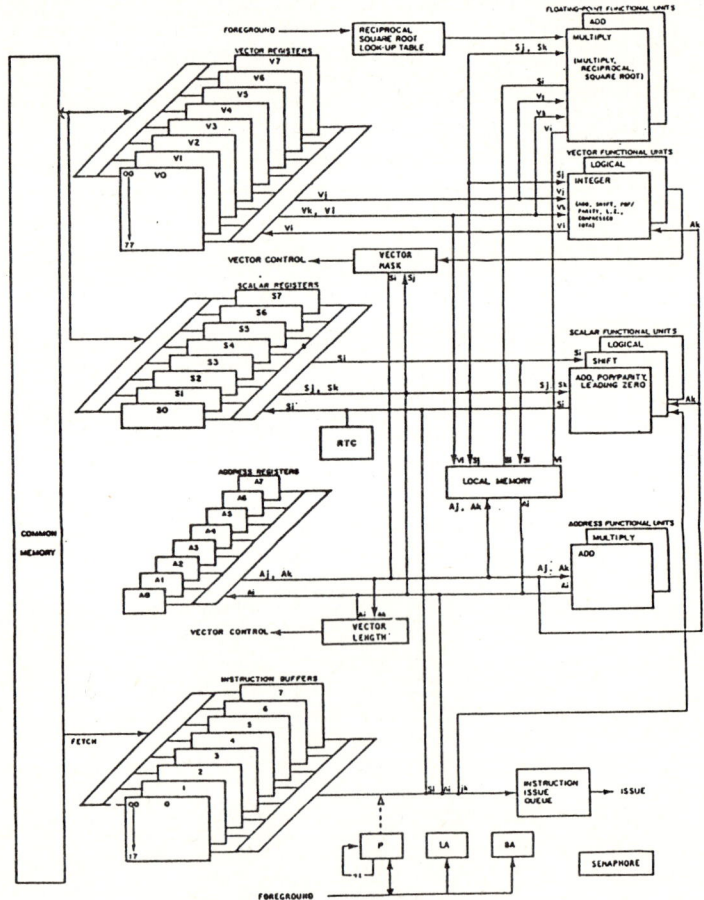

Background Processor Block Diagram   Figure 2

CPU has one port to the Common memory. There is a high-speed Local memory of 16K words within each CPU. This replaces the 128 B & T registers found in the Cray-1 and X-MP. There are 9 functional units per CPU, a simpler design than the 13 found in the Cray-1. The A registers for addressing are increased from 24 to 32 bits in width. An instruction can issue every other clock period.

The Cray-2 does not have chaining, but it does have functional unit overlap. Like the X-MP/48, the Cray-2 has hardware for gather/scatter.

A set of 8 semaphore registers is included for interprocessor communication (also possible through shared memory).

Each CPU has 2 floating point units, one for add and a second for multiply/ reciprocal/square root. Floating point numbers have a 48-bit mantissa, a sign bit, and a 15-bit exponent. The range is approximately $\pm 10^{-2466}$ to 10^{2466} with 14 decimal digits precision. Reciprocals and square roots calculated using an iterative scheme. Coefficients for the iterations are stored in a table lookup memory. In Table 1 we summarize key features of the Cray-1, Cray-XMP and Cray-2.

TABLE 1

CRAY ARCHITECTURAL SUMMARY

Machine	Year	Clock (ns)	Max. No. Processors	Max. Memory (mw)	No. Ports (ea processor)	Chaining	Cooling
Cray-1	1976	12.5	1	4	1	Yes	Freon
Cray X-MP	1982	9.5	4	16*	4	Enhanced	Freon
Cray-2	1985	4.1	4	256	1	No+	Fluorinert

* Secondary Storage (semiconductor memory) of 128 MW available
\+ Functional unit overlap

Architectural Comparisons: Cray-1, Cray X-MP, Cray-2

Software

The software provided with the Cray-2 includes the CX-OS operating system, based on ATT Unix System V (Release 2). An optimizing and auto-vectorizing Fortran compiler, CFT2, and a C compiler for system programming, as well as a high-level assembler, CAL2, are also provided.

Library support includes math and scientific libraries and a multitasking library. The multitasking library may be used to partition a single application across 2, 3, or 4 processors in the system. Task initiation, termination, event posting and waiting and lock facilities are provided in the multitasking library.

The Unix-based operating system is enhanced in several areas for the supercomputer environment. Foremost among these are I/O performance, networking and batch enhancements. Asynchronous and track-based I/O are included. Track-based I/O eliminates disk rotational latency by starting to fill (empty) a track-sized buffer at whatever point the read (write) head is located at the time the request is received. The first part of the buffer is filled by the time 2π of disk rotation has occurred. In addition, a single file may be striped (partitioned) across up to 7 drives, reducing I/O time by up to a factor of 7.

Network support includes a Cray proprietary Hyperchannel* driver. Additional protocol support, in particular a TCP/IP implementation, is planned for the near future. A Unix-to-Unix station to a DEC VAX acting as a front-end for terminal, file, and print traffic is available. Multiple front-ends or network connections are supported.

User processes or jobs may be run interactively through the Bourne shell or submitted to a batch facility. The batch facility is based on the Multi-Device Queuing System from the Army Ballistics Research Laboratory. All of Common memory is available to a single user if desired.

Early Installations

One processor prototypes of the Cray-2 were installed in August, 1984 at Cray's Software Development facility in Minneapolis and at MFECC in December, 1984.

* Hyperchannel is a trademark of Network Systems Corporation.

The first 4 processor machine was installed at MFECC in June, 1985. Since this was an early delivery, it's memory is 'only' 64 MW. This machine runs the CTSS operating system developed at MFECC.

The first 256 million word Cray-2 was installed at NASA Ames Research Center in Mountain View, California beginning September 30, 1985. This is also the first 4 processor running CX-OS, Cray Research's implementation of Unix.

There is also an installation scheduled for year-end 1985 at the University of Minnesota.

Performance

The Cray-2 is a new product, so its full capabilities are still being determined. Where the Cray-2 will really shine is in solving very large problems. It is its extremely large memory which is the most significant aspect of its power and the reason why it sets the new standard in supercomputing. Performance on problems larger than 10 million words or so is expected to exceed 20 times Cray-1 performance, since the problem can be memory-contained. For smaller problems, which are memory-contained on an X-MP, performance is expected to be roughly comparable or somewhat in excess of the X-MP on a per CPU basis. Problems characterized by long vectors will likely demonstrate superior performance on the Cray-2 even when memory-contained on the X-MP.

Certainly the peak rate of the Cray-2 (due to the faster clock rate) at 1.95 Gigaflops exceeds that of the four processor X-MP at 0.84 Gigaflops. Average relative performance between the machines is more comparable. This occurs for 3 reasons: (1) the lack of chaining on the Cray-2, (2) the greater number of memory ports on the X-MP and (3) the smaller number of segments (i.e. clock periods to complete an operation) in the X-MP floating point units. These factors are partially offset by the fast local memory on the Cray-2, which is much larger than the B and T registers on the X-MP.

Some initial results on several codes are summarized in Table 2. Average performance for the Livermore loops with the Cray-2 CIVIC compiler has been reported by Bruijnes (3). These are per CPU results and for the Cray-2 are on a single processor prototype. Unoptimized, the Cray-2 and X-MP results are very similar. With optimization via compiler directives (including the use of local memory in some cases) the Cray-2 is about 19% faster at 69 Mflops, average.

Table 2

CRAY-2 PERFORMANCE SUMMARY
-- Megaflops --

Code	CRAY X-MP	CRAY-2
Livermore Loops *		
Average	58	69
Harmonic Mean	12.7	14.6
Bucy convolution kernel	163	234+ (260)
Large Eddy simulation	71	82
Matrix multiply (4-processor throughput)	782	1640
FFT (256^3 complex, 32MW)		
1 processor	-	269
2 processors	-	459
4 processors	-	670
I/O Stream (20 DD-29s aggregate)		635 Mb/s

Results are all for one processor on either machine except where indicated.

* CIVIC compiler, with optimization via compiler directives
\+ Using local memory. With hand coding 260 Mflops is obtained.

Early Cray-2 Installations

The code BUCY is a convolution kernel which is the significant computational task in a non-linear filtering algorithm implementation (4), (5). Without the use of local memory the performance is just a bit better than the X-MP. It is an easy task, however, to place the most frequently accessed array (4917 words) into local memory. With this modification the code runs at 234 Mflops, or 44% faster than the X-MP. With hand coding we pick up another 11%.

The code LES is from the NASA Ames Research Center at Moffett Field, California. LES is a Large Eddy Simulation code for aerodynamics research. It runs at 82 Mflops on the Cray-2 compared to 71 Mflops on the X-MP, using 1 processor on each machine.

The highest performance thus far attained on the Cray-2 is from the matrix multiply (floating) algorithm, which makes good use of Local memory. A matrix-matrix multiplication where each is 512 x 512 runs at 1.64 Gigaflops throughput when 4 copies are run simultaneously (1 per processor). This is the first reported general purpose application to ever exceed 1 Gigaflop.

A very large FFT has been solved. A 256^3 complex FFT runs in 12.4 seconds on one processor. The problem requires 32MW and runs at 269 Mflops. A multi-tasked version runs on 4 CPUs at 670 Mflops.

It should also be remembered that the Cray-2 compiler is somewhat less mature currently than the X-MP compiler, so relative performance figures will increase with time.

Early results on the Cray-2 are certainly encouraging and show excellent potential. However much remains to be done and to be learned about the system, particularly its capabilities to solve very large problems. This will include usage of Local Memory, and memory access patterns in general as well as multi-tasking and traditional vectorization techniques. Careful instruction scheduling from compilers is necessary to ensure functional unit overlap, since chaining is not included.

Some of the most interesting tests remain, e.g. NASTRAN or a flow code on a 100 + MW problem. This type of capability brought to researchers and industrial science will justify the title "The New Standard in Supercomputing".

References

(1) R.M. Russell, "The Cray-1 Computer System" Communications of the ACM, 21, 1, 63-72, 1978
(2) S. Cray, internal memo, 1984.
(3) H. Bruijnes, The Buffer, National Magnetic Fusion Energy Computer Center, pp. 1-4, June 1985.
(4) R.S. Bucy and K.D. Senne, "Nonlinear Filtering Algorithms for Vector Machines", Computers and Mathematics, 6, 3, 317-338, 1980.
(5) S.C. Perrenod and R.S. Bucy, "Supercomputer Performance for Convolution", to be published in Proceedings of the First International Conference on Supercomputing Systems, 1985.

An Introduction to the ETA[10]

C.J. Purcell
ETA Systems
St. Paul, Minnesota

The ETA10 supercomputer is ETA Systems, Incorporated's initial product offering in the supercomputer marketplace. The ETA10 will have both general purpose features and high-speed calculation facilities. ETA Systems will add more features to the ETA10 as it is enhanced to meet growing customer needs.

There are five major functional elements in the ETA10 hardware architecture. These are:

- Central Processor Units

- Shared Memory

- Communication Buffer

- Input/Output Units

- Service Units

These functional elements combine to form a multi-processor system designed to provide a system-wide balance of data flow and processing capacity that exceeds the calculation speeds of existing supercomputers, and also extends the reliability and generality of supercomputers.

Each Central Processor Unit is actually a supercomputer on a single board. Each contains both a scalar and 2-pipe vector processor along with four million 64-bit words of Central Processor memory and ports to the Communication Buffer, the Shared Memory, and the Service

Units. Each Central Processor Unit operates independently at a peak speed of 1.25 gigaflops. The ETA10 can be configured with one to eight processors. Thus, a fully configured ETA10 provides 10 gigaflops of computing power. The smaller ETA10 configurations can be upgraded on site while the maching is running. Each Central Processor Unit contains a 128 word Vector Shortstop buffer to improve performance of the short vector construct. Figures 1 and 2 are diagrams of the ETA10 hardware architecture.

There are two significant technologies behind these single board Central Processor Units. First, the multi-layer printed circuit boards eliminate the necessity for interconnect coax cables as used in current Class VI supercomputers. The second innovation is the 20,000 gate CMOS chip. Both are designed by ETA Systems. An ETA10 chip dissipates less than 2 watts of heat and contains the equivalent logic of 80 chips used in today's supercomputers. An on-chip maintenance system called Built-in Evaluation and Self-Test (B.E.S.T*) allows complete functional testing of each individual chip in order to detect and isolate errors. The Service Unit can exercise and test each individual processor without the use of an experienced operator so that permanent on-site maintenance personnel are no longer required.

The ETA10 processor boards are submerged in a closed-loop liquid nitrogen system. The warmed liquid nitrogen gas is retrieved and cycled to a cryogenerator for reuse. When the chips are operated at liquid nitrogen temperatures, they perform at twice the speed of room temperature operation. In addition to increasing the processing speeds, the liquid nitrogen also increases the life of the processor boards, making an already reliable technology even more reliable.

ETA^{10} Hardware Architecture

As shown in figure 1, the ETA10 system has one and as many as eight, Central Processing Units (CPUs). Each CPU is connected to the large Shared Memory (up to two billion bytes) and the eight-million byte Communication Buffer. Also communicating with these large common memories are from 2 to 18 Input/Output Units (IOUs) that provide connection to and control of all ETA10 peripherals and network interfaces. A Service Unit (SU) is connected to all parts of the ETA10, and provides an operator console and maintenance connections for the system.

*B.E.S.T. is a trademark of ETA Systems.

peripherals and network interfaces. A Service Unit (SU) is connected to all parts of the ETA10, and provides an operator console and maintenance connections for the system.

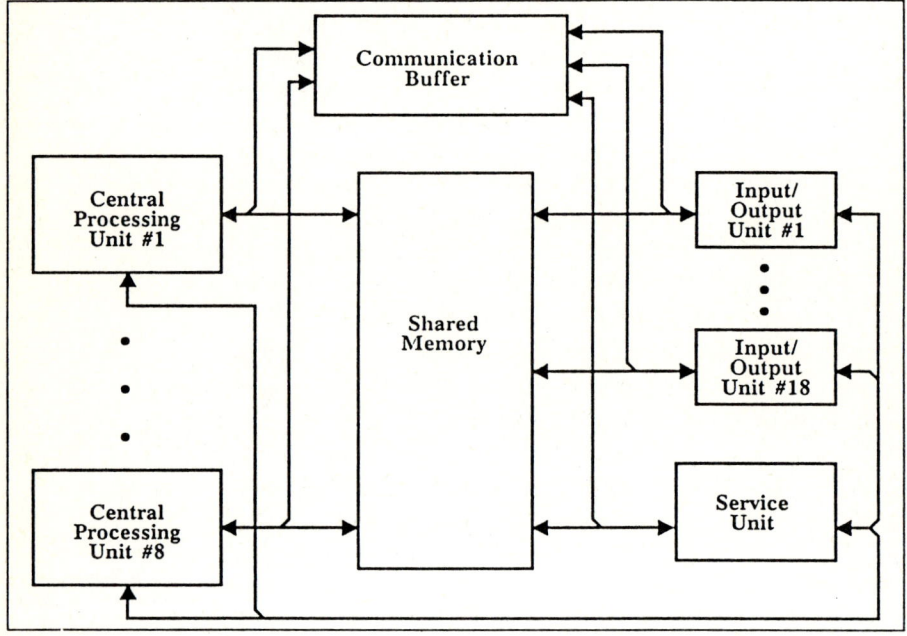

Figure 1. ETA10 supercomputer functional diagram.

Performance

The ETA10 system provides high performance for both computation and I/O, as described in the following subsections.

High Speed Computation

Each ETA10 CPU provides very fast scalar processing and vector processing. ETA FORTRAN provides state of the art optimization and automatic vectorization to system users. For applications with algorithms more readily expressed by vector notation, ETA Systems' ETA FORTRAN and Pascal compilers both will provide vector syntax.

The multiple processors of the ETA10 provide additional performance opportunities. Flexible system scheduling options allow the processors to be applied in parallel to provide very high performance for a single problem, or to be applied individually to sets of jobs to provide high system throughput. ETA Systems is developing techniques for the ETA FORTRAN compiler to perform automatic partitioning for multitasking of programs when a user selects this option.

Users who want to build explicit parallel operation into their programs also can use ETA Systems' multitasking library. Because not all programs naturally use the same model for parallel computation, this library contains several sets of calls, each of which provides a different way of expressing parallelism. One model is FORTRAN oriented, and avoids introducing shared data in a way that is contrary to FORTRAN's definition. Another model provides the counters and synchronization of the Industrial Real-Time FORTRAN subroutines. The programmer can select the model most natural and reliable for his or her application. ETA Systems will continue to add other models to this library.

High Performance Input/Output

The use of a large Shared Memory with a very high transfer rate between the ETA10 CPUs and disk subsystems provides the hardware needed to produce high overall I/O performance. Files being used are cached in the Shared Memory. The system selects buffer size, both in Shared Memory and the memory in each CPU, based on the user-chosen characteristics of each file. Users can provide file access hints to tailor the use of a file for higher performance by a specific program.

Hardware Components

Central Processing Unit

The CPUs provide the power of the ETA10 supercomputer. Each Central Processor of the ETA10 includes a scalar processor, a vector processor, a large register file, and interfaces to other system components. Each Central Processor fits on a single printed circuit board, and operates at a normal temperature of less than 100° K for enhanced performance. Each CPU is capable of issuing an instruction every clock cycle. The Central Processor of the ETA10 is instruction and data compatible with the CYBER 205, and has several new instructions for accessing the shared memories in the system.

Other CPU characteristics are:

- 64-bit word

- two's complement arithmetic

- bit, byte, half-word, and full-word operations

- high-speed, 256-word register file

- instruction stack

- virtual memory with 1K, 2K, or 8K word small page sizes; and 64K or 256K word large page sizes

The Central Processor Memory of each ETA10 CPU has a fixed size of four million virtually addressed words. CPM is constructed from 64K MOS Static Random Access Memory. The CPM bandwidth is 73 billion bits per second. Single error correction/double error detection (SECDED) protection is provided on each 32-bit half word. Access to Central Processor Memory is limited to the CPU with which it is associated, the maintenance port, and the shared memory port. The CPU diagram is shown in figure 2.

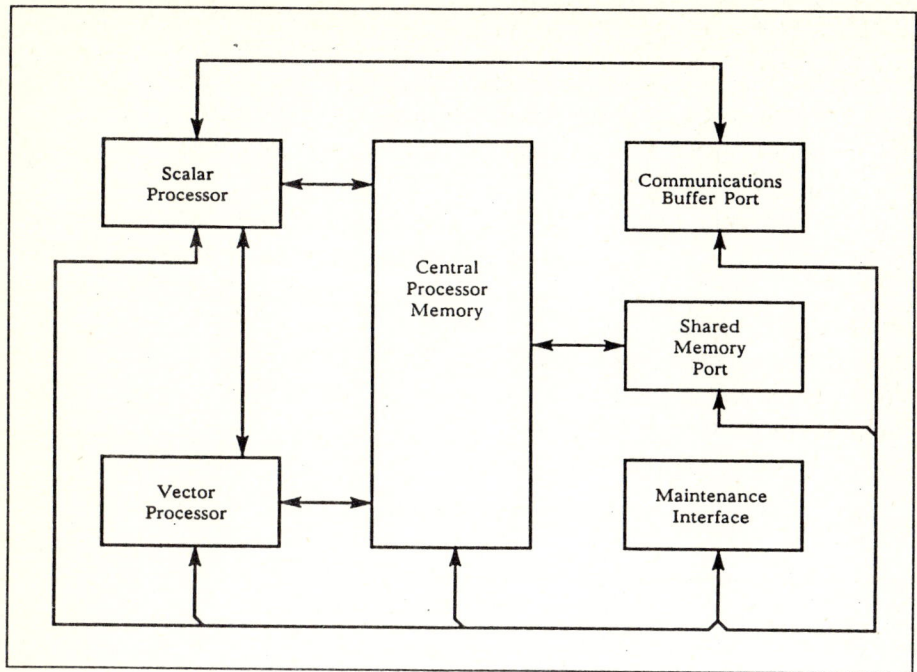

Figure 2. ETA10 Central Processing Unit.

The Shared Memory port and Communications Buffer port provide hardware interfaces from the CPU to each of those memories. The Maintenance Interface allows the Service Unit to connect directly to the CPU to perform diagnostic and maintenance functions.

Input/Output Unit

The Input/Output Unit provides the means to attach peripherals and networks to the ETA10 system. The base IOU consists of a cabinet, power supply, cooling, buses, maintenance interface, and Data Pipe Controller. Functional units that present a specific peripheral connection, or that provide a processor and memory increment, may be added to the base IOU. Each of these functional units provides a connection to disks, tapes, or networks. An IOU will hold up to eight functional units. All functional units in a single IOU share a Data Pipe to a Shared Memory low-speed port. Of the 20 Data Pipe Shared Memory ports, up to 18 may be assigned to IOUs. Figure 3 shows an internal diagram of the IOU.

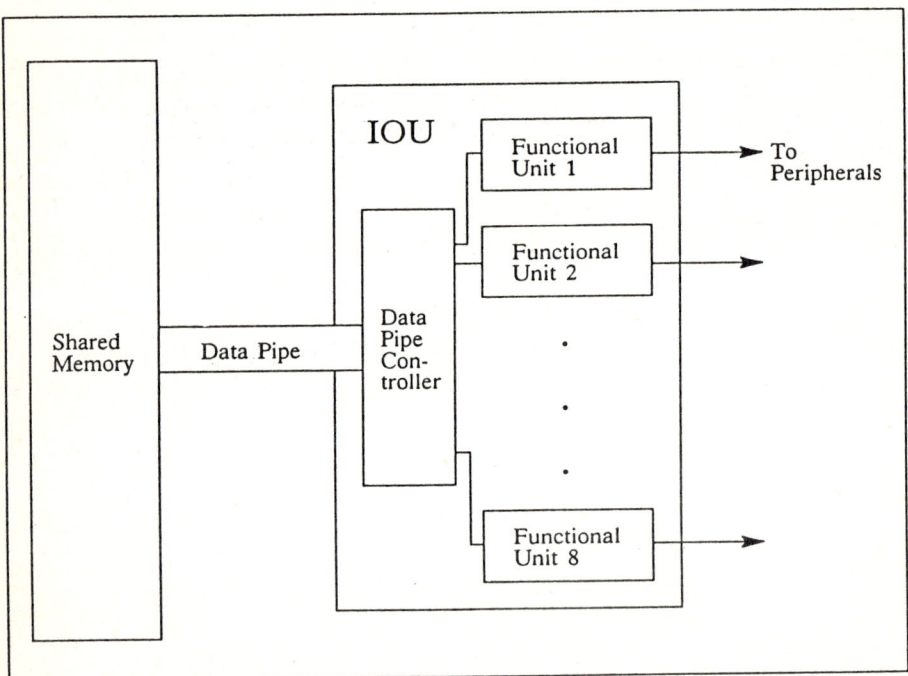

Figure 3. Internal diagram of the IOU.

Shared Memory Unit

The primary role of Shared Memory is to provide a large, high speed storage facility for active files. Shared Memory ranges in size from 64 million to 256 million words, in increments of 64 million words. Shared Memory is a 256K MOS Dynamic Random Access Memory. The Shared Memory Unit provides a total of 8 high-speed ports for CPU connection, with a sustained transfer rate of several billion bits per second per port; and 20 low-speed ports for IOU/SU connection with a sustained transfer rate of 350 million bits per second per port. The transfer size for a single request ranges from a half word to 65,536 words. SECDED protection at the 32-bit half word level is supported in Shared Memory. The system can be configured with degradable hardware so that during maintenance the Shared Memory Unit retains at least 50% of its normal operating capacity.

Communication Buffer

The Communication Buffer provides fast access to small shared data and synchronizing functions. The Communication Buffer has a fixed size of one million words. The Communication Buffer is constructed from 64K MOS Static Random Access Memory. The Communication Buffer bandwidth is 9.1 billion bits per second. The Communication Buffer provides unambiguous mutual exclusion operations for interprocessor synchronization. Access to the Communication Buffer and all its functions is available to all Central Processing Units, Input/Output Processors, and the Service Unit. The transfer size for a single request is a half word or a word. The Communication Buffer includes SECDED protection at the 32-bit half word level.

Service Unit

The Service Unit provides the ETA10 with operator consoles and system support tools. The Service Unit is a single network computer made up of two server nodes and two color graphics operator nodes. Up to six more (eight total) color graphics nodes may be attached to the network in order to provide additional operator consoles. These nodes are complete computer systems in themselves, and communicate with each other on a 12 million bit per second network. The SU also includes its own independent mass storage, which is shared by all nodes in its network.

The operator nodes connect to ETA Systems' Remote System Support Center by means of an attached modem. The modem supports 9600 baud communication over dial-up lines, and includes auto-dial and answer capabilities.

The Service Unit has the following peripherals: two 500M byte disk storage devices, one on each server node; one 86M byte Winchester disk with a built-in 62M byte, 1/4 inch streaming cartridge tape on each operator node; and one graphics printer.

The SU also includes a Power and Cooling Supervisor that collects and analyzes data about the power and cooling subsystems of the ETA10. In order to guarantee the safe and proper operation of the ETA10, the Power and Cooling Supervisor monitors and controls voltages, currents, pressures, temperatures, and other conditions.

Open Interconnection Network

The Open Interconnection Network supported by ETA Systems is based on the IEEE 802.3 standard for Ethernet. A single ETA10 Input/Output Unit (IOU) supports from 1 to 16 connections to the Ethernet cable(s). Each physical connection can support up to 128 logical connections to other devices on the network(s). Ethernet has a raw transfer rate of 10 million bits per second, and an effective applications data transfer rate of approximately 2 million bits per second.

The protocol supported over the Open Interconnection Network is the United States Department of Defense Standard TCP/IP protocol. This protocol facilitates the connection of a variety of devices to the Open Interconnection Network and the ETA10 system. The supported standard application protocols include File Transfer Protocol (FTP) and TELNET.

In addition to directly tapping an Ethernet Network, ETA Systems will offer a variety of devices that facilitate the connection of workstations, computers, terminals, and output devices to the network. These products will include:

- Protocol processing printed circuit boards and generic software for insertion into computers and workstations having an open architecture and a common bus interface, such as Multibus, Unibus, Q-bus, VME bus, or PC/AT bus.

- Terminal servers offering from 4 to 32 RS232, RS422, or V.35 ports for the connection of terminals, or for passthrough into other host mainframes supporting those terminals.

- Gateway servers supporting an X.25 interface, either to a public data network or to a host computer system supporting X.25 protocols.

- Bridges for connecting multiple Ethernet segments.

- Print stations and spooling software so print facilities are available directly from the ETA10.

- Network maintenance stations that provide control of network configuration, usage recording, directory services, and diagnostics.

The Open Interconnection Network also is designed to be compatible with other vendors' offerings that rely on Ethernet and TCP/IP. This design minimizes the constraints on customers in their selection of workstations to be used in conjunction with the ETA10. Some of the more popular workstations are certified by ETA Systems for operation with the ETA10.

Figure 4 depicts an example of an ETA10 system configuration with a variety of devices connected by the Open Interconnection Network. Nodes on the Open Interconnection Network can be reconfigured without disrupting other network activity. This includes reconfiguration around a malfunctioning node. Similarly, all maintenance and diagnostic activity can be accomplished without interrupting other nodes on the Open Interconnection Network.

As the International Standards Organization specifications for all seven layers of their Open System Interconnection model are implemented in the commercial marketplace, these standards also will be supported.

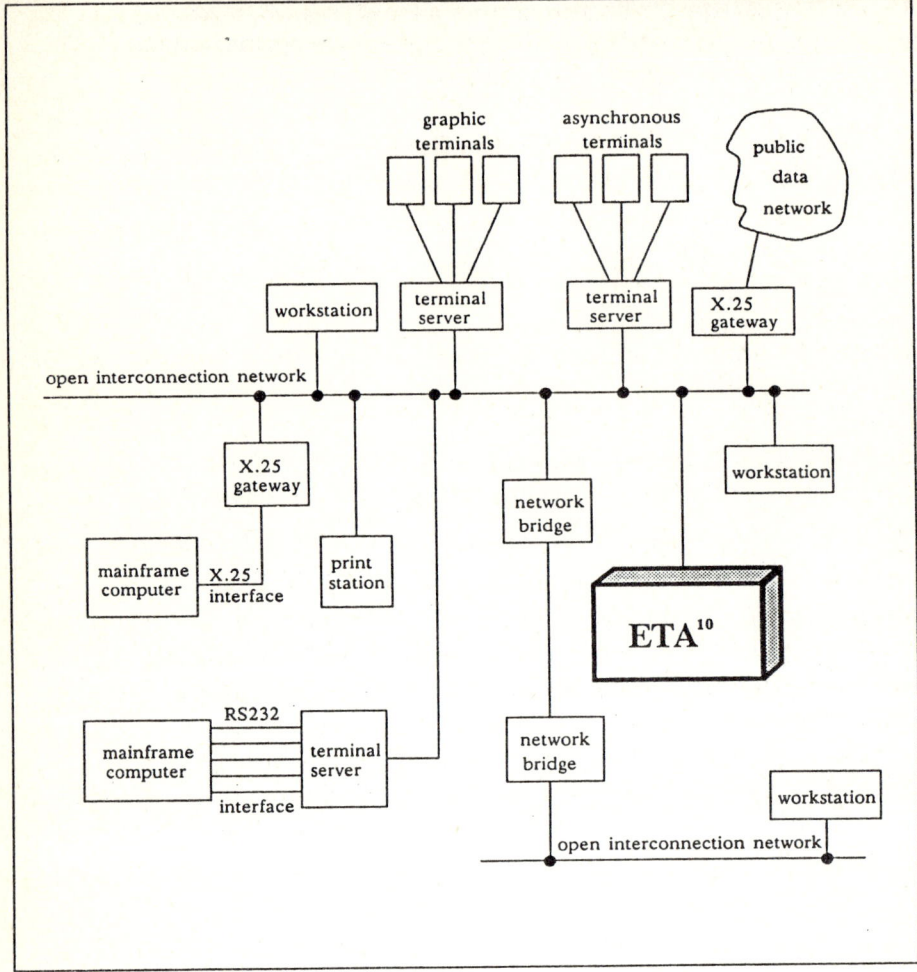

Figure 4. Example of an ETA10 system Open Interconnection Network configuration.

Loosely Coupled Network

The ETA10 system also can be connected to the Control Data Corporation Loosely Coupled Network (LCN). The LCN consists of various types of Network Access Devices (NADs) interconnected by coaxial cable using proprietary transmission mechanisms and protocols. NADs are available for connection to the following computer systems:

- CDC CYBER 170 and CYBER 180 series running NOS version 2.3
- CDC CYBER 205 running VSOS version 2.1.6

Connections to the these other computer systems will be verified later:

- IBM 303X and 43XX running MVS/SP version 1.3 with JES2/JES3
- DEC VAX models running VAX/VMS version 4.2

A NAD connects directly to a single channel on the CDC and IBM computer systems. The NAD model that interfaces to a VAX requires one slot in the VAX Unibus for access to memory. It can support up to four VAX machines.

A NAD can connect to as many as four different coaxial cables (trunks). Any single trunk can be up to 3000 feet in length or connect to as many as 28 NADs. The NADs provide contention-free transport services to the connected hosts, with a single NAD supporting up to 128 different virtual circuits. Figure 5 illustrates an example of an LCN configuration. LCN has a raw transfer rate of 50 million bits per second, and an effective transfer rate of up to approximately 6 million bits per second. (The effective transfer rate is dependent on the host system.)

The basic transport service provided by LCN is augmented with Remote Host Facility (RHF) applications running on each connected host computer. RHF provides for the copying of any file from any host to any other host. Copy modes can automatically perform character and record conversion to the native mode of the receiving host, or transfer the file as a transparent bit stream without conversion. RHF also supports entering a job into the input queue of a connected host, and returning output to the submitting host. Files also can be directed to particular output devices on any host.

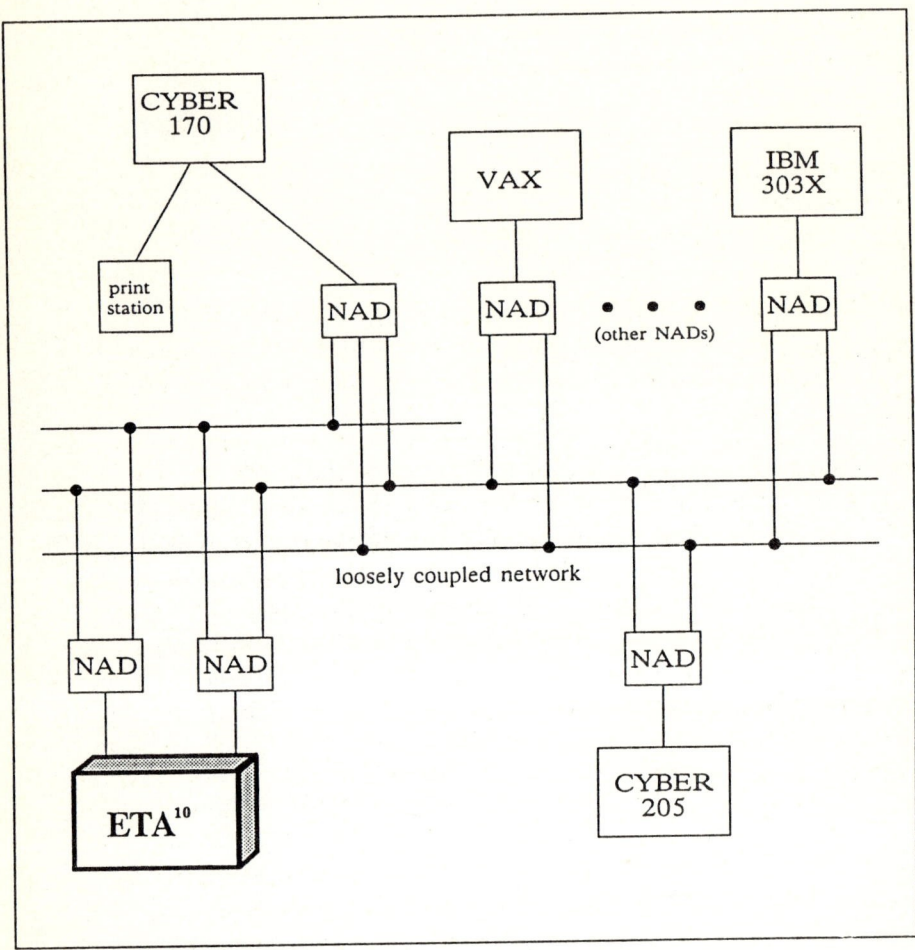

Figure 5. Example of a Loosely Coupled Network configuration.

Programming Environments

To help programmers create applications for the ETA10 supercomputer, the system provides two different programming environments: UNIX, a highly portable and widely used environment; and VSOS, the user interface of the CYBER 205. When programmers submit jobs or start interactive sessions, they choose one of the environments (or use the default the installation has assigned to them) for their particular jobs or sessions. Each of these environments provides the command language, tool sets, and the most important programming languages to which current users of these standard systems are accustomed. Both these environments also have access to a set of ETA Systems products that are environment-independent.

UNIX Programming Environment

ETA Systems has chosen to support a UNIX programming environment for several reasons: (1) it is compatible with many types of workstations, minicomputers, and microcomputers; (2) its user community is large and growing; many people know UNIX and write applications for a UNIX programming environment; and (3) it has a rich set of software development tools. The UNIX environment on the ETA10 is a full-featured software development environment, which emphasizes completeness and compatibility with the UNIX definition.

The UNIX programming environment on the ETA10 is based on AT&T System V, Release 2, with some Berkeley extensions. It has both the Bourne and C shells. Almost all the utilities and routines included in UNIX System V are supported, including the standard UNIX kernel calls. Additional networking facilities and accounting information also are available for users who wish to access them. As described later in this section, products common to all environments, including the numeric and multitasking libraries, also are available for use with the UNIX programming environment.

VSOS Programming Environment

The VSOS programming environment is provided on the ETA10 for compatibility with the CYBER 205. It is less full-featured than the UNIX environment, but the VSOS environment presents a straightforward system interface that is more explicitly tuned for batch performance than the standard UNIX interface.

The VSOS programming environment is based on the CYBER 205 VSOS Release 2.2. It has been enhanced in several ways. It provides richer interactive features, such as improved job control language with procedure file capabilities and multiple parallel sessions per user. The user interface also has been simplified by removing some CYBER 205 paging file limits and other file system limitations. Jobs have the ability to maintain file position from one task to another, simplifying the processing of input and output files. The owner of a file specifies the type of access allowed to the file, including multiple readers or multiple writers, if desired.

In addition to the common product languages described in the next subsection, the CYBER 205 FORTRAN200 compiler is provided in the VSOS programming environment for compatibility.

Also available on the ETA10 are many of the CYBER 205 System Interface Language (SIL) routines that provide an interface to operating system functions. This interface is conveniently callable by higher level languages. Most of the CYBER 205 SIL routines are provided; the exceptions are those that are dependent on CYBER 205 internal system table formats.

Products Usable from Either Environment

Several ETA Systems software products are designed to be used with either programming environment. For this reason, they are called common product languages or common product tools. These products include the standard programming languages (ETA FORTRAN, C, and, in the future, Pascal), multitasking capabilities, and some program development tools (debugging tools, for instance).

While these common environment products are functionally defined independently of the environments, they do use some of the environmental definition for context. For example, a user working in the UNIX environment can expect the standard debugger on the ETA10 to use the UNIX file search algorithms to locate requested files.

Programming Languages

In the first ETA10 system release, there are two common product programming languages: ETA FORTRAN and C. Pascal will be added later. ETA Systems sees FORTRAN and C as the early, most important languages for adapting applications for the ETA10 or for developing new applications.

FORTRAN

The ETA FORTRAN compiler supports the ANSI 78 standard language and anticipated array notation of the next ANSI standard. The compiler also supports some of the most popular language extensions from other major vendors, including BUFFER IN/BUFFER OUT, CYBER 205 FORTRAN vector syntax, IBM-compatible arithmetic type statements, and multiple assignment statements.

There are two ETA FORTRAN compilation modes on the ETA10: production and development. The production mode stresses execution speed and provides a variety of optimizations and vectorization. The development mode emphasizes compilation speed and extensive diagnostics. Users may select the compilation mode most appropriate for their needs.

Extensive scalar optimization is available to compiler users. The compiler provides common subexpression elimination, redundant load and store elimination, constant folding, removal of invariant code from loops, inner loop optimization, global register allocation, instruction scheduling, and other optimizations for scalar code.

A state-of-the-art automatic vectorizer also is included in the ETA FORTRAN compiler. The vectorizer not only finds the vector operations already in the code, it also applies numerically sound transformations to create additional ones. It recognizes vectorizable constructs in both DO and IF loops. When beneficial to execution speed, it will interchange loop indexes to create longer vectors or promote scalars to vectors. It also flags program statements where users can add directives to supply more information, allowing more vectorization than could safely be done automatically.

The compiler also provides limited automatic partitioning of programs in preparation for execution using multiple processors.

C

The C language, as defined in *The C Programming Language*[1], is fully implemented on the ETA10 system. The C compiler emphasizes compatibility with other portable C compilers, fast compilation speed, and diagnostics.

Pascal

A full implementation of Pascal, as defined in the *Pascal User Manual and Report*[2], will be available after the first release of the ETA10 system. The language will be extended to include a vector notation. The Pascal compiler will emphasize fast compilation speed and good diagnostics.

---

[1] Brian W. Kernighan and Dennis M. Ritchie, *The C Programming Language* (Englewood Cliffs, NJ: Prentice-Hall, 1978).

[2] Kathleen Jensen and Niklaus Wirth, Pascal User Manual and Report (New York: Springer-Verlag, 1985).

Lecture Notes in Engineering

Edited by C.A. Brebbia and S.A. Orszag

Vol. 1: J. C. F. Telles,
The Boundary Element Method
Applied to Inelastic Problems
IX, 243 pages. 1983.

Vol. 2: Bernard Amadei,
Rock Anisotropy and
the Theory of Stress Measurements
XVIII, 479 pages. 1983.

Vol. 3: Computational Aspects of
Penetration Mechanics
Proceedings of the Army Research
Office Workshop on Computational
Aspects of Penetration Mechanics
held at the Ballistic Research Laboratory
at Aberdeen Proving Ground, Maryland,
27–29 April, 1982
Edited by J. Chandra and J.E. Flaherty
VII, 221 pages. 1983.

Vol. 4: W.S. Venturini
Boundary Element Method in Geomechanics
VIII, 246 pages. 1983.

Vol. 5: Madassar Manzoor
Heat Flow Through Extended
Surface Heat Exchangers
VII, 286 pages. 1984.

Vol. 6: Myron B. Allen III
Collocation Techniques for Modeling
Compositional Flows in Oil Reservoirs
VI, 210 pages. 1984.

Vol. 7: Derek B. Ingham,
Mark A. Kelmanson
Boundary Integral Equation
Analyses of Singular, Potential,
and Biharmonic Problems
IV, 173 pages. 1984.

Vol. 8: Linda M. Abriola
Multiphase Migration of Organic
Compounds in a Porous Medium
A Mathematical Model
VIII, 232 pages. 1984.

Vol. 9: Theodore V. Hromadka II
The Complex Variable Boundary
Element Method
XI, 243 pages. 1984.

Vol. 10: C. A. Brebbia, H. Tottenham,
G. B. Warburton, J. M. Wilson, R. R. Wilson
Vibrations of Engineering Structures
VI, 300 pages. 1985.

Vol. 11: M. B. Beck
Water Quality Management:
A Review of the Development and
Application of Mathematical Models
VIII, 108 pages. 1985.

Vol. 12: G. Walker, J. R. Senft
Free Piston Stirling Engines
XIV, 286 pages. 1985.

Vol. 13: Nonlinear Dynamics
of Transcritical Flows
Proceedings of a DFVLR International
Colloquium, Bonn, Germany, March 26, 1984
VI, 203 pages. 1985.

Vol. 14: A. A. Bakr
The Boundary Integral
Equation Method in Axisymmetric
Stress Analysis Problems
XI, 213 pages. 1986.

Vol. 15: I. Kinnmark
The Shallow Water Wave
Equation: Formulation,
Analysis and Application
XXIII, 187 pages, 1986.

Vol. 16: G. J. Creus
Viscoelasticity – Basic
Theory and Applications
to Concrete Structures
VII, 161 pages. 1986.

Vol. 17: S. M. Baxter
C. L. Morfey
Angular Distribution
Analysis in Acoustics
VII, 202 pages. 1986.

Vol. 18: N. C. Markatos,
D. G. Tatchell, M. Cross, N. Rhodes
Numerical Simulation of Fluid Flow
and Heat/Mass Tranfer Processes
VIII, 482 pages. 1986.

Vol. 19: Finite Rotations
in Structural Mechanics
Proceedings of the Euromech
Colloquium 197, Jablonna 1985
VII, 385 pages. 1986.

Vol. 20: S. M. Niku
Finite Element Analysis
of Hyperbolic Cooling Towers
VIII, 216 pages. 1986.